Women of Vision, Women of Peace

Women of Vision,
Women of Peace

Nancy D. Potts, Ed.D.

Peace Publishing
Austin, Texas

COVER DESIGN BY LaVONNE PROSSER
COVER LOGO BY SANDIE ZILKER

98   97   96   95   94   5   4   3   2   1

Library of Congress Cataloging-in-Publication Data

Potts, Nancy D.
  Women of Vision, Women of Peace/Nancy D. Potts-1st ed.
  Includes bibliographical references and glossary.
  ISBN 0-9640010-0-4   CIP 94-65675
  1. Spirituality.   2. Women's Studies.   3. Inspirational.

Printed by Morgan Printing & Publishing, Inc., Austin, Texas 78756

For additional copies, write:
Peace Publishing
303 Camp Craft Rd., Suite 250
Austin, Texas 78746

CONTENTS

LIST OF ILLUSTRATIONS

Acknowledgments

Writing is a solitary adventure, undertaken on faith, usually with little awareness of how much time it will require. But it is also a collaboration of people whose help is crucial. I want to thank these people—one by one—for the gift of their talent and time. This book is an example of people coming together to work for the good of the whole, in the spirit of cooperation. In that regard, it is a small step toward peace.

My deepest appreciation to Marilyn Hamor, a senior student, friend, assistant, and tireless worker who has been a wellspring of energy for this book. Marilyn has been an integral part of the work for twenty years—she has offered not only encouragement and research, but she also typed, edited, and contributed to the birth of my first book years ago. She was there for the original conception and planning of *Women of Vision, Women of Peace*; she then transcribed and typed long hours of interview tapes followed by preparation of the initial drafts of the manuscript. She was the first person to read and comment on the completed manuscript. Thank you, Marilyn. May all that you have so generously given be returned to you in blessings and contentment.

The coordination of the entire self-publishing project was left in the trustworthy and capable hands of Ann Mellor. With great skill and attention to detail, she managed to do all the computer work, provide proofing and deadline schedules, and had input on each phase of development. Senior student and friend in the work of The Peace Institute of Universal Christianity, Ann brought years of computer experience and organizational ability to this project as well as a deep appreciation and enthusiasm for the subject matter. Thank you, Ann, for blessing this work with enormous skill, humor, love, and discipline. May your generous service in this labor of love bless you in unseen ways.

To Shirlene Bridgewater, a senior student, writer, editor, and friend in the work of The Peace Institute, my deep gratitude. In the service of author and reader alike, she brought her previous journalistic experience to *Women of Vision, Women of Peace* and enhanced the text with her expert editorial improvements. Since the first draft of the book was written, significant revisions have been made. Therefore, Shirlene, in essence, edited not one, but two books using her graceful yet astute skills. Thank you, Shirlene, for being a superb editor and advisor. May this labor of love bring blessings to you and encouragement for what is possible.

Peace Publishing, a nonprofit branch of The Peace Institute, was enthusiastically encouraged and organized by Janet Leubner, a friend and senior student of The Institute. With advanced training and experience in marketing, Janet has blessed the new self-publishing venture with her expertise, love, and humor. She has sensitively combined her marketing skills and commitment to service to ensure that the book might effectively reach those whose hearts yearn for a deeper spiritual life. Thank you, Janet, for all that you bring to this effort and for the gift of yourself. May you receive the continual blessings that come from service for the highest good.

To LaVonne Prosser and Sandie Zilker, my heartfelt gratitude for a beautifully designed cover and logo. Both women are talented artists, each in her own unique way, who came together to create an elegant "home" for the written text. Senior students and friends of The Peace Institute, LaVonne and Sandie have generously given their time and talent to this labor of love, as they have on numerous other occasions. Thank you, LaVonne, for the gentle and graceful skill with which you create visual images. Deep gratitude to you, Sandie, for giving so freely of your talent in various media. May all that you have so selflessly given be returned to you with joy and love.

To the wonderful volunteers who proofed every word and comma, each footnote and capital letter—thank you. For always so graciously giving your time, attention to detail, and love—thank you: Linda Berthelsen, Sharon Bradford, Lanette Buehler, Bethany Cunha, Marilyn Hamor, Alyse Kyriay, Janet Lake, Mary Jane Lamonte, Janet Leubner, Peggy Post, Karin Runciman, and Trish Taylor.

To Janet Lake and Mary Jane Lamonte, senior students and friends in the work of The Institute, my deepest gratitude for help in the final preparation of the manuscript for publication. Warmest thanks to Mary Jane for her skilled attention to the reference material of this book. Thank you, Janet, for the efficient administrative support in the office and for dedicated work on this book as well as other projects.

To the Friends of The Peace Institute whose generous financial contributions have made this book possible, my everlasting gratitude.

The members of our spiritual family at The Peace Institute have helped with this project more than they will ever know: especially Lois Arcure, Sharon Bradford, Shirlene Bridgewater, Bob Buehler, Lanette Buehler, Carlton Cook, Bethany Cunha, Glen Dorries, Marilyn Hamor, Elisabeth Juen, Alyse Kyriay, Janet Lake, Mary Jane Lamonte, Janet Leubner, Ann Mellor, Pam Padgett, LaVonne Prosser, Karin Runciman, Faye Smith, Trish Taylor, and Sandie Zilker. Thank you, one and all.

It is also important to acknowledge those who have taught, encouraged, and provided a link in our understanding and development. We each stand on the shoulders of those who came before us. In a book which celebrates the interconnection of life, this gratitude seems especially appropriate. To those who have served as teachers and/or consented to interviews, my heartfelt gratitude and love: Elizabeth MacDonald Burrows, Elisabeth Kubler-Ross, M.D., Gweneth E. Robinson, and Bernadette Roberts.

A special gratitude to Elizabeth Burrows for the rich heritage of the Christian mysteries that she so generously shared.

To Gweneth Robinson, a homeopath in England, my deep gratitude for her wisdom, love, and support.

To Morgan Printing's Nick Denner, Mike Morgan, Terry Sherrell, and Dawn McGehee, grateful acknowledgment for the important assistance, advice, and guidance we received on this project.

Grateful acknowledgment for excerpts quoted from published material and unpublished interview transcripts is made to the following:

Ann and John Rush of the Peace Pilgrim Center in Hemet, California, for a delightful interview regarding Peace Pilgrim and for their gracious hospitality. To photographer Carla Anette in Honolulu, Hawaii, for kind permission to use her photograph of Peace Pilgrim in the book.

Heartfelt gratitude to Irina Tweedie for our long afternoon interview in London, England, which began with a cup of tea and progressed to a discussion of the deepest Truth of the heart. Grateful acknowledgment also to Llewellyn Vaughn-Lee for our meeting after the previously mentioned interview.

To AP/Wide World Photos for permission to reprint a 1979 photograph "Mother Teresa Receives Nobel Peace Prize." Special gratitude to Sister Mary Jo McFarlane of the Sisters of the Holy Family in San Francisco and to Sister Patricia, O.C.D., of Carmel of Reno for their time and sensitivity in locating the appropriate photograph of Saint Teresa of Ávila.

Grateful acknowledgment is made to publishers and authors for use of quotes cited in the text. Bibliographic references are provided in the list of Notes at the end of the volume. Use of the following is cited with appreciation: E.P. Dutton for *Cosmic Consciousness* by Richard M. Bucke, M.D.; ICS Publications for *Saint Teresa of Ávila: A Spiritual Adventure* by Tomas Alvarez, C.D., and Fernando Domingo, C.D., translated by Cristopher O'Mahony; Bear and Company for *Meditations with Teresa of Ávila* by Camille Campbell; Paulist Press for *Purgation and Purgatory: The Spiritual Dialogue* by Saint Catherine of Genoa, translated by Serge Hughes in *Classics of Western Spirituality: A Library of the Great Spiritual Masters*; Harper and Row Publishers, Inc., for *Mother Teresa: Her People and Her Work* by Desmond Doig; Ignatius Press for *Fire Within* by Thomas Dubay, S.M; Nilgiri Press for *Love Never Faileth* and *Words To Live By: Inspiration for Every Day* by Eknath Easwaran; Paulist Press for *The Essential Sermons, Commentaries, Treatises, and Defense* by Meister Eckhart, translated by Edmund Colledge, O.S.A., and Bernard McGinn in *Classics of Western Spirituality: A Library of the Great Spiritual Masters*; Doubleday, Image

Books for *Such A Vision of the Street: Mother Teresa—The Spirit and the Work* by Eileen Egan; Doubleday, Image Books for *The Little Flowers of Saint Francis* by Saint Francis of Assisi; New American Library, Mentor Books for *The Varieties of Religious Experience* by William James; Institute of Carmelite Studies Publications for *Collected Works of St. John of the Cross* by Saint John of the Cross, translated by Kieran Kavanaugh, O.C.D., and Otilio Rodriguez, O.C.D; Doubleday, Image Books for *Dark Night of the Soul: St. John of the Cross* by Saint John of the Cross, translated and edited by E. Allison Peers; Paulist Press for *John of the Cross: Selected Writings* by Saint John of the Cross, edited by Kieran Kavanaugh, O.C.D. in *Classics of Western Spirituality: A Library of the Great Spiritual Masters*; Ave Maria Press for *Imitation of Christ* by Thomas à Kempis, translated by William Casey; Doubleday, Image Books for *The Story of a Soul: An Autobiography* by Saint Thérèse de Lisieux, translated by John Bieners; The Liturgical Press for *Teresa of Ávila's Way* by Mary J. Luti; Paulist Press for *Meister Eckhart: Teacher and Preacher*, edited by Bernard McGinn, with Frank Tobin and Elvira Borgstadt, collaborators in *Classics of Western Spirituality: A Library of the Great Spiritual Masters*; Harper and Row Publishers for *A Gift for God: Prayers and Meditations* by Mother Teresa; Harper and Row Publishers, Inc., for *Life in the Spirit: Reflections, Meditations, Prayers* by Mother Teresa, edited by Kathryn Spink; Harper and Row Publishers, Inc., for *The Love of Christ* by Mother Teresa, edited by Georges Goree and Jean Barbier; Ballantine Books for *My Life for the Poor: Mother Teresa of Calcutta* by Mother Teresa, edited by José Luis González-Balado and Janet N. Playfoot; Doubleday, Image Books for *Prayer Times with Mother Teresa: A New Adventure in Prayer Involving Scriptures, Mother Teresa, and You* by Mother Teresa, edited by Eileen Egan and Kathleen Egan, O.S.B.; Harper and Row Publishers, Inc., for *Something Beautiful for God: Mother Teresa of Calcutta* by Malcolm Muggeridge; Ocean Tree Books for *Peace Pilgrim: Her Life and Work in Her Own Words*, compiled by some of her friends; Eerdman Publishing Company for *Mother Teresa: Early Years* by David Porter; Shambhala for *The Experience of No-Self: A Contemplative Journey* by Bernadette Roberts; Shambhala for *The Path to No-Self: Life at the Center* by Bernadette Roberts; M. Boens, Publisher for *What is Self?: A Study of the Spiritual Journey in Terms of Consciousness* by Bernadette Roberts; ICS Publications for *The*

Collected Works of St. Teresa of Ávila, Vol. 1 by Teresa of Ávila, translated by Kieran Kavanaugh, O.C.D., and Otilio Rodriguez, O.C.D.; ICS Publications for The Collected Works of St. Teresa of Ávila, Vol. 2 by Teresa of Ávila, translated by Kieran Kavanaugh, O.C.D., and Otilio Rodriguez, O.C.D.; Paulist Press for The Interior Castle by Teresa of Ávila, translated by Kieran Kavanaugh, O.C.D., and Otilio Rodriguez, O.C.D. in Classics of Western Spirituality: A Library of the Great Spiritual Masters; Penguin Books for The Life of Saint Teresa of Ávila by Herself by Teresa of Ávila, translated by J. M. Cohen; Doubleday, Image Books for The Life of Teresa of Jesus: An Autobiography of Saint Teresa of Ávila by Teresa of Ávila, translated and edited by E. Allison Peers; Doubleday, Image Books for The Way of Perfection by Teresa of Ávila, translated and edited by E. Allison Peers; Element Books for The Lover and The Serpent: Dreamwork Within A Sufi Tradition by Llewellyn Vaughan-Lee; Element Books for The Chasm of Fire: A Woman's Experience of Liberation Through the Teachings of a Sufi Master by Irina Tweedie; and finally, excerpts reprinted from Daughter of Fire: A Diary of a Spiritual Training with a Sufi Master by Irina Tweedie, published by Blue Dolphin Publishing.

Lord make me an instrument of thy Peace;
Where there is hatred, let me sow Love;
Where there is injury, Pardon;
Where there is doubt, Faith;
Where there is despair, Hope;
Where there is sadness, Joy;
Where there is darkness, Light;
O Divine Master,
Grant that I may not seek to be consoled, as to console,
To be understood, as to understand,
To be loved, as to love;
For it is in giving that we receive,
It is in pardoning that we are pardoned,
It is in dying that we are born to Eternal Life.

Saint Francis of Assisi

Preface

Why write a book about women who are at an advanced stage of the spiritual journey? First, most writings, with the exception of those about women Christian saints, are about men and their process of growing up spiritually. Second, three of the women profiled here are alive or recently deceased; they grew up in our time in history. The other wrote a classic in mystical theology. Third, while there is more emphasis today on understanding women's spiritual experiences, these women live in a spiritually *mature* state of consciousness. They are beyond what Christianity refers to as the awakening, transforming union, and the early years of the unitive life. Consequently, they see the spiritual journey from a different vantage point. And, fourth, it is hoped that the book will inspire others to grow up spiritually. As a result, people will become less self-centered and more concerned with the well-being of everyone in the world family.

This book is also written as an act of service to show that there *are* contemporary women who have traveled up the steep path of the mountain of Truth and have marked the passage for those who follow in their footsteps. Each of us makes the journey alone, in our own time. Nevertheless, it is inspiring to know others who have made it to the summit of spiritual maturity. Advanced spiritual travelers do not put their names in lights, however. Instead, they simply love God and work humbly, often without public notice. Consequently, I am certain others, as well as those profiled here, live at the summit. But these women do provide a rich perspective of the spiritual journey—one grew up without formal religious training, one is a contemplative, another a Christian mystic, and one a Sufi.

An interview was conducted with Irina Tweedie and excerpts are in the biographical chapter of her life. Her remarks were edited to reduce repetition; otherwise the richness of the stories remain in her own words. The chapter on Peace Pilgrim includes previously unpublished background information from long-time friends and family, as well as a discussion between Peace Pilgrim and John and Ann Rush, founders of the Peace Pilgrim Center. Mother Teresa's health prohibited a personal interview, but well-documented books about her life and work are quoted in the chapter on her; and the introduction quotes from a letter she wrote about this project. Saint Teresa's life and spiritual journey are well-documented in her writings. But she is included here as a link in a rich spiritual heritage of women saints and contemplatives who lived in inner transcendent freedom. Her life and work, considered in twentieth century language, is a beacon of light to those who wish to live in the integrity of their own inner depths.

Now, it is a thorny problem to decide which pronouns to use these days. The feminist movement has performed a great service in pointing out how language, as well as actions, reveal prejudice against women. On the other hand, we are stuck with pronouns which are gender specific. I have used feminine pronouns and the plural "we" and "us" with two exceptions. First, quotes from men spiritual writers naturally require masculine pronouns. Rare gems of spiritual wisdom are quoted without regard for what kind of body—male or female—the soul happened to wear. Truth is Truth. So, quotes are selected for their unique ability to highlight the journey, whether spoken by a man or woman. In reality, the *soul* is not male or female, and growing up spiritually is difficult regardless of whether we experience it as a man or woman. In advanced states, we grow beyond male and female identity and embrace our eternal identity.

The second use of the masculine pronoun is in reference to God or Ultimate Reality or Truth. By whatever name, It that is That is beyond gender pronouns. We project our own labels to make Ultimate Reality or God personal to us. And so it should be. Some refer to God or the Divine as He or She. Yogananda, a great Indian saint, called God the "Divine Mother." Whatever makes God personal to us, a living presence, is the name we choose. In ancient times, the masculine pronoun was used to refer to God as the creative principle in the universe, not to gender identity. Hence, the choice of He or His in this book refers to that living principle of creation.

Now, we begin an extraordinary journey. Because this book is for everyone who longs for a deeper meaning in life, it is dedicated to those who, with love and humility, seek God.

Nancy D. Potts
Austin, Texas
March 1994

Introduction

This is a book about four women whose work in the world is an expression of their love for God. These women are not humanitarians or social workers. Nor do their acts of peace originate from a commitment to reform or serve their communities. Everyone—as members of the world family—has a responsibility to be kind and helpful to others. But, for these women, it is far more than trying to create a better world.

What transformed these women into living examples of selfless charity? What kind of love creates a revolution in mind and soul, unites us to the Divine, and remakes us? It is said that each of us is a stream whose source is hidden. These women discovered the source and their union with it.

They are spiritual travelers who climbed the mountain of Truth and reside at its summit. For over twenty years, each woman has lived in the unitive state of consciousness. Their vantage point of the spiritual journey and its landmarks, pitfalls, and experiences is from the perspective of seasoned veterans of the mature spiritual life.

****

Most people write and speak about their spiritual experiences before union with God or right after the revelation of union. They bask in exalted feelings and relish their expanded awareness. Some admire their own virtues and conceive of themselves as having a halo. Dazzled by the reflection of God in other souls, they wear their "halos" with pride, competing with other seekers. But spiritual pride and ambition consume the soul's

1

humility. Experiences are overrated or misunderstood; *effects* of the Divine are misinterpreted *as* the Divine.

This state of the soul passes, but writings undertaken at this stage are immature, just as the twenty-five year old who writes about life has a different interpretation than someone who is fifty-five. Both have stories to tell, but one is more experienced in life's ways. Perhaps it is better to silence pen and voice until we live the mature spiritual life long enough to see the journey in retrospect.

The high mountain with its distant summit is an exquisite symbol of the spiritual quest to union with God. At the beginning of our climb, we carry our cherished beliefs with us and are susceptible to the changing climate of our senses. The mind creates its own image of the Divine and envisions a journey of emotional highs and spiritual nuggets of truth. Later we discover the mirages in our thinking.

From a vantage point halfway up, however, our view is more complete and our foggy perception clears, but only of the path just traveled. We cannot see higher than we are standing. But with our backs to the summit, we can look down and track our formidable climb, unmasking some of our false expectations about ourselves and the journey. We realize we overvalued some of our experiences, misunderstood others, and frequently were ambushed by our vivid imagination. Nevertheless, our vague yearning draws us further up the mountain, where perhaps we receive a fleeting glimpse of the hidden summit.

Now we must stay centered on the path ahead and not be distracted by toys of the senses or the thrill of side trips. By the grace of God, the hardy soul reaches closer to the mountain's edge. Whatever baggage unnecessary for our destination has been discarded along the way.

There never is—never has been—any going back for the soul seeking God. The immense beauty and stark emptiness of higher altitudes are beyond the mind's comprehension, yet we are pulled as magnets to mountain peaks where we breathe divine air. It is a journey that defies description. We search for words to describe this inner transformation, but come up empty. It is beyond translation; the journey must be lived to be understood.

At some mysterious point, after we have exhausted our means to climb steadily higher, God takes over. Through His grace, we reach the summit. But the journey is not over. It is another beginning. Now without map or compass, another phase begins—we live at the summit in full unitive consciousness, stretched to the limits of our human potential.

****

The major world religions have always known about the ascent of the mountain of Truth and about the summit of spiritual maturity. In their mystical teachings, they describe the landscape of the mountain and provide disciplines for the advanced spiritual traveler in pursuit of the Divine. Each religion may emphasize different landmarks, however, and call God by different names. Some spiritual traditions insist on the value of altered states of consciousness in order to discover a transcendent vision of life. In moments of profound awakening, beyond ordinary consciousness, the false self is transcended. The "dark nights" of Christian prayer refer to these mountaintop experiences. Other spiritual paths seek to bring the mountaintop to each moment. Transcendence is "here and now"; each moment is filled with the light of the sacred. Both approaches can be transforming, peaceful, and joyous. Both ways have their dangers and delusions as we navigate uncharted realms of consciousness. But, by whatever path, by whatever name we call God—Beloved, Truth, Ultimate Reality, Yahweh, Allah—our destination is the same: union with God.

Mysticism is the art and science of the soul's journey to permanent, supernatural union with God. Today, however, the word "mystical" is used to describe everything from psychic phenomena to the "mystical experience" of driving a car or entering a passionate relationship. As the world awakens to the next stage of evolution—spiritual consciousness—classical descriptions of the spiritual journey, once reserved for earnest seekers in monasteries and convents spring from behind protective walls to find new life in the public domain. This is as it should be as we grow up spiritually and hunger for Truth. The drawback, however, is that words denoting specific experiences and phases of the journey have become diluted and misapplied. Thus, while all experiences of the Divine may be called mystical, the classical definition of a mystic is one who pursues union with God. And God is beyond all the experiences that may accompany spiritual awakening and development—trance or ecstasy, voices or visions, prophecy or healing, and even the emotional fire of religious exaltation. These are transient experiences, according to Saint John of the Cross, nonessential aspects of the journey and certainly not to be sought. God, and our union with Him, is the destination.

While religion explains our divine heritage and ultimate destiny, Western psychology does not usually mention the path of grace. Instead, it focuses on uniting conscious with unconscious and healing psychological pain. Yet any psychology which does not take into account the divine promise in every human being is not a mature psychology. God transcends the unification of the psyche or consciousness. God is the center of the soul. True psychology begins with the divine center and understands the evolutionary mechanism which exhorts us to grow to higher stages of development. Psychological symptoms are the result of consciousness trying to become harmonious with its true nature and developmental course. We can seek the Divine or flounder in self-centered cravings.

Psychology, originally the science of the soul, is in its infancy. Psychology of the future must account for the evolutionary destiny of the human race and explore the effects of our transition into spiritual consciousness. Richard M. Bucke, in *Cosmic Consciousness: A Study in the Evolution of the Human Mind*, says:

> . . . Just as, long ago, self-consciousness appeared in the best specimens of our ancestral race in the prime of life, and gradually became more and more universal and appeared in the individual at an earlier and earlier age, until, as we see now, it has become almost universal and appears at the average of about three years—so will Cosmic Consciousness become more and more universal and appear earlier in the individual life until the race at large will possess this faculty. The same race and not the same; for a Cosmic Consciousness race will not be the race which exists today, any more than the present race of men is the same race which existed prior to the evolution of self-

consciousness. The simple truth is, that there has lived on earth, "appearing at intervals," for thousands of years among ordinary men, the first faint beginnings of another race; walking the earth and breathing the air with us, but at the same time walking another earth and breathing another air of which we know little or nothing, but which is, all the same, our spiritual life, as its absence would be our spiritual death. This new race is in act of being born from us, and in the near future it will occupy and possess the earth.[1]

Spiritual consciousness, our next stage of development, is only beginning. Though more people experience illumination, or cosmic consciousness, it is a partial or temporary state. We receive only a glimpse of the destiny of the human race. Such a glimpse, however, is life-changing. Before, we felt separate from the world. Now we experience the universe as a living presence, permeated by the essence of the Creator.

We swim in a deep ocean of joy, ecstatic about life. Sorrow ends. We are free of our fears of death and evil. Our sense of immortality is no longer a conviction, but a reality in which we live. Finally, we comprehend that love, the glue of the cosmos, stretches golden fingers of light within and around us.

This is a higher form of consciousness than that possessed by ordinary men and women. It is beyond self-consciousness, subjective and objective, and represents the new woman, the new man—the consciousness of the future in which the lower mental faculties subside. Now, the old gives way to the new. Outdated priorities of wealth and subtle forms of materialism are shed as old clothes, too small to contain the new growth.

The glimpse of new humanity is accompanied by a moral elevation, greater capacity for learning, and increased powers. It is as though uncaged lightning has struck the mind, illuminating consciousness with everything worth knowing.

The human race is gradually developing this kind of consciousness, far advanced of our self-centered existence. It will lift us beyond instincts, fears, ignorance, selfishness, and the brutalities of today's world. A glimpse of destiny gives us hope and rekindles a sense of wonder in our world-weary hearts.

There are those, however, who not only have experienced the

illuminative states of the spiritual journey, but also, emptied of self, live in full, supernatural, permanent union with God. They have grown beyond the infant and adolescent stages of spiritual consciousness and live in spiritual and psychological maturity. They have lived on the mountain's summit for many years.

God's direct invasion of the soul is the beginning of the unitive life and advanced spiritual and psychological development. The will becomes totally conformed to divine will, and we discover our true identity by self-loss in Him. This passage through consciousness to permanent union with God is an extraordinary process directed by the Divine. It is beyond a partial illuminative experience. Neither is it a materialistic achievement nor a drug-induced altered state of consciousness. There is no quick fix road to spiritual maturity. Quite the contrary—it is a hard, slow process to grow up spiritually. And while the ego may set its sights on spiritual experiences rather than God, ambition will not open the door to the Divine. Sooner or later, we discover that our attempts to live beyond our current development and character send us sliding to our former stage to complete the missed steps in our growth.

In the mature spiritual life, however, we live by the strength of apparent emptiness. We escape from rigid habits, religious dogma, and self-idolatry. Character and moral development steadily increase. Thus, while the destiny of the human race is continued improvement, we grow little by little rather than by leaps and bounds. In the process, we lose interest in the external self and our own significance. The path of grace to union with God is borne of love and pours humility into a soul once filled with treasures of the self.

In the full unitive state, our lives express selfless charity, and we see the divine center of love in everyone regardless of religious, social, cultural, or political differences, or self-centered ways.

The spiritually mature do not seek fame or fortune, but selflessly work at their appointed mission. Consequently, they are not necessarily well-known unless their work is accorded public recognition, thereby furthering the mysterious ways of God in the world.

****

The four women profiled here have climbed the mountain on different paths, reached the summit, and lived fully their permanent union with God. Their stories serve as inspiration to all spiritual travelers; their process of development underscores the need for understanding this advanced stage of consciousness in the framework of normal human development.

Chapters 1 and 2 describe the ascent of the mountain and the view from the summit. From beginning to end, our whole human experience is a journey to spiritual and psychological maturity. Chapter 1 describes our part in the journey from awakening through what Saint John of the Cross refers to as the "first dark night." Chapter 2 describes the process when God takes over, thrusts us into training, and remakes us to live our full human potential in Him. *This spiritual process and its psychological effects will be the developmental psychology of the future.* (A full psychological treatment of this process is in a larger work-in-progress.) But to better understand the women profiled, a thumbnail sketch of the process is provided in Chapters 1 and 2. The language and symbolism is drawn from Christian mysticism and from the writings of spiritual giants of past centuries. It bears repeating, however, that the major world religions describe the journey, the disciplines, and milestones using language and metaphors that are understood culturally.

The profile of each woman begins with an overview of her work—her mission or calling. With deep love and a will conformed to divine will, each one works as though she is nothing— God is all. The second section describes her formative childhood years, the threads of which are later woven into a divine tapestry of love and charity. The third section reveals a unique spiritual journey, the work of God in the soul. There is nothing that we can do to persuade God to reveal Himself. This divine transformation is an awesome, eternal act of grace.

The first profile is of Peace Pilgrim, a woman who spent her retirement years as a penniless pilgrim walking for peace. She began her pilgrimage in 1953, on foot and in faith, and crisscrossed the country seven times before her death in 1981. In her "Steps to Inner Peace," she describes the slow dying of the self-centered nature and the freedom of living totally in the God-centered nature.

Mother Teresa, in the second profile, exemplifies selfless charity-in-action. In a letter written in regard to this book, she said, "I assure you of my prayers that all will go well for the greater glory and honour of God." That also sums up her life as an "instrument of His peace." When Mother Teresa renounced her will and her life for God, she left everything to serve in India. Her childhood, however, provided unique experiences which prepared her to serve the "poorest of the poor." Nevertheless, the call to leave the convent and live among the poor came twenty years after she became a nun—twenty years of spiritual preparations came first. Mother Teresa, emptied of self, is a pure reflection of God's love.

Irina Tweedie is a Sufi. She is eighty-six years old, and when asked if death was near, she replied: "Yes. I feel I am just treading water now. My work is just about finished." Today when "freedom" is a newspaper headline, Mrs. Tweedie defines *true* freedom as something earned through spiritually-guided disciplines. She was born in Russia in 1907, educated in Vienna and Paris, and lived in England with her naval officer husband. His death prompted her deep search for meaning and her eventual meeting with the Sufi teacher who dramatically changed her life. Mrs. Tweedie was the first Western woman to be trained in this ancient yogic lineage, the journey to the "heart of hearts." Bhai Sahib, her teacher, requested that she keep a diary of her spiritual training. It is an amazing five-year record of her spiritual transformation. After her teacher's death, she returned to England to daily teachings in her London home and lectures in the United States and Europe. During our interview, she said: "My Teacher once said that I love beauty too much— the birds, flowers, trees, pretty colors, everything beautiful. Now at the end of my life, I am going blind. I will not be able to see beauty. It is alright. There is only one love—the love for the Beloved (God). Always there are spiritual lessons, you see."

The fourth profile is of Saint Teresa of Ávila, a Christian mystic and Catholic Saint. Her path of conversion began in 1555 at the age of forty, transforming an insecure, head-strong woman into a spiritually mature, psychologically integrated servant of God. In her book, *Interior Castle*, Saint Teresa recorded the stages of prayer and an elegant, trustworthy analysis of the inner life and exalted states.

Each woman is a profile of peace. Although the world family has extraordinary hopes for peace, it is not the enduring kind. *True peace will never be a military cease-fire or a negotiated settlement. We will not have peace among nations until we have peace within families. And we will not have peace in families until we have peace within individuals. Peace must first come in our own hearts.* Until then, we dump our inner projections of aggression, greed, and self concerns on those around us.

True inner peace—peace of soul—occurs when we spiritually grow up. We become like a glass emptied of self-will and filled with the pure love of God. In the full unitive state we are like a window pane cleaned of dirt and grime, which reflects the sun, to later vanish into its light. It is a remarkable journey of grace.

The four women profiled here live in divine union. From the top of the mountain, they bear the vision others less mature cannot see. Their continuous peace of soul, unruffled by changing circumstances, is like a light which radiates peace to a darkened world. They are women of vision, women of peace.

Chapter I

Growing Up Spiritually

The caterpillar's metamorphosis into a butterfly has long served as a metaphor for spiritual transformation. The caterpillar sacrifices her life to undergo a mysterious transformation—alone and in the solitude of a dark cocoon—to reenter the world as a butterfly. Nature dresses the butterfly in beauty, but it is not her elegance that is important, but what her life has become. Never again will she return to caterpillar life. Now, free from encumbrances, she flies fleetly into the wind to begin a new phase of life in which she will fulfill her destiny as a butterfly. Later, she will die to her butterfly life, and begin yet another phase of life.

God did not discuss His plan with the caterpillar. He simply hid His original design in her nature, and she unknowingly fulfilled her purpose. God left people free, however, to discover our true identity and to choose whether to work with Him in the creation of our life. The question, "Who am I?" cannot be answered by us alone, though we make a conscious endeavor to know ourselves and the workings of our psyche. Because the secret of our true identity is hidden in God, the only way we can discover self is to discover God, and only God can show us Himself.

We make a choice—to live behind the masks we wear, absorbed in a false, immature self, or to respond to God's call from the inmost center of our being. Our self-will can wallow in self-centeredness or follow its natural developmental direction and seek God and our highest good.

The Caterpillar Stage: The Self-Centered Life

The caterpillar stage is symbolic of our self-centered life in which we either cater to the desires, passions, and ambitions of the false self, or we direct our energy towards God and the discovery of our true self. Traditionally, the false self has been given numerous names—the lower or lesser self, the self-centered nature, the egoic self—and the true self has been called the higher, deeper, or real self.

Our false self is the mask we wear into the world. We believe it to be our true self, so we use up our life fulfilling its desires for love, approval, power, security, pleasures, and assorted experiences. We devote all our energy to the false self's well-being and clothe ourselves in superficial accomplishments. Success and pleasure, honor and power will not last, however, for they are surface clothes which will fall away, revealing our naked emptiness. But, until then, we live as captives imprisoned in a protective cell, a stranger to our highest destiny. We are prisoners in a mistaken identity, devoured by activities and strangled by accomplishments.

We are not very good at recognizing our masks and illusions. The false self has overshadowed us since birth, and we have modeled our lives after others who indulge their cravings and accumulate pleasures. Accurate observation shows people wanting bigger houses, faster cars, greater prestige, classier clothes, and intense sensual experiences. We compare ourselves and our collected goods against our neighbor's—who has more, who has less—building walls and divisions between us. Admiring the distance, we evaluate our progress: we are popular, you are not; we are successful, you are a failure; we are rich, you are poor. Our divisions are comfortable, familiar, a barrier between ourselves and other people. We hide in our disguises so easily—pride masquerades as humility, envy hides in love, service shrouds self-admiration, excellence conceals competition, works for God veil desires for feeling good about self. We wear our masks as though parading through a costume ball, seeing ourselves as others see us. No one pierces beneath our disguise. In time, even we wonder who we are. We have forgotten we are heaven-born as well as earth-born. We have a divine heritage and are one family, members of one another.

To begin the spiritual journey, we must see the false self for what it is: self-centered and ruthless in pursuit of its desires. When thwarted, it flails about in anger, revenge, or some other form of tantrum behavior. *The energy of a will focused on itself creates a roller coaster of emotional extremes, and deep spiritual and psychological suffering.* The false self builds an altar to itself, adorns it with experiences, and worships it as an idol. It uses anything—people, things, perceptions, knowledge, feelings—in its effort to grab what it wants. In extreme form, the false self harasses everyone in its presence with its tantrums and demands. Wars and inhumane suffering are inflicted by a false self's fury.

As consciousness unfolds, however, we become aware of the Divine, and go in search of our true identity hidden in the love of God. *That is our vocation, our intended destiny—to seek God and discover our true identity in Him.* The true self is like a treasure waiting to be lifted from the bottom of the sea. To draw it up requires sacrifices, risks, and an openness to God as He reveals the mystery of Himself in every circumstance.

We sense the deep treasure long before we are ready to pursue the voyage to its hiding place. But our frantic lives are too noisy and congested with activities to heed the divine call. Nevertheless, the love of God seeks our awakening, though we may fear His coming in proportion to our attachment to the false self. The trinkets of the world enchant us while the Divine is an experiential mystery. We face a crossroads: Do we pamper the false self and perpetuate its cravings or seek the Divine? Do we fill up our lives trying to please other people or discover our true identity? Do we wind down our well-worn path of distractions or set the compass for an unknown region under God's direction?

To awaken to God is a gift of love from Him who is love. It is like opening a window to inhale the clear air of a fresh morning in a newborn world. He has sprinkled dew on all creation, and we are awed by the sacredness of life. All that lives bears God's holy imprint. The embryo morning light reveals nature's wonder, and we see with new eyes—every plant, every animal, every person is our family. Each flower that raises its tiny face to the sun is a reminder of God's love. We behold the beautiful tapestry of life in and around us, and it is as dear as breath to the body. The divine insight lingers on an authentic spiritual world which has overemphasized material existence.

When God initially reveals Himself, often through some supernatural power, the ego, or the energy of self-will, is pulled toward the Divine as though attracted by a magnet. We seek God with all our energy; the pull to Him is overpowering.

Now, we long for serenity instead of chatter, and simplicity rather than a scattered mind chasing diversions. It is a call for solitude, a drawing into our inner world. In the past, we may have feared solitude. Thus, our interior world has remained a foreign country, unvisited and unknown, awaiting the courageous traveler. We have known our interior resides safely below our surface existence, but do we want to travel there? God comes to us, however, in the solitude of our inner life. To be receptive to Him, we must cultivate solitude in the center of our souls. The spiritual traveler does not want to live on the surface of life. So, we reverently seek solitude as a pilgrim who finds a road to climb which will lead to the gates of heaven. We pray for strength to wait for Him in silence.

Solitude is essential. Yet how often it is misunderstood. It is not self-hypnotism; it is not feelings or thoughts or reactions; it is not a narcissistic reflection on our self; it is not a refuge from problems for they will follow us; it is not a barrier between ourselves and others. True solitude is our home where we enter the sanctuary of the soul for communion with the Divine.

"Seek ye first the kingdom of heaven, and all else shall be added unto you," says the Gospel According to Saint Matthew. We enter our place of worship—perhaps a corner in a room that we have created as a place of prayer—and we seek God. We enter daily, at the same time, and we come alone, quiet, with reverence. Prayer and meditation are the cornerstone of the spiritual life; through them we express our humble love for God. And it is through meditation that we reach at-one-ment with God as He reveals our union with Him.

At first our meditation is like drinking from a shallow stream, but in time we penetrate the surface and drink steadily deeper. It requires commitment, devotion, complete concentration. Eventually, our meditation is like being at the bottom of the ocean— quiet, peaceful, beyond sensory awareness. The splashing waves and strong currents overhead do not reach us; they remain at another level of consciousness. Here, we love God with an undivided heart.

In the beginning, however, our undisciplined faculties rebel and angrily taunt us to abandon meditation. They plague us to take up a more worthwhile pastime, something more suitable to their passions, activities, and greed for experiences. Whatever consumes us during the day follows us into meditation and steals our attention from God. But, we must not yield to our faculties and attachments. We master them by refusing to feed them. Otherwise we leave the center of our spirit to serve the restless mind and imagination; we scatter and fragment our attention away from God. It is comparable to wearing an inflated inner tube while struggling to dive below the stream's surface to greater depths awaiting us. We discover we cannot indulge our faculties' whims and earnestly seek the kingdom of heaven. As long as we are caught in selfish attachments, we are unable to live in constant awareness of the divine unity of life.

Before long, we unearth layers of attachments, both respectable and trivial. We are tied down to everything from houses and people, to prestige and power, to memories and dreams. Our biggest fear is our loss of things we deem indispensable. Yet whatever we cannot live free of, binds our heart. Whatever we cling to replaces God in the center of our souls. Our attachment is actually to the false self. We replace God with an impostor:

> The soul that is attached to anything, however much good there may be in it, will not arrive at the liberty of divine union. For whether it be a strong wire rope or a slender and delicate thread that holds the bird, it matters

not, if it really holds it fast; for, until the cord be broken, the bird cannot fly.

Saint John of the Cross

On one hand I felt the call of God; on the other, I continued to follow the world. All the things of God gave me great pleasure, but I was held captive by those of the world. I might have been said to be trying to reconcile these two extremes, to bring contraries together: the spiritual life on the one hand and worldly satisfactions, pleasure, and pastimes on the other.

Saint Teresa of Ávila

Saint John of the Cross and Saint Teresa of Ávila, Christian contemplatives and Spanish writers, were giants of the spiritual life. Both emphasize that we go wholeheartedly to God or not at all. It took Saint Teresa twenty years, however, to move beyond her doubts and struggles and become established in God. Everyone begins with doubts and conflicts and attachments. One of the requirements of this stage is not to be disheartened but patient; not to evaluate our progress, but become as little children growing up in the delight of God. We must be faithful and persistent to our course, come what may:

He who interrupts the course of his spiritual exercises and prayer is like a man [woman] who allows a bird to escape from his hand; he can hardly catch it again.

Saint John of the Cross

The journey to the hidden treasure requires a change in lifestyle. An occasional prayer and the lapse of time are insufficient to reach our destination. We simplify our lives, removing what clutters our time and attention, to meditate and read spiritual writings, and to practice the presence of God. Everything we do is for God—our time of prayer, carpools for children, office and volunteer responsibilities, the clatter of preparing meals in the kitchen. Our house is without a steeple, but it is our church just the same. We live the spiritual life in the ordinary of our days.

Most people are sound asleep to their true nature, so our changing lives may be viewed with question, even suspicion. Living the spiritual life requires a nobler conduct and more self-discipline than the world demands or can appreciate. But we cannot tread in the slush of opinions and appearances or coast on the breeze of popularity. The wind blows in another direction for one earnestly seeking God. The curious will ask about our changes, but the spiritual life is not an afterdinner conversation for those seeking novelty. It is the essence of who we are.

As our awareness and understanding of the spiritual life deepens, we begin to discriminate as to what we put into our own consciousness. We have been passively receptive to images from television, videos, movies, and books which court the false self's passions. But now evening television is traded for solitude and prayer. Meaningless activities are surrendered for time to study inspirational books. Self-control is stretched to its limits as we learn to say "no" to whatever tugs us toward our selfish appetites. It is too expensive to succumb to the ways of the world; we allow the "bird to escape" from our hand. We also know our true treasure rests at the bottom of the sea of consciousness, not in the world's priorities.

We plod along led by some inner imperative which exhorts us to grow, feeling exhilaration, joy, clarity, well-being, and confidence followed by periods of aridity and loss. At other times, we feel crushed beneath the tension between our outer journey and our inner journey; it is a tug-of-war which saps our energy. Our thoughts are like sudden bends in the river—quick, shallow, unexpected. They are too easily out of control rushing after their own pursuits. And our unhealed psychological splits rear their heads as projections onto other people—in them, we see our unresolved conflicts. Blind to ourselves, others serve as handy hooks for our criticism, anger, worries, and sorrows.

It is now that we must not quit—now when our meditation is sometimes dry, friends and family may not understand, and we feel off-balance by the change of direction from the outer life to the inner life. Saint John of the Cross calls this the *active* dark night, when we do our part to reach God, and the things of the world lose their hold on us. Later, by His grace, the *passive* night begins: God does His work in us in the "night of the senses" and "night of the spirit." Meanwhile, we rely on His love and remain faithful to the journey.

This is a major milestone. We feel the spiritual journey costs us everything. Saint Teresa, writing to her nuns, says:

> Do not be dismayed, daughters, at the number of things which you have to consider before setting out on this Divine journey, which is the royal road to Heaven. By taking this road we gain such precious treasures that it is no wonder if the cost seems to us a high one. The time will come when we shall realize that all we have paid has been nothing at all by comparison with the greatness of our prize.

The Gospel According to Saint Matthew says, "Ask, and it shall be given you; seek, and ye shall find; knock, and it shall be opened to you." We have received a glimmer of understanding about the spiritual journey; He said He would come to us. By grace, when we yield to His love, offering Him our whole being as our most precious gift, He promises to come.

For those who seek God, we repeatedly go to the edge of our experience and fall off. Our fears, out-worn concepts, and self-imposed limitations float to consciousness. We come face to face with our prized delusions. *To move along very far on the spiritual journey, we must discover a sense of our own being, and live with dignity and integrity, strong enough within ourselves not to be influenced by others' expectations for us.* We outgrow the need to over-involve ourselves in others' lives as a way to shadow our own dependencies and insecurities. Nor do we use spiritual development or its disciplines to repress psychological problems. We must resolve psychological patterns and addictions which entrap us, creating a stronghold on our interior life. Our self-defeating behavior patterns show themselves in perfectionism, relationships that do not work, the need to control others and always be right, and in our addictions to excitement, crisis, and drugs or alcohol. If we are totally lost to ourselves, we find it impossible to make decisions or even know what is best for us. The domain of psychology has been to heal the splits within ourselves, but has too often only encouraged the perfection of the false self. Yet, what we yearn for cannot be found in the struggles of our false identity. The recurrence of anger, confusion, loss, and ambition indicates our readiness to understand the root cause of these emotional forces. In time, we discover that each is propelled by fear. We are afraid to be open, to change, to embrace life as a human dance of cycles, and to live fully in our true nature. But, as we compassionately touch the face of our false self, we see how it controls our life until we awaken. In the spirit of adventure and pilgrimage, we learn to release that which binds our heart and transform the energy for good use. In so doing, profound healing occurs, resulting in a sense of wholeness.

The spiritual journey to God and our true self requires that we not be blinded by the mad scramble of the false self. Rather, in sweet simplicity, we give ourselves just as we are to God just as He is. We seek forgiveness when we hurt ourselves and others, and amend our less than noble conduct. We confront our behavior honestly and assume responsibility for our feelings, thoughts, and actions. In the process, we develop an inner resiliency to pick ourselves up by our own bootstraps when necessary and leave behind the treasures of the false self. With singleness of heart and simple humility, we embark on an extraordinary journey of the human spirit.

It is difficult enough to grow up physically and psychologically, but it is immeasurably more difficult to grow up spiritually. It is essential not to confuse psychological maturity—our union in ourselves, whereby we heal the splits within, and unite conscious and unconscious—with spiritual maturity and our union with God. These are two distinctive rites of passage. Psychological maturity in and of itself does not lead to spiritual maturity. But, union with God—which is an advanced stage along the spiritual path—is accompanied by psychological integration. It is a parallel process, an effect of transforming union. When we yield to the love of God, our union with Him supersedes psychology, philosophy, and all other forms of intuition, experiences, or ways of knowing.

The spiritual path is not an escape from ourselves. Quite the contrary, we discover our true self in union with God. On the path of grace, there are summits of new and higher mountains on which God reveals Himself and what we are created to be. For our part, we surrender to the only One who can take us from here, the One who created us. We pray for strength for a later day when, by His grace, we shall know by unknowing and die to the self as we enter a higher life beyond.

The Spiritual Path to Union with God

To return to God, to the Source of love, is the whole meaning and heart of life. Our destiny is to go beyond everything and discover our true being in the One who created us. Spiritual transformation is a profound process in which we commit our heart, mind, and soul to this hidden mystery.

The great spiritual traditions offer through prayer, meditation, selfless service, and devotional practices a way to awaken our heart to its true nature. We cannot, however, merely sample the disciplines and practices of various traditions and expect our development to penetrate to deeper levels. Sooner or later, we must commit fully to the way that is true to our own heart and follow it through all difficulties as they lead us to greater understanding and growth. By whichever way, it will require all that we have to give. But true love has no second thoughts. We go forward like rushing water casting aside our childish ways and fears.

To mature in the spiritual journey requires the dedication of our whole heart. On wings of aspiration we fly to the gate of our inner sanctuary, bidding it to open before us. We ask to know the secrets of God, in humility and self-forgetfulness.

In today's Western culture, however, we often confuse numbness with self-emptiness and meaninglessness with non-attachment. Spiritual development becomes a mask to shield our vulnerability and disconnected sense of self. With no sense of self, however, we have no self to give. We may experience the peace and calm of meditational states; through the force of love, we may have entered the unitive way. But the effects are unintegrated in our lives. Cut off from ourselves, we are resentful, inflexible, controlling, and angry. We confuse our roles with our identity and we devalue our feelings, experiences, and intuitions. Unable to trust ourselves, we fear the unknown. Whenever we have been abused or cut off from ourselves, we must reclaim and heal our mind, heart, and soul. Our childhood environment and birth temperament may have created a wounded, inauthentic connection with ourselves, reinforced by social and educational experiences. Healing that which is wounded within us becomes a parallel task of the spiritual journey. Healthy development seeks to strengthen, through patient training, qualities of faith, respect, wisdom, courage, kindness, and compassion. The fertile soil of consciousness grows seeds of wholeness, connectedness, and a reverence to honor our personal destiny. Wings of aspiration, now strong and expansive, fly through an open door to the unsettled wilderness between our everyday consciousness and the Divine.

The journey to perfect union with God through love is the aim of the spiritual life, according to Saint John of the Cross. But before we examine how the voracious caterpillar is transformed into a butterfly, we must understand the concept of union, for then the path to the summit of the spiritual life is more intelligible.

Saint John refers to a supernatural union, and not the union by which God is ever present, preserving our life. Thus, it is a habitual state of supernatural and total union, produced by the love of God, which makes the soul resemble Him—the soul and God "seem to be one." To illustrate union, Saint John describes the sun (God) shining on a window (the soul):

> A ray of sunlight shining upon a smudgy window is unable to illumine that window completely and transform it into its own light. It could do this if the window were cleaned and polished. The less the film and stain are wiped away, the less the window will be illumined; and the cleaner the window is, the brighter will be its illumination. The extent of illumination is not dependent upon the ray of sunlight but upon the window. If the window is totally clean and pure, the sunlight will so transform and illumine it that to all appearances the window will be identical with the ray of sunlight and shine just as the sun's ray. Although obviously the nature of the window is distinct from that of the sun's ray (even if the two seem identical), we can assert that the window is the ray or light of the sun by participation.
>
> The soul upon which the divine light of God's being is ever shining, or better, in which it is always dwelling by nature, is like this window, as we have affirmed.[1]

According to the Saint, the soul must purify itself, clean the windows of their grime, so that God may transform it, by the force of love. Such purifications are an act of love, and "to love," asserts the Saint, "is to labor to divest and deprive oneself for God of all that is not God." This is not to imply, however, that the body, mind, ego or self are dirty or bad. We are children of God who naturally yearn for the source of our original goodness. We become transparent to the light which is forever shining, and our hearts open to the voice of wisdom. The spiritual journey is like looking into a mirror in which we resume our true nature while passing through all our familiar thoughts, images, beliefs, and frames of reference. Ultimately, we see with the heart of love rather than with the mind that compares. We discover what we were seeking outside has always been inside. In the traditional language of Saint John, we are "purified and transformed."

Saint John of the Cross divides the soul into sensory and spiritual parts, each possessing its own powers. The sensory part has exterior sense faculties of sight, hearing, smell, taste, and touch and inner faculties of fantasy and imagination. The spiritual part of the soul contains the intellect, memory, and will—a will which can cultivate sense objects or God.

The path to God, declares the Saint, is a dark night of two distinct parts. To attain union with Him, the soul must pass through both the *active* and *passive* nights, or purifications, which clean the sensual and spiritual windows of the soul.

In the *active night of the senses*, we renounce our "voluntary appetites" or attachments, desires, hunger for things, and anything we make the center of our world. In the *active night of the spirit*, we struggle to seek the will of God and make Him the center of our love. We travel by faith alone, resting on nothing— not what we understand, taste, feel, or imagine. All that is not God is stripped away, including images, forms, and ideas which help us in meditation. It appears to be a forlorn world within our soul, a night of emptiness and storms, yet it is the path to eternal day. But for now, as we become increasingly freed of binding sense objects and passions of the false self, we live by the three virtues—faith, hope, charity—in darkness. All that we feel, know, and imagine is dark in the active night:

Faith causes darkness and a void of understanding in the intellect, hope begets an emptiness of possessions in the memory, and charity produces the nakedness and emptiness of affection and joy in all that is not God.[2]

Saint John of the Cross

We live only on faith, accepting the difficulties of this first dark night, without expectation of any light reaching us. Slowly, we enter a deeper contemplation, beyond the images and forms of our early meditation. We experience peace, joy, and blessed quiet. Our whole value system has undergone a silent transformation. For so long, we spent our energy on scattered interests and loves. Now a profound change has occurred—we are not scorched by the heat of possessing. Released from binding attachments, we are calmer, more accepting of life's windstorms, and more in harmony with ourselves. Vagrant thoughts are removed. Our once scattered will is focused. We experience a great inner freedom and serenity while living in a restless world.

Our painful self-simplification process has opened our eyes to a more valid life. Our priorities, ideas, and actions are more in harmony with the spiritual world in which we dwell. Even our work and how we spend our time takes on new meaning. Now, regardless of our occupation, it becomes an act of service.

We have become increasingly aware of the divinity expressed all around us: the hills drenched in moonlight, the wind singing its harmonies to forests splashed in autumn gold, the river glistening in the sun as it rushes to its source. With new eyes, we watch as a storm rolls in, cleansing the Earth's face with raindrops while thunder and lightning proclaim God's wonder. We are filled with joy and delight as our love expands to include a universe once unknown to us. The shell that enclosed our love is broken; we touch the transcendent mystery of life, and our silent heart hears God in the voice of His creatures. Now, we see our fellow-travelers with attentive eyes—from the birds in migratory flight to the cat sleeping on her back with paws outstretched to the tree as it presents the divine cycle of seasons. All are manifestations of that invisible divine spirit. We have seen it all before. But now we look with the eyes of a friend. We accept both life and death, beauty and suffering into our conscious awareness as we connect with the spirit of life. Joy and sorrow are inseparable; together, they live in nature's invisible pattern of life. And our love, once narrowly focused, has increased to include all life as our family as we continually cast away barriers between us. Our deepest communion occurs as heart, mind, and will stretch out with expanded attention to pour love on Divine Reality. But our journey is not over. It is ever-deepening toward a new beginning.

Our journey has brought us to the shadow of a mountain, where one day by grace, we shall arrive at the summit as a guest of God. *The second phase of the journey, however, is by divine intervention; whereas the active night occurs through the soul's own efforts in our love for the Divine.* This second phase—the passive night—does not necessarily immediately follow the soul's active night, but occurs later, often years later.

While the active night is initiated by us, the passive night occurs when God directly intervenes to further purify the soul, and bring its faith and love to perfection. Initially, God communicates to the soul through the senses; then He purifies them and communicates without the aid of the senses. The Saint calls this direct communication to the soul "inflow," "infusion," or "illumination." A new world has risen in this second night, one in which communication is more than the morsels received in meditation; now the infusions of love are more abundant. The senses, now bypassed, are dry and gain no satisfaction in meditation or from things of the world. It is reminiscent of the active night, but this is the *passive* night of the senses. It is the necessary gate which leads to the "purgation of spirit."

The dark night of the soul begins with this passive night of sense. At first we experience the Divine only in flashes which tantalizingly appear and disappear by grace. Each time it disappears, our first reaction is dryness and longing. We feel like we are in a spiritual wasteland. All the pretty images of God have vanished; prayers are hollow echoes; we cannot think or even meditate. We are tortured by our imaginations and our worries that we have offended God. We can squeeze no feelings out of ourselves—no delights, no joys, and precious little interest in spiritual activities. This phase passes away, however, and is followed by an illuminative one in which we are joyous, productive, and peaceful. Our negative patterns and selfish ways gently drop away as leaves from a tree in autumn. We have the sunny assurance that the Divine is real, and for the first time, perhaps, we are aware of our original goodness. But the peace which seeped into our soul evaporates, and our self-centered nature resumes control. The illumination period is followed by another period of darkness. Although this phase brings unhappiness, even depression, to the soul, it serves to intensify our aspirations for the Divine and decrease our interest in worldly pursuits. In blind trust, we remain still, sensing peace in the heart of this silent darkness. Somehow, we recognize God is the source of this purification process and our periods of joy and dryness.

If we do not run away or fill the emptiness with pleasures, but let God lead us through this desert, we will be led to our habitual union with Him. But we must totally abandon all spiritual progress to God and travel on pure trust in Him alone.

Many experience this "night of the senses" in the passive night, and many come to a standstill. They are not ready to surrender everything or live too long away from warmth and comfort. The emptiness and sterility of their interior world is devastating. Finally, they flee the darkness seeking any ray of light to fill the emptiness. Their progress up the mountain path is traded for relief. This is another turning point, a major milestone. "Many are called, few are chosen"; most turn back from the hardships.

Others are drawn further into the wasteland where a greater trial awaits. So great is the sacrifice that even personal happiness must be offered up. *It is an advanced stage along the spiritual path, so rigorous that it is reserved for those who totally surrender to God, leaving nothing for the self.* During this period, we feel forsaken, emotionally depressed, mentally fatigued, and paralyzed in our spiritual progress. Yet, our spiritual development is directed by God, where by grace, our sublime union with Him is revealed, and we enter the second passive night—the "dark night of the spirit." We are plunged into new experiences, tests, and further purifications.

The dark night of the spirit is marked by a definitive stroke of the Divine. For some, it may follow a period of great illumination but, nevertheless, it is an awesome intervention by God, impossible to confuse with any other previous experience. It is the beginning of the unitive life, from which we will never be cut off.

Now, the soul travels blindly, ever deeper into the sanctity of desolation. Only in retrospect will we be able to trace the windings of a course unimaginable to us now. The web of destiny is woven, and the caterpillar enters the cocoon for "transforming union," and a new life in God.

Chapter II

Spiritual Maturity: The Unitive Life

To the informed quester, the dark night of the spirit is just another stage of growth. Until now, our spiritual life has contained both dryness and sudden inpourings of light. Moments of illumination have gently come and departed as silently as a cloud, transcending all previous ways of knowing. In such times, all multiplicity and disunity ceases. There is nothing left to desire or be. We are not the same person, yet are more ourselves than ever.

The caterpillar has done everything she can to reach God through disciplines and meditation. She has received God's grace and enjoyed her emotional ecstasies. She may even think she is already in habitual, supernatural union with God. Many mistakenly believe they have entered the spiritual door when, in reality, they are still outside it. Others seek entrance from spiritual ambition rather than humble love. They shall remain outside, waiting. Some simply misinterpret their experiences, not realizing there are still higher stages of growth. Since we can interpret another's experience only by our own, we are blind to what awaits us down the road.

At some critical moment, after we have reached the limits of what we can do, the Divine initiates a sudden, irreversible breakthrough deep in our unconscious, revealing our union. Now the Divine takes over all purification, searing to the unfallowed depths of our being. *This is the beginning of the dark night of the spirit and the unitive state of consciousness. It is a point of no return.*

The caterpillar then enters the cocoon governed by a higher will. Helpless and dependent on God, she begins a passage which contemplative literature calls "transforming union," a journey inward and downward to the depths of being. All our work in the active night of sense and spirit, however, could not alone bring us to this cocoon stage. Nor is the passive night of sense sufficient. It provides a cleansing of consciousness—of thoughts, emotions, even physical condition—to be ready to receive the inflow of Spirit. Consciousness becomes like a clean chalice rather than a dirty, small, and weakened vessel.

Thus, the dark nights are essential steps in the journey to grow up spiritually. But the disciplining of the self can go on and on. Eventually, the ego, or self-will, which is behind all the improvement, must be removed from its station in front of the spiritual door. The self, however, cannot liberate itself, only God can. Only God can prepare us to fulfill life's higher purpose. And we are only beginning to grasp the beauty of the destiny that awaits us:

> Most people live, whether physically, intellectually or morally, in a very restricted circle of their potential being. They make use of a very small portion of their consciousness, and of their soul's resources in general, much like a man who, out of his whole bodily organism, should get into a habit of using and moving only his little finger.
>
> William James

Transforming union trains us for the mature spiritual life and the fulfillment of our soul's potential. Though we do not wish to belabor the difficulties of growing up, adolescence is made more bearable when we understand its purpose and demands. We are also better prepared when the spiritual landscape is marked.

The passive night of spirit is initiated and directed by the Divine alone. Silently, without warning, the Divine invades our consciousness, revealing our deepest union with Him, in a *sudden, permanent* change of consciousness to which we must adjust. The Divine plumbs the depths of our psychological being. Our task is to trust with passive abandon His work in our soul. This initial, quick stroke of the Divine has been called the descent of the spirit, our possession by God, and the falling away of the ego-center (self-will). It is the first stage of the unitive life.

Elizabeth Burrows describes two phases in the descent of the spirit:

> First, I felt something like stardust, or tiny, little stars, penetrate my skin. It was bearable, but two to three months later in the middle of the afternoon, a crown of thorns descended around my head. Though unseen by others, it is a constant tight band that has never left. That's when the spirit descended to live in the flesh. It brought an agony of purgation. There were no holds barred in the scrubbing of consciousness. I reeled under the impact.[1]

Kitamura Sayo was a Japanese peasant woman known to her followers as O-gami-sama (Great Goddess). She referred to the descent of the spirit as possession of the soul by God. In 1944, Sayo received her first divine inspiration that a Shinto deity, the Heavenly Goddess, dwelled in her body and was the same God of the Christians and Buddha. In 1945, she received an explanation of the nature of the deity:

> The male God Katai-Jin, who descended into Your body on November 27 last year, and the Female God Amaterau Meokami who descended on August 11, have united as one God, making Your body a temple, and thus forming the "Trinity"![2]

Kitamura Sayo rejected the values of the world, and taught that everyone must surrender the ego and become reconciled with God. The self must be emptied for selfless service in oneness with the Absolute.

Bernadette Roberts, a contemporary Christian contemplative, who writes about the stages of the unitive life and the no-self experience, describes her entry into the dark night of the spirit as a "merciless milestone":

I had been reading in the garden when I felt an invisible film, or thin veil, come down over my head, and shroud my mind. . . . Swiftly and decisively, all had been done in silence; yet, however simple and innocent its quiet descent, this act was, in effect, terrible and awful—the Almighty had simply lowered the boom.

The first thing I noticed was that I could no longer see the words on the page; suddenly, they had become characters without meaning. It was several days before I could read again, and then it was totally without meaning. For years afterward, I could only derive meaning when and where God permitted some understanding to break through; these breakthroughs would shed light on the mystery of God's ways in my soul, in creation, or in his great plan for man. . . . Apart from the practical knowledge necessary for daily living (horse sense), my mind was plunged into darkness, wherein the only way of knowing was by this special light; I had to trust in it implicitly, because there was no other way of seeing.

. . . Although the mind is now left in a painful, empty void, this symptom is actually the lesser of two that mark this phase of the dark night. If it is dark and empty "above" (in the mind), so too, it is dark and empty "below" (in our interior). After the descent of the veil, I looked inward to encounter not the usual, obscure presence of God, but a gaping black hole where He had been and on seeing this, there arose from this center a pain so terrible, so enormous, that I wondered how it could be contained. It was the feeling of being cauterized, branded by God in the depths of my being—depths I never knew I had till then. The pain was beyond control, verging on the limits of human endurance with no escape or cooperation possible; in a word, the pain was all! For the next nine months, this pain came and went as it pleased, in daily bouts, several times a day. My understanding was that God had some merciless work to do here, and would not relent until His mysterious job was done. . . .

Eventually, I learned that the best protection against this pain was to fully accept it, and that by virtually sinking into it, sinking into my feeling of utter misery and nothingness, the pain lost much of its punch. It seems that a deep submissiveness is essential here, because, with the increasing ability to hold still, let go, sink in, and thereby come to naught, the pain subsides, and eventually disappears. After this came peace of soul, though it was initially loveless and joyless, it was nevertheless, as painless and restful as the calm after a great storm. Then, from out of this nothingness, this ash-heap of misery, there gradually emerged a whole new life.[3]

After the descent of the spirit, the caterpillar enters the yawning darkness of the cocoon for a divine training program in which our self-will is conformed to divine will. Never again will we be able to go against our highest good. Now the soul is purified, tested, and prepared for a later stage when she emerges as a butterfly. Much later, she will thank God for this hidden act of grace. But today, she feels shipwrecked in a strange land with no compass to get her bearings.

Characteristics of Transforming Union

Transforming union is like an underground mining operation in which all aspects of self are unhinged, purified, and reintegrated. This process is not to be confused with various psychological conditions. It is not an intense cyclic variation in moods which may indicate a manic-depressive condition. It is not a lifelong depression or chemical imbalance. Neither is it the result of intense grief work, physical suffering, personal pain, or psychosis. It is not psychological, but an act of grace.

Initially, the dark night of the spirit is painful. The quest seems lost; our meditation is dry and barren. No intellectual theory can bring solace. Emotions are starved of joy and peace. Even personal resourcefulness is to no avail. There is no consolation from people, books, activities, or from our inner life. All spiritual joys have died off. We live in unbearable emptiness, seemingly with no freedom of choice. The effect stuns us.

Mentally, we are in a prolonged stupor where sustained thinking is a drain. Nothing seems to matter; all appears aimless or trivial. Emotionally, we are flat, leaden. Our listless will swats at fears—our biggest one is that this could be a permanent state. We feel doomed forever.

Worse still, our spiritual life is bankrupt. There is no fire in our heart, only darkness and ashes where once there was light. God seems so far away—even the stars seem closer—so why speak out, we are not heard. Yet we cannot and will not give up our meditation and prayer. Our past intuitions now seem unreal; our present inner life is destitute; and hope for the future withers.

We force ourselves to continue outside activities, but we are spectators to a meaningless life. It seems futile to pursue our active life and old social responsibilities. We have no interest in art, work, literature, self-improvement, or whatever else once appealed to us. What do we do when nothing seems worthwhile? How do we continue with only lukewarm determination? Do we just play out our roles as mechanical robots? The futility of it all is oppressive.

Such is the dark night of the spirit. We are outcasts; we cannot return to caterpillar life; we are not ready to fly with the butterflies. It does not seem like God wants us either. Our patience is stretched to the limits as we are pushed to the end of our endurance, over and over again. Previous psychological problems and dark nights do not hold a candle to our entry into the cocoon of transforming union.

Our task is to submit and accept this work of the Divine and admit our helplessness. By our own powers, we can do nothing. It is useless to complain, though we do. The moment we gave our heart to Him, we invited the onset of the dark night, whether or not we knew. Sooner or later, we would arrive at this day. Now, we are completely in God's hands, and we will emerge at the time set by His wisdom. Nevertheless, we can take solace in the words of Comte de Saint Germain: "Every tunnel has its end."

Purifications, Tests, Psychological Effects

It is a paradox that as beginners in the spiritual life we feel close to God and receive dazzling illuminations, while in transforming union we feel God is absent, as light is experienced as darkness. Spiritual joys may entice us on the journey, but they are sacrificed as we progress. All stumbling blocks to our full union with God, including the ego's relish of spiritual experiences, are withdrawn. And, once the ego itself is removed from its post in front of the spiritual door, so is our previous way of knowing the Divine. Then, in transforming union, we enter a state of passive suffering that revamps our whole being—character, intellect, emotions, and will:

> A human being has so many skins inside covering the depths of the heart. We know so many things, but we don't know ourselves! Why, thirty or forty skins or hides, as thick and hard as an ox's or a bear's, cover the soul. Go into your own ground and learn to know yourself there.
>
> Meister Eckhart

Our journey to God is a passage through our layers of skins. We travel through consciousness confronting instincts, memories, repressed cravings, inner conflicts, and archetypes of pure energy. There is no hiding place for the soul being transformed by God, no skeletons in the closets of consciousness. Once the Divine invades our being, the light shines in the house of the soul, revealing all that is hidden. Previously, we gazed out the window, captivated by scenes in our surface consciousness. Now, we turn away from the window to see what creeps in the shadows behind us. It is a deep searching introspection, a more intense purification of our layers of consciousness.

We have sheltered splits within ourselves and given refuge to desires, sorrows, insecurities, and passions. Once more they well up to the surface of consciousness, surprising us by their strength. It seems that overnight, dormant seeds have sprouted to full-grown plants; we cannot avoid facing ourselves as we really are. Even what was suppressed during our practice of spiritual disciplines parades before us. Now we confront those aspects of self once and for all.

Exposed to light, our personality excesses are intensified. We discover what we depend on for security—we tricked ourselves into thinking we had no crutches, only our love for God. Now, we discover deep, subtle dependencies on people or prestige, ambition or money. Even habits and ways of thinking about God are safety nets when our equilibrium flounders. We are purified of limiting thoughts and decaying habits as we remain passive to God's work in the soul. Fighting it only increases the suffering.

We make new discoveries: of deceptions, large and small, past and present; of negative attitudes we rationalize as truth; of selfish motives in our common acts of life. Our masks are cracked, and hidden faults and weaknesses exposed. It is not a journey for the timid. We confront each aspect of ourselves, release it, and are strengthened in the process.

Our inner purification evokes a full range of emotional reactions. At first, our emotions whip up a storm in consciousness, but as we stay centered in God, they subside. The unconscious produces fantasies and dreams so we can resolve the splits within ourselves at the symbolic level. If that does not work, a crisis is generated to force us to face ourselves and heal the splits. Our emotions have too often been given free reign without examination. As we keep a watchful eye on our motives, we discover even despair and melancholy are self-serving. Thus, we curb emotional undercurrents by refusing to dawdle in their downswings.

The light of the Divine reaches deep into our consciousness; no weakness is able to wiggle away from its searching gaze. If we accept this inner scourging as purification necessary to make us more "fit to love," we more readily persevere in this trauma to consciousness. If we lust for comfort and peace, we discover yet another desire to be tamed:

> Some people want to see God with their eyes as they see a cow, and to love Him as they love their cow—for the milk and cheese and profit it brings them. This is how it is with people who love God for the sake of outward wealth or inward comfort.
>
> Meister Eckhart

Our inner transformation by grace brings us to our knees, humbled that the Divine comes to such a soul. This is a quiet cleansing process, not of the personality that the world sees, but in the hidden, inner chambers of consciousness.

Our task is to acclimate to this interior work and sudden change in consciousness. We get accustomed to seeing in the dark by not struggling against the work of grace. There will finally come a time when we hit rock bottom in what seems like a descent through darkness to a bottomless pit. As we travel below the level of thoughts and emotions, we reach the depths of our being. Now we are in the center of our house, but there is no peace or joy here—only calm. From here, we watch as thoughts and emotions pound the doors and windows trying to overrun our calm center. Much later in the journey, the restless mind and emotions will rattle the doors and windows to no avail. But, for now, we are grateful for some measure of calm and a new strength within.

The more we adjust to our inner renovation, the greater our understanding of the ways of the Divine. No level of consciousness is untouched; the invasion of our psyche is total. During the initial months or years, our threshold of consciousness is everchanging, allowing distinct states of consciousness to arise, each with its own qualities. As physical energies, emotions, and thought patterns surface and are released, new levels of the unconscious appear in our awareness to take their place, followed by powerful altered states of body, mind, and heart as spiritual development deepens. Our climb up the ladder of consciousness reveals the transient nature of all experiences; the self owns and controls nothing. Life, like shifting sand, dissolves into tiny moments of experience, arising and passing before us. Even our exalted states of consciousness are impermanent. As we fly over the mountains of divine knowledge, our elegant meditative states of calm, joy, clarity, and peace pass away, like dew evaporating in morning light. A major turning point occurs as we cease to grasp for exalted states or use them to create a new spiritual sense of self. *Lights, raptures, and energy releases do not in themselves produce or indicate wisdom.* Initially, we may have thought the goal of meditation was to experience these dazzling side-effects. Now, in darkness, we know the illusion of our thoughts and self-identified goals. We humbly withdraw our attachment to these positive effects of God. The heart seeks what is beyond all transient identities.

The journey is long and cannot be tread by thought or self-interest. To navigate these deeper realms, we must passively submit, with humility and grace, as our changing sea of consciousness washes ashore all that is hidden below the surface. Even primitive qualities rise within us, like waves darting to the sandy shore. We discover that basic instincts can still overpower us if we let down our watchful guard. Survival, fear, and self-interest concerns of our primitive human heritage are still with us, only in disguised form.

Pride, anger, envy, avarice, sloth, gluttony, and lust, the seven deadly sins of Christian ethics, represent instinctive energies which float to consciousness. They are subtle, more sophisticated expressions of our distant past when survival, safety, and sexual reproduction were our only concern. We witness our modern disguise in our greed for money, security, and sexual excesses. A more elevated form of our basic instincts masquerades as spiritual pride. It takes a long time to recognize and sublimate impulses from our early stages of development to more civilized ways of expression. Prior to transforming union, our rational mental life tries to subdue and channel instinctive desires, but history is deeply embedded in consciousness, slow to be transformed. Spiritual consciousness, the next state in human potential, is yet in its infancy, and spiritual maturity is still rare. Only God can purify His creation and bring her to full maturity.

Our rational mind and instincts are both guests in the house of the soul. Neither is to be dishonored or repressed. Instead, we harness the energy of consciousness and wed it to a higher purpose than self-interest—to a more universal concern. We remain vigilant to the growls and passions within us, acknowledge them, and elevate our creative energy to serve on the spiritual level. It is a major task of transforming union:

> Set me free from evil passions, and heal my heart of all inordinate affection; that being inwardly cured and thoroughly cleansed, I may be made fit to love, courageous to suffer, steady to persevere.
>
> Thomas à Kempis

Transforming union is the beginning of our God-directed journey through consciousness to Him. The lower planes are purified of forces and instincts of our primitive, more aggressive nature. It may be accompanied by phenomena, fears, morbid fantasies, and voices. They result from a deep cleansing of the unconscious. In this, the ultimate fire of self-disclosure, we learn what it is to grasp at nothing yet meet the stream of life with an open heart. We stay centered in God during these bone-rattling times. And, though prayer and meditation are difficult, we find solace in the beauty of nature, inspirational books, and a constant awareness that this is the Divine at work. It helps to follow healthy routines, eat nutritious foods, exercise, breathe fresh air, and work diligently at our appointed tasks. The worst choice is to become a recluse, pampering our changing moods. We crush the inclination to become self-absorbed either in the "stuff" thrown up from unconscious realms or in divine archetypes.

Though the Divine is doing its work in the soul, *we* are not the Divine. But it is possible to be overrun by an archetype of the Divine which makes us believe we have come to save the world, found a new world order, or redeem the world family. We must stay centered in God and keep our feet on the ground. The Divine archetype will be unmasked for what it is. Our experience *of* the divine is not the same as *being* Divine.

In transforming union, we are cleaned up, purified, and trained to function and be as God originally designed His creation. All elements of consciousness, discordant in themselves, become one melody. Intellect, instinct, feelings, thoughts, and will, unite and conform to the will of God.

But for all its darkness, transforming union provides some brilliant rays of sunshine. Our heart is cleaned as a sanctuary for God, and the soul's natural beauty shines throughout. We learn humility, obedience, and wisdom that cannot be taught. We experience the mysteries of life, unfathomable before God took over our soul, and the truth of death. Our destiny is revealed and the way prepared to fulfill it. We have been transformed by an Artist. We are the canvas, and God has painted His picture. Now, for the first time, we truly see, but not with our physical eyes.

At some point, our deepest divine center of being is revealed. Oneness with God is totally secure. We rejoice in the absolute freedom of the egoless condition, and feel brand new:

> As iron put into the fire loseth its rust and becometh clearly red-hot, so he that wholly turneth himself unto God puts off all slothfulness, and is transformed into a new man [woman].
>
> Thomas à Kempis

Our love of God, once a flame burning brightly, now flares into overflowing. Our past acts of charity and kindness seem nothing compared to God's love for us. Now we want to serve God in more selfless ways. Later, we discover we express love best if we fully live what He has created us to be:

> Love feels no burden, thinks nothing of trouble, attempts what is above its strength. . . . It is therefore able to undertake all things, and it completes many things, and warrants them to take effect, where he who does not love, would faint and lie down.
>
> Thomas à Kempis

Now we begin to understand how Joan of Arc, Saint Teresa, Florence Nightingale, Mother Teresa, and all others of spiritual maturity can defy all practical considerations. They are fueled by love. Adjusted to a different interior world, they no longer follow the path dictated by society, self-image, former beliefs, or habitual ways of life. They have transcended psychological and self-centered experiences. The gates of the human heart are open and love flows out, touching all in its path.

We are now in the full unitive state, ready to begin the next stage of spiritual maturity. It is time to leave the cocoon to begin life as a butterfly. But, in retrospect, we see that the effects of transforming union are extraordinary. Slowly, imperceptibly, our character has improved, consciousness has been purified, and we live according to the highest ethical and moral conduct. The purification of consciousness, particularly those aspects of self for which we were ashamed, has altered our perceptions of others. Aware of our own shadow side, how can we possibly judge another? Everyone grows up in her own way, in her own time. We are all works in progress.

Love is the sentinel on duty during this dark night of the soul, standing watch through a process of death and dissolution to all that we have known. Transforming union is a profound life and death cycle experienced in various forms as restlessness, oppression, dryness, painful sorrow, etc. From it, the sun of understanding melts our hardened heart, and we see the profound sufferings of life. As our old identities unravel, we have firsthand experience that life, as we have known it, is like quicksand; it is not solid or familiar. With an acute awareness that life is fragile, we focus with laser-beam concentration on endings within and around us. Attuned to finalities, we notice people, music, our past, the cycles of seasons, goodbyes to friends. We may even become overly-concerned about our own physical death.

Out of the birth and death cycles within our own consciousness, we experience a deep sympathy and compassion for all life's sufferings. The world is a house of sorrows with hidden pain in adults, children, families, communities, the planet itself. Even clouds seem to weep tears of sorrow over our treatment of the Earth and all who live here. We have opened to death in all its disguises as we travel through each new level of consciousness, poignantly realizing that all passes away. With our heart wide open, we face fear and joy, and grasping neither, live in our true nature.

Sooner or later, we discover that other realms experienced by consciousness do not provide freedom or permanence. As we understand these dimensions, we outgrow the playthings of spiritual infancy. No longer are there any desires, if there ever were any, to play with the energies of the psyche. Dabbling in psychic activities, channeling, and exploring visionary realms of existence that constitute both beauty and horror are revealed for what they are. These realms are the play of consciousness itself and are transient in nature. They can easily hide the fears and desires still residing within us. The experience of these realms does not indicate wisdom. Misunderstood, they may foster pride, illusion, and self-inflation. Each person must knock on the door of God and seek a deeper reality, one that requires self-dissolution rather than self-expansion. God-drenched souls need no activities of the self. They pray. People often want to hold onto experiences more than they want God. They are simply greedy for spiritual experiences. Yet, there is no goodness without sacrifice:

> True love grows by sacrifice and the more thoroughly
> the soul rejects natural satisfaction the stronger and more
> detached its tenderness becomes.
>
> Saint Thérèse of Lisieux

Everything not of God is removed, including experiences that are mingled with the self's ambition and satisfactions. Mother Teresa was once asked about prophecies and succinctly responded with the essence of Truth:

> "Mother Teresa, do you have any prophecies for the future?"
> "Who am I to prophecy?," asks Mother Teresa, "I am nobody. I know only one thing. If people only had more love for each other, our life would be better. If more people realized that Jesus was in their neighbor, and they would help, things would be much better than they are."[4]

Transforming union is a tremendous learning process on multiple levels. We have been preparing each step of the darkened way for our work in His service. Our mind and heart are given everything necessary to fully express our destiny as a butterfly. The Divine shapes, by fire and illumination, "an instrument of peace."

Now the purified soul leaves the cocoon to begin a new life, exercising her full potential. She entered the cocoon feeling shipwrecked in a strange land. On wings of light, she exits her darkened hideaway, "shipwrecked into life again."

The Butterfly Stage: The Full Unitive State

The caterpillar has undergone a spectacular transformation in preparation for her new life as a butterfly. As she leaves the cocoon, she tests her wings on an unmarked trail of flight, to begin yet another phase of growth. Now she lives the ego-less life of a butterfly, and gives her self away in a selfless life of charity.

The soul, in spiritual maturity, experiences her greatest human potential. She has suffered the trials and tribulations of transforming union to emerge with expanded creativity and heightened intelligence. A fresh life has been infused into the soul, an enormous energy and vitality, unsolicited but humbly accepted. Supernatural illumination enhances natural abilities, completes all ideas of the mind, and makes strengths out of weaknesses. All categories of time and space and personality have been swallowed up by unifying love. The soul is sensitive, compassionate, loyal, gentle, kind, self-giving—the abundant life resulting from the Divine at work in her soul. She is God's unitive partner, sharing in creation, and ready to embark on the next phase of the journey.

Characteristics of the Full Unitive State

We experience absolute freedom and confidence in the full unitive state, secure within divine union. Situations which previously evoked emotional responses, now elicit compassion. Feelings of anger, jealousy, revenge, hate, greed—calling cards of our self-centered nature—no longer disturb us. They can beat at the windows and doors of the soul, but they cannot come inside. We live at a deeper level than our emotional nature. Calm and peace permeate our being, rather than occurring periodically as an emotional reaction:

> When the soul is naughted and transformed, then of herself she neither works nor speaks nor wills, nor feels nor hears nor understands; neither has she of herself the feeling of outward or inward, where she may move. And in all things it is God who rules and guides her, without

the mediation of any creature. And the state of this soul is then a feeling of such utter peace and tranquility that it seems to her that her heart, and her bodily being, and all both within and without, is immersed in an ocean of utmost peace. . . . And she is so full of peace that though she press her flesh, her nerves, her bones, no other thing comes forth from them than peace.

Saint Catherine of Genoa

Neither do we see or experience evil in other people. What others call evil, we accept as spiritual immaturity or ignorance, even when people take advantage of the soul's goodness and trust. *Whatever happens—joy or sorrows, acceptance or rejection, love or hate—the soul united with God experiences compassion.* Each act is unquestionably accepted as God's will in the grand scheme of life.

The soul perfects the science of love. She sees God in others, so loves unconditionally, for it is He that she loves in people. It is to others' highest good that she is devoted, however, rather than to feelings originating from the emotional plane of consciousness. Pure love and compassion are polished diamonds in the crown of the soul.

The butterfly's vocation and the course of her destiny is selfless giving. For the remainder of her life she will actualize love and wisdom in the world. Perhaps it will be in heroic action, perhaps by small endeavors in home and office, classroom or street corner, hospital or next door. She will work to awaken people to spiritual Truth. Life has an inviolable sacredness, and it must be nurtured. In living charity, the soul will mend what is broken, befriend the forsaken, hold the hand of the lonely dying. It is her purpose. The soul's loving attention brings Truth from its hiddenness before the eyes of others.

But it is not altruistic service. There is no personal fulfillment; love is the water of life given to all who thirst. The soul is simply expressing her love for God; it is her true identity in Him. And in His mysterious ways, God is using up self-consciousness, preparing the soul for a time of no duality.

The soul for all its beauty, however, has no outward symbol of this divine metamorphosis: no badges, no signs denoting her fearless courage, not even a sterling personality universally loved. Society's standards of success measured in money, prestige, and power are without meaning to a soul sharing the divine life. Some people mistakenly believe the soul in union with God will be publicly honored and become famous. In reality, there are usually no songs of praise, no tributes. Instead, people may turn their heads away and condemn her message. The thorns of misunderstanding, however, do not wither the flowering soul. She serves obediently, in conformity with the word of God, in the face of all criticism. She is a servant of God, and a servant neither boasts of her spiritual estate nor retreats from adversity. The transformed soul knows each receives light according to the degree in which we live in Truth. She understands the way of the world:

> ... the butterfly can never rejoin the caterpillar as long as he lives. The butterfly is not an extraordinary caterpillar; rather, he is a different type altogether.
>
> When the butterfly returns, the caterpillars do not recognize him anymore: he is an outsider. Nobody wants what he has to give; nobody is interested in his new knowledge. If the butterfly tries to give them some perspective on their creeping lives they are outraged, call him a fraud, and bring him down. They may even put him to death. Because the butterfly has returned full and overflowing, being dismissed, ignored, and misunderstood is a bewildering predicament. Like Santa Claus returning with good things for all men, he discovers he cannot give anything away. What we have here is no success story; there will be no glory in this unitive life. It will not be easy—Christ lasted only three years among the caterpillars. Yet to be put down, put out, and put away is the way it is supposed to go. To be rejected is the way forward now; it is the essence of the new movement, and what will demand the exercise of the full unitive life.[5]

The soul finally discovers she cannot give the divine spark to others. The butterfly flies higher and sees a different vision that cannot be shared with earthbound travelers. We are powerless to give God to others; only He can give Himself. The vision must be borne alone, in the solitude of our heart.

In the full unitive state, self-satisfaction is extinct; it was sacrificed for real love. Yet, we experience difficulties common to everyone in the human family—financial pressures, physical pains, fatigue, etc.

The soul in full spiritual maturity may be burdened by the weight of this suffering, but her inward security never ceases. Her union with God is true and constant, withstanding all indifference, misunderstanding, and criticism. The peaceful center holds, unmoved. All that opposes and grieves the soul increases her absolute dependence on God. The last smears on the window of the soul are being wiped clean; there are no more subtle dependencies on anything but the Divine. Now we stand only in the abiding love of God, in this world but not of it.

The View From the Summit

The summit of the high mountain of Truth provides a clearer vision of the path of grace than can any spot along the upward climb. In retrospect, looking back down the mountain, the milestones and landscape of the path traveled stand in bold relief.

We discover it has been a constantly repetitive journey, experienced from ever-deepening levels of consciousness. It is not a straight line movement, but a spiral in which increasingly subtle aspects of self are revealed, transformed, and reunified as we journey to God and live in full union with Him.

The world, however, is the same; but our response is one of compassionate understanding. Cooked in the fires of love, our emotions are now quiet, not swayed by every gust of passion. We live and experience a deeper level of Reality than our emotional system. Flights of imagination and fantasy are grounded to the anchor of Truth. We are totally present to every moment, not revelling in the past or creating an imaginative future.

Our mind, sharpened as His instrument and infused with light, pierces veils of ignorance. It easily unravels the tangles in the world's priorities and corrupted values, seeing them for what they are, and pointing the way to eternal values. Mystics, saints, and world religions are right: the path is narrow. *There is no balancing act between God and the rest of our life. God is the first priority*. Sometimes the world, in its confusion, places love of people, experiences, and things first.

Our passage to God is a journey through the contents and energies of consciousness. From instincts to archetypes, nothing escapes the blinding gaze of Truth—everything is unmasked, transformed, and unified. It is a slow reorganization of our entire being, a unification of character. *Our personality, however, remains the same. The Divine is interested in deeper aspects than the quirks and preferences of personality.*

During the journey, psychological structures are repeatedly broken down creating disequilibrium, followed by peace. Recurring disruption, adjustment, and peace accompany each movement to a deeper level of consciousness. Beliefs, thoughts, constructs about God, judgments, prejudice, emotional blocks, patterns of thinking and living are continually unhinged from their secure place and refined. Antique behavior patterns reflective of earlier stages of development are discarded. Now all behavior is directed into one stream of purpose.

We have been released from egocentric judgments. We no longer ask questions like, "What does it mean to me?", "What do I want?", "What would make me feel better?", "How can I show I am better than you?", "What can I accomplish?". These are questions of spiritual immaturity. There is nothing left to become, no expectations to build. The world is our family; wherever we happen to be is home. We live in the full unitive state, accepting our humanity and living to our full potential united to God in the deepest center of our being.

We have undergone a complete transformation of consciousness—all because God revealed our union with Him and made us partners in the divine life. Only now, living many years on the summit in the full unitive state, do we fully understand what this means. We thought we knew before, but it was a partial understanding. Now it is a knowing, borne of experience, which we live with fearless abandon. We have adjusted to the Divine on its ground, rather than knowing God through the ego's receipt of sensory data.

Life at the summit is not abstract or dreamy, neither is it a hibernation from the world. It is a full integration of active and contemplative life, of our outer and inner world. We know that in its essence, life is love. Secure in divine union, we live in the center of a love that transcends all diversity. This union of love in the heart of God overflows to practical acts of love guided by wisdom, scattered wherever there is need. Life becomes one continuous act of charity.

The spiritual journey is a pilgrimage home to God in the center of our soul to then live selflessly as a co-creator with Him in the world. It is a passage of grace in which the Divine purifies by fire, then weaves love, wisdom, and peace into the fabric of our being. We are humbled, joyous, and obedient to His will—we could not do otherwise. Then, after long years of sharing the divine life in the unitive state, we transcend self-consciousness and go beyond the self to our final destiny. In Christianity, Christ shows us the way and takes us to our ultimate stage of development.

The unitive state with God can only be known through experience, yet only when we reach the summit will we *know* what we experienced. But we can get a glimpse of other pilgrims who have made the journey. We can see the outward effects, or the fruits, of the unitive state. And we can touch the spirit of grace as we see it expressed in His "instruments of peace."

Peace Pilgrim (1908-1981)

Chapter III

Peace Pilgrim

I am a pilgrim, a wanderer. I shall remain a wanderer until mankind has learned the way of peace, walking until I am given shelter and fasting until I am given food.[1]

For twenty-eight years, Peace Pilgrim lived this pledge. She began her walk across the United States on January 1, 1953, when she set out, penniless, from the Tournament of Roses Parade in Pasadena, California:

I walked ahead along the line of march, talking to people and handing out peace messages, and noticing that the holiday spirit did not lessen the genuine interest in peace. When I had gone about half-way a policeman put his hand on my shoulder and I thought he was going to tell me to get off the line of march. Instead he said, "What we need is thousands like you."

What happened to me in the Los Angeles area in the beginning was almost miraculous. All channels of communication were opened to me, and my little peace

49

message. I spent hours being interviewed by newspaper reporters and being photographed by newspaper photographers. The story of the pilgrimage and even my picture went out over all the wire services. Besides doing two live television programs, I spent hours recording for radio and the television newscasts.

Newspapers all along the line from Los Angeles to San Diego were interested. In San Diego I did one television program and four radio shows. The head of the San Diego Council of Churches approved of my message and my three petitions, and they were widely circulated in the churches.[2]

Of her pilgrimage, she said, "A pilgrim is a wanderer with a purpose. A pilgrimage can be to a place—that's the best known kind—but it also be for a thing. Mine is for peace, and that's why I am a Peace Pilgrim." She walked "as a prayer" and the chance to inspire others to pray and work for peace: "when enough of us find inner peace, our institutions will become more peaceful, and there will be no more occasion for war."

Peace Pilgrim wore a navy blue shirt and slacks, tennis shoes, and a short tunic with pockets all around the bottom. Everything she needed, all her worldly possessions, was carried in these pockets: comb and folding toothbrush, ballpoint pen and current correspondence, and copies of her peace message: "This is the way of peace. Overcome evil with good, falsehood with truth, and hatred with love." To make contacts in the "kindest way," her tunic had PEACE PILGRIM printed in white letters on the front and 25,000 MILES ON FOOT FOR PEACE on the back.

Even in the early years when Peace Pilgrim was unknown, she never missed more than three or four meals before someone offered her food. She found shelter in haystacks or bus stations, in drainage pipes or under bridges, on beaches or road sides, in cemeteries or wheat fields. Sometimes a friendly sheriff unlocked an empty jail cell in which she could rest. And once, she slept on the seat of a fire engine in Tombstone, Arizona. As strangers became friends, they invited her into their homes and arranged speaking engagements for her, often a year or more in advance.

This foot traveler walked with tireless energy, averaging twenty-five miles a day, and sometimes as many as fifty miles, to arrive at speaking engagements on time. Her routes carried her north in summer and south in winter to avoid the worst weather. When cold, she stuffed newspapers under her tunic to keep warm and slept under a stack of leaves. In harsh cold, she walked all night. After walking 25,000 miles, which took from 1953 until 1964, she stopped counting miles. Speaking became her priority, and she often accepted rides to keep her appointed schedule.

Peace Pilgrim initially began speaking to groups almost on the spur of the moment:

> While passing through San Diego that first year I was introduced into public speaking. A high school teacher approached me on the street and inquired if I would speak to her class. I told her in all fairness that as Peace Pilgrim I had never spoken to a group before. She assured me that it would be fine and asked only that I would answer the students' questions. I agreed. If you have something worthwhile to say, you can say it. Otherwise, why in the world would you want to be speaking?
>
> I have no problem speaking before a group. When you have completely surrendered to God's will, the way seems easy and joyous. It is only before you have completely surrendered that the way seems difficult. When I speak, energy flows through me like electricity flows through a wire.
>
> In the beginning, my speaking engagements were often arranged on the spur of the moment. As I was walking past a school the principal came out and said, "My students are looking at you from the windows. If you would come in and talk to them we'll gather them in the gymnasium." So I did.
>
> Then at noon, a man from one of the civic clubs approached me and said, "My speaker disappointed us. Will you come and speak at our luncheon?" And of course I did.
>
> The same afternoon a college professor on the way to his class stopped me and asked, "Could I take you to my students?" So I spoke to his class.[3]

Peace Pilgrim willingly accepted speaking engagements to spread her peace message. In every situation she saw the seed of a spiritual lesson. She also graciously accepted the hardships and tests along the way.

She was arrested twice for vagrancy, and once told her interrogators, "You can imprison the body, but not the spirit." Behind bars but spiritually lifted, she led songs and talked to her cellmates about inner peace. No one had ever seen the likes of this woman! The judge dismissed the case the next day, and she was officially released as a "pilgrim with a religious purpose." Officers, won over by her attitude and cheerfulness, drove her back to the highway to the exact spot of her arrest so she could continue her pilgrimage.

On another occasion, a psychologically ill teenage boy, startled by a thunderstorm, beat her. But Peace Pilgrim did not lift a hand. The boy suddenly stopped and fell to the ground sobbing, genuinely remorseful. Peace Pilgrim said, "A spark of good is in everyone, no matter how deeply it may be buried." In that moment, it had been reached in the boy and serious harm was avoided.

In her most difficult test, she defended a terrified eight-year-old girl against a large man who intended to beat her:

> I was staying at a ranch and the family went into town. The little girl did not want to go with them, and they asked, since I was there, could I take care of the child? I was writing a letter by the window when I saw a car arrive. A man got out of the car. The girl saw him and ran and he followed, chasing her into a barn. I went immediately into the barn. The girl was cowering in terror in the corner. He was coming at her slowly and deliberately . . . I put my body immediately between the man and the girl. I just stood and looked at this poor, psychologically sick man with loving compassion. He came close. He stopped! He looked at me for quite a while. He then turned and walked away and the girl was safe. There was not a word spoken.
>
> Now, what was the alternative? Suppose I had been so foolish as to forget the law of love by hitting back and relying upon the jungle law of tooth and claw? Undoubtedly

I would have been beaten—perhaps even to death and possibly the little girl as well! Never underestimate the power of God's love—it transforms! It reaches the spark of good in the other person and the person is disarmed.[4]

Peace Pilgrim said that she never experienced any real danger on her walks. Once a man in a speeding truck threw something at her. It turned out to be a fistful of crumpled dollar bills, which she donated to the next church in which she spoke. Occasionally, there were extreme weather conditions. She walked in a dust storm in blowing winds too strong to stand against, and dust too thick to see ahead:

> A policeman stopped alongside me, threw open his car door and yelled, "Get in here, woman, before you get killed." I told him I was walking a pilgrimage and did not accept rides (at that time). I also told him that God was my shield and there was nothing to fear. At that moment the winds died down, the dust settled and the sun broke through the clouds. I continued to walk. But the wonderful thing was that I felt spiritually lifted above the hardship.[5]

People scoffed at Peace Pilgrim when she began her pilgrimage. Friends counseled against it. Family members worried. One said she would die within the first year. She was undaunted. Her pilgrimage began in an era before peace marchers, before there was much concern with inner peace. By the late sixties and seventies, however, more people were interested in peace and spiritual growth. Yet, Peace Pilgrim did not try to persuade these new enthusiasts to make a pilgrimage. Instead, she inspired them to live their lives in harmony with divine purpose. She once wrote, "Some people have asked if I accept disciples. Of course, I do not. It is not healthy to follow another human being."[6]

Many were inspired to change the direction of their lives after talking with Peace Pilgrim. Others, though enthusiastic about the pilgrimage, were entangled in a self-made web of false success:

I remember one day as I walked along the highway a very nice car stopped and a man inside said to me, "How wonderful that you are following your calling!" I replied, "I certainly think that everyone should be doing what he or she feels is the right thing to do."

He then began telling me what he felt motivated toward, and it was a good thing that needed doing. I got quite enthusiastic about it and took it for granted that he was doing it. I said, "That's wonderful! How are you getting along with it?" And he answered, "Oh, I'm not doing it. That kind of work doesn't pay anything."

I shall never forget how desperately unhappy that man was. In this materialistic age we have such a false criteria by which to measure success. We measure it in terms of dollars, in terms of material things. But happiness and inner peace do not lie in that direction. If you know but do not do, you are a very unhappy person indeed.

I had another roadside experience when a fine car stopped with a well-dressed couple inside who began to talk to me. I started to explain to them what I was doing. Suddenly, to my amazement, the man burst into tears. He said, "I have done nothing for peace and you have to do so much."

And then there was the time when another man stopped his car to talk with me. He looked at me, not unkindly, but with extreme surprise and curiosity, as though he just glimpsed a live dinosaur. "In this day and age," he explained, "with all the wonderful opportunities the world has to offer, what under the sun made you get out and walk a pilgrimage for peace?"

"In this day and age," I answered, "when humanity totters on the brink of a nuclear war of annihilation, it is not surprising that one life is dedicated to the cause of peace—but rather it is surprising that many lives are not similarly dedicated."[7]

At the time of her death, Peace Pilgrim was on her seventh journey across America. She had walked through the McCarthy era, the Korean War, the Cold War, the Vietnam War, and beyond. She had walked through all fifty states, and had visited the ten Canadian provinces and parts of Mexico. Although invited to India and Europe, she felt her work was in the United States. She believed that if this country learned the way of peace, people in other countries would be inspired to peace. While she focused primarily on inner peace, Peace Pilgrim was concerned about peace on all levels:

> My pilgrimage covers the entire peace picture: peace among nations, peace among groups, peace within our environment, peace among individuals, and the very, very important inner peace—which I talk about most often because that is where peace begins.[8]

On her first walk across America, Peace Pilgrim spoke and gathered signatures for three petitions. One was to end the Korean War which was partially accomplished before the first year of the pilgrimage was over. The second petition was directed to the President of the United States to request the establishment of a Peace Department. Years later she wrote a follow-up letter:

LETTER TO PRESIDENT, VICE-PRESIDENT, CONGRESSIONAL LEADERS:

Dear Friend:

I'm writing you, and some of our other leaders, about a suggestion for a step toward peace.

I've been walking and speaking throughout our country for almost 25 years, and the more I learn to know it, the more I learn to appreciate it. We've gone through a good cleansing in the past few years, and it may not be over yet, but our basic values still remain—our kind hearts, our individual democracy, our political democracy. In many ways we can still be an example to the world.

Let us lead the world toward peace by establishing a Peace Department in our government. I see such a department as having three main functions, as follows:

It would do extensive research on peaceful ways of resolving conflicts—realistic research for the age in which we live.

It would deal with our national problems in connection with world disarmament and world peace, like the adjustment of our economy to a peaceful situation.

It would be an example—it would be established with some fanfare, and we would ask every other nation to establish a similar department and work with us for peace.

This is a time for great decisions which future generations will bless us for.

Sincerely and peacefully, *Peace Pilgrim*

P.S. - Also let us ask in the United Nations for the establishment of a world language, to be taught as a second language. I believe this would be the biggest single step we could take toward world understanding—and a long stride toward world peace.[9]

The Cabinet level Peace Department has yet to be established.

The third petition was to the United Nations and world leaders:

If you would find the way of peace you must overcome evil with good and falsehood with truth and hatred with love. We plead with you to free us all from the crushing burden of armaments, to free us from hatred and fear, so that we may feed our hungry ones, mend our broken cities, and experience a richness of life which can only come in a world that is unarmed and fed.[10]

She presented the signed petitions from individuals, peace groups, churches, and organizations to officials at the White House and the United Nations at the conclusion of her first walk. This pilgrim of peace delivered in tangible form the hopes of Americans for a peaceful world.

Peace Pilgrim walked cross-country year after year and talked about peace. In the early years, her feet were her sole means of transportation. She walked alone, on faith, amidst the beauty of nature—emerging stars, the moon, reflections of trees in glassy lakes, fields of wild flowers, the spring song of birds—all God's signature of love. To Peace Pilgrim, nature was a living sanctuary in which she walked in prayer.

While others crept out of crowded houses for office or school or to attend some pleasure, Peace Pilgrim lived in the still silence that answers loudly to those who listen. She had inner peace, and it radiated out to all she met.

Beyond the chatter of voices and lives made unnecessarily complex, she lived simply and in harmony with all living things. Peace Pilgrim would not think of wounding one of nature's creatures. She valued all God's offspring.

Throughout the pilgrimage, God provided the creature comforts she needed—cold water from a spring, wild berries for food, star lamps at night. Sometimes this chilled traveler slept nestled under God's bedclothes—the fallen leaves. He always provided.

Through the years she observed the evidence of peace everywhere—in the colors of morning and evening, in sunset clouds, in summer leaves scattered in the wind, in the brisk breeze of a new autumn day. Nature's ways were a constant reminder of God's peaceful, orderly universe. Peace Pilgrim loved nature's eloquence; it was her home.

When her first cross-country walk ended, Peace Pilgrim "was thankful she had not failed to do what she had been called to do":

> I either said or thought to myself, "Isn't it wonderful that God can do something through me!"
>
> Afterward I slept at the Grand Central Station railroad terminal in New York City. When I came into the state between sleep and wakefulness, I had an impression that an indescribably beautiful voice was speaking words of encouragement: *"You are my beloved daughter in whom I am well pleased."* When I came into full wakefulness it seemed as though a celestial orchestra had just finished playing in the station, with its echoes still lingering on. I walked along the cement sidewalk, but I felt I was walking on clouds. The feeling of living in harmony with divine purpose has never left me.[11]

Peace Pilgrim "made the glorious transition to a freer life" on July 7, 1981, near Knox, Indiana. She died instantly in a head-on collision with an inebriated truck driver as she was being driven to a speaking engagement.

Messages of condolence came from across the country. Those who knew her felt they had lost their best friend. They remembered "her love and easy laughter, her ready wit and contagious zest." They had been touched by one who spoke with simple yet profound wisdom, and who served with a cheerful obedience to her calling. It was ironic that friends knew so much about her but knew nothing of her past. Only when her physical body died did they learn that her name was Mildred Norman and that the "friend" in Cologne, New Jersey who forwarded her mail for twenty-eight years was her sister, Helen.[12*]

"This is the way of peace. Overcome evil with good, falsehood with truth, and hatred with love." A simple message, but not a new one. What was extraordinary was the stunning example of one woman who lived spiritual truth as a practical way of life. The day before her death, she concluded a radio interview in Knox, Indiana by saying, "I certainly am a happy person. Who could know God and not be joyous? I want to wish you all peace." Peace Pilgrim, in her own words, summed up her life, her message, and her wish for the world.

The Making of a Pilgrim

Mildred Norman never revealed her given name or details about her past. She believed her message to be more important than her pre-pilgrim life. Born in 1908 in Egg Harbor City, New Jersey to Ernest and Josephine Norman, she was the oldest of three children. For the first twenty-five years of her life, Mildred lived on the family poultry farm, often plucking chicken feathers with her sister for a penny a chicken. It was a sparsely settled area, without municipal water and sewage. The family may have been poor, but Mildred felt rich with woods to play in, a creek to swim in, and daily exercise from the two-mile walk to school. It

---

*Footnotes 12-14, 16-18 are from a personal interview with John and Ann Rush conducted by the author at the Peace Pilgrim Center in Hemet, California on July 20, 1989.

was a close family, and she remembered her childhood as a happy time.[13]

Although Mildred had no religious training as a child, she was brought up with strong principles. Good conduct was a way of life with the Normans. Her father, whom she adored, was a building contractor respected for both his skill and his honesty. Thus, when Mildred was short of money, she bought whatever she needed on credit. Townspeople knew that the family always paid their debts.

The extended family had a strong influence on Mildred. Four aunts and an uncle, all unmarried, lived near the Norman house. They were pacifists, and believed in educating people rather than fighting with them. Mildred's early education in peace and nonviolence began with lengthy discussions with her aunts and uncle.[14]

Her sister and brother remember Mildred as a spirited child with a presence that made other children listen to her. She was captain of the high school debate team. She loved to dance at the Grange Hall dances, and she acted and directed the town theatrical group plays. Unlike the simply dressed Peace Pilgrim, Mildred liked fancy clothes, and even traveled to Atlantic City for shoes to match her hat and gloves.

Considered serious and strong-willed, though mild-mannered, Mildred was unacquainted with fear and defeat. A frequent daredevil, she dived off a tall bridge into the river, though warned of the dangers.

In contrast to her later vegetarian diet, the young Mildred craved meat and potatoes, and hated all vegetables except green beans. When offered second helpings at dinner, she called for "more meat." While in her pilgrimage years, she ate only healthy foods; as a youth, ice cream sundaes were a lunchtime ritual. And, while she was never ill as the Peace Pilgrim, she continuously had tonsillitis and headaches as a child.

Her message of peace emphasized tolerance ("Be concerned that you do not offend, not that you are not offended"), but as a teenager she disapproved of her sister's friends, especially those of different races and classes.

During her senior year in high school, Mildred began her search for God. Later she said:

I went about inquiring, "What is God? What is God?" I was more inquisitive and I asked many questions of many people, but I never received any answers! However, I was not about to give up. Intellectually, I could not find God on the outside, so I tried another approach. I took a long walk with my dog and pondered deeply upon the question. Then I went to bed and slept over it. And in the morning I had my answer from inside, through a still small voice.

Now my high school answer was a very simple answer—that we human beings just lump together everything in the universe which is beyond the capacity of all of us, and to all those things together some of us give the name of God. Well, that set me on a search. And the first thing I did was to look at a tree, and I said, *there's one*. All of us working together couldn't create that one tree, and even if it looked like a tree it wouldn't grow. There is a creative force beyond us. And then I looked at my beloved stars at night and *there's another*. There's a sustaining power that keeps planets in their orbit.

I watched all the changes taking place in the universe. At that time they were trying to keep a lighthouse from washing into the sea. They finally moved it inland and said they had saved it. But I noticed all these changes and I said, *there's another*. There is something motivating towards constant change in the universe.

When I reached my confirmation from within I knew beyond all doubt that I had touched my highest light.

Intellectually I touched God many times as truth and emotionally I touched God as love. I touched God as goodness. I touched God as kindness. It came to me that God is a creative force, a motivating power, an over-all intelligence, an ever-present, all pervading spirit—which binds everything in the universe together and gives life to everything. That brought God close. I could not be where God is not. You are within God. God is within you.[15]

In 1933, Mildred Norman eloped with a man of whom her family disapproved, and moved to Philadelphia. Disinterested in homemaking and rearing children, she hungered for learning and improving herself. Two nights a week, she attended courses in psychology and public speaking. When her husband worked the late shift and left home at three o'clock in the afternoon, Mildred walked out the door behind him and attended evening Quaker meetings. Frequently, the meetings concluded with late night coffee and further discussions about peace.[16]

The day her husband entered military service was the day their marriage died. And when Mildred discovered a portion of her income tax paid for war armaments, she resigned her job, and found work as a twelve-dollar-a-week bookkeeper. Her income was then insufficient to be taxed. Mildred's principles were firm: she would not pay for war or visit her military husband who supported the war effort. He, eventually, was stationed overseas, and later they divorced.[17]

As time passed, Mildred became increasingly distressed about the impoverishment in the world. Some had so much; others were literally starving. That, coupled with her strained marriage and her father's death in an automobile accident, created considerable inner distress. It culminated in an all-night walk in the woods "in desperation and out of a very deep seeking for a meaningful way of life." During her all-night vigil she had a revelation that her life would be devoted to service:[18]

> I came to a moonlit glade and prayed. I felt a complete willingness without reservation to give my life—to dedicate my life—to service. "Please use me!" I prayed to God. And a great peace came over me . . . .
>
> . . . However, there's a great deal of difference between being willing to give your life and actually giving your life, and for me fifteen years of preparation and inner seeking lay between.[19]

In the beginning of the preparation years, Mildred helped people in simple ways such as reading to the recuperating ill and visiting the elderly. Later she worked with troubled teenagers, emotionally disturbed adults, and the physically impaired. Off and on for ten years, she did volunteer work with various peace groups including the American Friends Service Community, the Women's International League for Peace and Freedom, and the Fellowship of Reconciliation. At the same time, Mildred underwent a rigorous inner transformation as she began to mature spiritually. Then in 1953 the pilgrimage began. The silver-haired woman became Peace Pilgrim, spending her retirement years as a "penniless pilgrim on a journey undertaken on foot and in faith."

Spiritually Growing Up

Peace Pilgrim was poor, with little education, and, according to her, had "no special talents." Yet, she underwent a complete spiritual and psychological transformation that was beyond the comprehension of those who knew her.

It began during her all-night walk when she totally surrendered to God. There were no promises or bargains; nothing was held back. It was an absolute surrendering of the heart. From that moment, she began leaving the self-centered nature and entering the God-centered life:

> Spiritual growth is a process the same as physical growth or mental growth. Five-year-old children do not expect to be as tall as their parents at their next birthday; the first grader does not expect to graduate into college at the end of the term; the truth student should not expect to attain inner peace overnight. It took me fifteen years.[20]

Peace Pilgrim later referred to this slow evolutionary process as her "steps to inner peace."

STEPS TO INNER PEACE

> I was not far down the spiritual road when I became acquainted with what psychologists refer to as ego and conscience, which I call the lower self and the higher self, or the self-centered nature and the God-centered nature. It's as though we have two selves or natures or two wills with two contrary viewpoints . . . .
>
> Your lower self sees you as the center of the universe—your higher self sees you as a cell in the body of humanity . . . .
>
> The body, mind and emotions are instruments which

can be used by either the self-centered nature or the God-centered nature. The self-centered nature uses these instruments, yet it is never fully able to control them, so there is a constant struggle. They can only be fully controlled by the God-centered nature.

When the God-centered nature takes over, you have found inner peace. Until that time comes, a partial control can be gained through discipline. It can be discipline imposed from without through early training which has become a part of the subconscious side of the self-centered nature. It can be discipline undertaken voluntarily; self-discipline. Now if you are doing things you know you shouldn't do and don't really want to do, you certainly lack discipline. I recommend spiritual growing—in the meantime self-discipline.

During the spiritual growing up period the inner conflict can be more or less stormy. Mine was about average. The self-centered nature is a very formidable enemy and it struggles fiercely to retain its identity. It defends itself in a cunning manner and should not be regarded lightly. It knows the weakest spots of your armor and attempts a confrontation when one is least aware. During these periods of attack, maintain a humble stature and be intimate with none but the guiding whisper of your higher self.

The higher self has been given many wonderful names by religious leaders, some calling the higher governing power the *inner light*, or the *indwelling Christ*. When Jesus said, "The Kingdom of God is within you," he was obviously referring to the higher self. In another place it says, *Christ in you, your hope of glory, the indwelling Christ*. Jesus was called the Christ because his life was governed by this higher governing power.[21]

Peace Pilgrim gave voice to her spirit, in simple words which would quietly wind their way into her listener's heart. She bore witness to a profound Truth that answered the deep hunger of the soul. Her lovely, silent walks brought this noble truth to the farmer on a warm, dark night; to the housewife as rain caressed the lofty oaks in crimson foliage; to the college student nestled in the halls of knowledge, eager for learning. She wandered up and down the country in blessed joy and peace, a presence of simplicity. Her words are now a written prayer of how to discover life.

As we read her simple words on "preparation, purification, and relinquishment," an inner clarity explodes our habitual way of thinking. As if now a witness to life, we receive the benediction of greater wisdom, an impersonal truth so different than the mental whirlpools and enslaving desires which pull us away from the deepest longing of our heart. Life not built on a solid foundation splinters into undercurrents of conflicting passions and darkness. Peace Pilgrim's words pierce the night, leaving footprints of light in the soul, as radiant as a deep snow sparkling in the moon. Her message is a wayshower to a life which transcends all separation and division. But it all began with what Peace Pilgrim simply calls "preparations":

Preparations

I would like to mention some preparations that were required of me. The first preparation is to take a *right attitude toward life*. This means, stop being an escapist! . . . Be willing to face life squarely and get down beneath the surface of life where the verities and realities are to be found.

. . . If only you could see the whole picture, if you knew the whole story, you would realize that no problem ever comes to you that does not have a purpose in your life, that cannot contribute to your inner growth. When you perceive this, you will recognize that problems are opportunities in disguise. If you did not face problems, you would just drift through life. It is through solving problems in accordance with the highest light we have that inner growth is attained.

The second preparation has to do with *bringing our lives into harmony with the laws that govern this universe*. Created are not only the worlds and the beings, but also the laws that govern them. Applying both in the physical realm and in the psychological realm, these laws govern human conduct. Insofar as we are able to understand and bring our lives into harmony with these laws, our lives will be in harmony. Insofar as we disobey these laws, we create difficulties for ourselves by our disobedience. We are our own worst enemies. If we are out of harmony through ignorance, we suffer somewhat; but if we know better and are still out of harmony, then we suffer a great deal. Suffering pushes us toward obedience . . . .

There is a third preparation that has to do with something which is unique for every human life, because every one of us has *a special place in the Life Pattern* . . . . There is a guidance which comes from within to all who will listen. Through this guidance each one will feel drawn to some part in the scheme of things . . . .

You begin to do your part in the Life Pattern by doing all of the good things you feel motivated toward, even though they are just little good things at first. You give these priority in your life over all the superficial things that customarily clutter human lives . . . .

There is a fourth preparation. It is *the simplification of life*, to bring inner and outer well-being, psychological and material well-being, into harmony in your life. This was made very easy for me. Just after I dedicated my life to service, I felt that I could no longer accept *more* than I need while others in the world have *less* than they need. This moved me to bring my life down to *need level*. I thought it would be difficult. I thought it would entail a great many hardships, but I was quite wrong. Instead of hardships, I found a wonderful sense of peace and joy, and a conviction that unnecessary possessions are only unnecessary burdens . . . .

Purifications

Then I discovered that there were some purifications required of me. The first one is such a simple thing: it is *purification of the body*. This had to do with my physical living habits. I used to eat all the standard foods. I shudder now to think of what I used to dump into this temple of the spirit . . . .

Now I eat mostly fruits, nuts, vegetables, whole grains (preferably organically grown) and perhaps a bit of milk and cheese. This is what I live on and walk on . . . .

I realized that I was disobeying my rule of life which says: *I will not ask anyone to do for me things that I would refuse to do for myself.* Now, I shouldn't kill any creature—and therefore I stopped immediately eating all flesh . . . .

The difficulty is we have not learned to stop killing *each other* yet. That's our present lesson—not to kill each other. To learn the lesson of sharing and the lesson of non-killing of man by man. The lesson of non-killing of creatures is a little bit into the future, though those of us who know better need to live up to our highest light . . . .

There is a second purification: *purification of thought.* If you realized how powerful your thoughts are, you would never think a negative thought. They can be a powerful influence for good when they're on the positive side, and they can and do make you physically ill when they're on the negative side. I don't eat junk foods and I don't think junk thoughts . . . .

If you're harboring the slightest bitterness toward anyone, or any unkind thoughts of any sort whatever, you must get rid of them quickly. They are not hurting anyone but you. It isn't enough just to do right things and say right things—you must also *think* right things before your life can come into harmony . . . .

The third purification is *the purification of desire* . . . . Since you are here to get yourself in harmony with the laws that govern human conduct and with your part in the scheme of things, your desires should be focused in this direction. It's very important to get your desires *centered* so you will desire only to do God's will for you. You can come to the point of oneness of desire, just to know and do your part in the Life Pattern . . . .

There is one more purification, and that is *purification of motive.* What is your motive for whatever you may be doing? If it is pure greed or self-seeking or the wish for self-glorification, I would say, *don't do that thing.* Don't do anything you would do with such a motive. But that isn't easy because we tend to do things with mixed motives . . . .

. . . The motive, if you are to find inner peace, must be an outgoing motive. Service, of course, *service.* Giving, not getting. Your motive must be good if your work is to have good effect. The secret of life is being of service . . . .

Relinquishments

. . . Once you've made the first relinquishment you have found inner peace, because it's *the relinquishment of self-will.*

You can work on subordinating the lower self by refraining from doing the not-good things you may be motivated toward—not suppressing them, but transforming them so that the highest self can take over your life . . . .

The second relinquishment is *the relinquishment of the feeling of separateness.* We begin feeling very separate and judging everything as it relates to us, as though we were the center of the universe . . . . In reality, of course, we are all cells in the body of humanity. We are not separate from fellow humans. The whole thing is a totality. It's only from the higher viewpoint that you can know what it is to love your neighbor as yourself. From that higher viewpoint there becomes just one realistic way to work, and that is for the good of the whole.

Then there is the third relinquishment, and that is *the relinquishment of all attachments.* No one is truly free who is still attached to material things, or to places, or to people . . . . Anything that you cannot relinquish when it has outlived its usefulness possesses you, and in this materialistic age a great many of us are possessed by our possessions. We are not free . . . .

There is another kind of possessiveness. *You do not possess any other human being,* no matter how closely related that other may be . . . . When we think we possess people there is a tendency to run their lives for them, and out of this develops extremely inharmonious situations . . . .

In our spiritual development we are often required to pull up roots many times and to close many chapters in our lives until we are no longer attached to any material thing and can love all people without any attachment to them.

Now the last: *the relinquishment of all negative feelings.* I want to mention just one negative feeling which the nicest people still experience, and that negative feeling is *worry.* Worry is not *concern,* which would motivate you to do everything possible in a situation. Worry is a useless mulling of things we cannot change.

... No outward thing—nothing from without—can hurt me inside, psychologically. I recognized that I could only be hurt psychologically by my own wrong actions, which I have control over; by my own wrong reactions (they are tricky, but I have control over them, too); or by my own *inaction* in some situations, like the present world situation, that needs action from me. When I recognized all this how free I felt! ...

These are my steps toward inner peace .... There is nothing new about this. This is universal truth. I merely talked about these things in everyday words in terms of my own personal experience with them.[22]

Toward the end of the fifteen years, Peace Pilgrim had more fully acclimated to a state of consciousness which led to a complete readjustment of her inner life. Less and less of the self-centered nature was present. "There was a time—when I attained inner peace—when I died, utterly died to myself." Total energy and dedication were focused on serving God. The year before her pilgrimage began, her mission became apparent:

There were hills and valleys, lots of hills and valleys, in that spiritual growing up period. Then in the midst of the struggle there came a wonderful mountaintop experience—the first glimpse of what the life of inner peace was like.

That came when I was out walking in the early morning. All of a sudden I felt very uplifted, more uplifted than I had ever been. I remember I knew *timelessness* and *spacelessness* and *lightness*. I did not seem to be walking on the earth. There were no people or even animals around, but every flower, every bush, every tree seemed to wear a halo. There was a light emanation around everything and flecks of gold fell like slanted rain through the air. This experience is sometimes called the illumination period.

The most important part of it was not the phenomena: the important part of it was the realization of the oneness of all creation. Not only all human beings—I knew before that all human beings were one. But now I knew also a oneness with the rest of creation. The creatures that walk the earth and the growing things of the earth. The air, the water, the earth itself. And, most wonderful of all, *a oneness with that which permeates all and binds all together and gives life to all.* A oneness with that which many would call God.

I never felt separate since. I could return again and again to this wonderful mountaintop, and then I could stay there for longer and longer periods of time and just slip out occasionally.

The inspiration for the pilgrimage came at this time. I sat high on a hill overlooking rural New England. The day before I had slipped out of harmony, and the evening before I had thought to God, "It seems to me that if I could always remain in harmony I could be of greater usefulness—for every time I slip out of harmony it impairs my usefulness."

When I awoke at dawn I was back on the spiritual mountaintop with a wonderful feeling. I knew that I would never need to descend again into the valley. I knew that for me the struggle was over, that finally I had succeeded in giving my life or finding inner peace. Again this is a point of no return. You can never go back into the struggle. The struggle is over now because you *will* to do the right thing and you don't need to be pushed into it.

I went out for a time alone with God. While I was out a thought struck my mind: I felt a strong inner motivation toward the pilgrimage—toward this special way of witnessing for peace.

I saw, in my mind's eye, myself walking along and wearing the garb of my mission . . . . I saw a map of the United States with the large cities marked—and it was as though someone had taken a colored crayon and marked a zigzag line across, coast to coast and border to border, from Los Angeles to New York City. I knew what I was to do. And that was a vision of my first year's pilgrimage route in 1953!

I entered a new and wonderful world. My life was blessed with a meaningful purpose.[23]

On January 1, 1953, Peace Pilgrim celebrated her spiritual birthday, "the period when she was merged with the whole." It was also the beginning of her pilgrimage, when she became a wanderer relying on the goodness of others. The pilgrimage birthplace was the city of Angels—Los Angeles—and all claims to name, personal history, affiliations, and possessions were left behind.

Peace Pilgrim's appointed work was to awaken the divine nature within people. She tried to arouse people from apathy to seek the ultimate good: union with God. She often said religion is not an end in itself, but a stepping stone to God. And as is characteristic of the unitive state, she said that she had "no more feeling of need to become." She was content to be, and to "keep on growing—but harmoniously." She respected all religions, even though her path was not religious training:

> I believe Jesus would accept me because I do what he told people to do. This doesn't mean, though, that all who call themselves Christians would accept me. Of course, I love and appreciate Jesus and I wish Christians would learn to obey his commandments. It would mean a most wonderful world.[24]

She exemplified the way of love that emerges from union with God: "Pure love is a willingness to give, without a thought of receiving anything in return":

> I see the divine spark in people, and that's what I concentrate on. People look beautiful to me; they look like shining lights. I always have the feeling of being thankful for these beautiful people who walk the earth with me.[25]

Peace Pilgrim described living in the unitive state, the mature spiritual life, when she said:

> ... It's as though the central figure of the jigsaw of my life is complete and clear and unchanging, and around the edges other pieces keep fitting in. There is always a growing edge, but the progress is harmonious. There is a feeling of always being surrounded by all of the good things, like love and peace and joy. It seems like a protective surrounding, and there is an unshakableness within

which takes you through any situation you may need to face.

The world may look at you and believe that you are facing great problems, but always there are inner resources to easily overcome the problems. Nothing seems difficult. There is a calmness and a serenity and unhurriedness—no more striving or straining about anything. . . .[26]

Looking through the eyes of the divine nature you see the essence within the manifestation, the creator within the creation, and it is a wonderful world.[27]

A friend once asked Peace Pilgrim what to do with the printed copies of her peace message after her death. Peace Pilgrim nonchalantly replied, "Oh, just take what's here and send it out." She had no organizational support and no plans for her work beyond her lifetime. After she made her transition, five of her friends compiled her teachings in a book, *Peace Pilgrim: Her Life and Work in Her Own Words*, which is sent to whomever writes and requests a copy.

Someone asked Peace Pilgrim: "If you have grown up spiritually, how come you are not famous?" She replied, "Most people who have attained inner peace are not famous." Her message, however, has become far-reaching. Her book is now in over 104 countries, including China, the Soviet Union, Middle Eastern countries, India, Africa, Central America, and Europe. There is at least one copy on Maurituis, an island between Africa and India. The book is requested by people representing all religious faiths and by those who claim no religious affiliation at all. Letters from grateful readers, inspired by her message, have claimed that Peace Pilgrim must have been Catholic, Jewish, Christian, Buddhist, Hindu, or Islamic. Others are certain that she was a licensed psychologist. She was not a member of any religious faith or any organization. She was a penniless pilgrim teaching the way of peace that transcends all differences among people.

Mother Teresa (1910-   )

Courtesy AP/Wide World Photos, 1979.

Chapter IV

Mother Teresa

O God through free choice and through your love, I want to stay here and do your will. No, I cannot go back. My community are the poor. Their security is mine. Their health is my health. My home is the home of the poor: not just the poor, but of those who are the poorest of the poor. Of those to whom one tries not to get too close for fear of catching something, for fear of the dirt, or because they are covered in germs and disease. Of those that do not go to pray because they can't leave their house naked. Of those that no longer eat because they haven't the strength. Of those that fall in the street, knowing that they are going to die, while the living walk by their sides ignoring them. Of those who no longer cry, because they have no tears left. Of the untouchables.[1]

Mother Teresa, the frail Roman Catholic nun, has been called a contemporary saint. Her door opens to a vast sea of suffering humanity in cities crowded with the forgotten, the lonely, and the dying. In evening shadows, the poorest of the poor seek their night's lodging on the streets. Their bodies stumble against invisible chains of disease; their hearts hunger for a kind word, a gentle touch. Yet, while other people may turn their faces away as a shield of silent reproach, Mother Teresa advances in the spirit of love of He who created us. She opens the door of her soul, pouring love on the wounds of "Jesus in his distressing disguise." Mother Teresa sees the world that Love created, where every cry is heard and each private agony is in God's care. She is a messenger of love in the midst of suffering.

But she is not a humanitarian. Rather, she is directed by an inner experience revealed in the sacrament of Holy Communion. At the Last Supper, Jesus gave us one of the great mysteries of faith, the effects of a mystical union with Christ. In the fullness of this sublime mystery, we are one heart, one mind, one spirit with Christ. Lost in mystical union as a drop becomes lost in a chalice of wine, we yield completely to the mystery of Christ's love and are transformed in Him. With an enlightened heart, we know the charity of Christ which surpasses all understanding.

In active-contemplation, Mother Teresa labors in the world in the spirit of charity, obedience, simplicity, humility, and great purity of heart. That which contemplates within her, however, is He, who in the beginning bathed the horizon in golden light and flung stars into the night. As a contemplative-in-action, Mother Teresa works with God. She does not lose herself in activity, however, but abandons self to the will of God. Self-sacrificing action is an expression of love, and love is a release of spiritual energy through the invisible power and presence of God. Each day becomes a sanctuary in which the secret of life is fully lived, with the results of all labors left to the Divine alone. It is His work, and she is an instrument through which love finds expression. Over the years, others have joined Mother Teresa in the work with the poorest of the poor; today hands of love reach into most countries of the world.

Mother Teresa founded the Missionaries of Charity after going alone to work in the slums of Calcutta. Only one consecrated to God in unified love, however, would have ventured into a city of unmasked horrors to see Jesus in the "poorest of the poor."

During this century, all means of human destruction has visited Calcutta. Religious clashes, Hindu-Moslem bloodbaths, famines, and massacres—only a few of India's violent convulsions—left in their wake starving people, homeless children, and blood-stained bodies lying where they fell in the streets. In unimaginable agony, street people lived and died amidst flooded sewers of filth in a country where extreme poverty and riches coexist. Gandhi's nonviolent campaigns and historic Salt March focused the world's attention on the cruel indignities suffered by the people of India. In applying the Spirit of Truth to all situations of life, he sought to stir the conscience, transform political atrocities, and calm interreligious storms through love and peaceful nonviolence.

Embers of trouble still burned when Mother Teresa walked into the streets of Calcutta to answer a call within a call from God. The slums were filled with destitute street people and disease. Faces revealed an intimate experience with sorrow and despair; all around were people whose eyes were closed in death.

By living among and attending to the poorest of the poor, Mother Teresa answered the call to share the love of One who took up His cross and told others to put their feet on the Way and follow. "Come follow me" is a journey of faith. For Mother Teresa and the sisters, the journey has taken them to the doorstep of the world. Since its founding in 1949, the Missionaries of Charity Sisters and Brothers has grown to over 430 missions in 95 countries on five continents. They care for and run leper colonies, schools, AIDS facilities, soup kitchens, and homes for the dying.

From New York to Ethiopia, "over 126,000 families are being fed, 14,000 children are being taught, 186,000 leprosy victims are being treated and 22,000 dying and destitute are being cared for daily. All of this work is without government funds, grants, or solicitation of any funds. Mother Teresa says: it should be the spontaneous giving of those who are not afraid to love until it hurts."[2]

There are three groups of helpers who actively "love until it hurts." The Co-workers are 40,000 lay persons who meet regularly in their communities. They pray, prepare bandages, and minister to the needs of poor children. They join Mother Teresa in the worldwide work for God. Another group of over 800 people, called the sick and suffering, offers their pains for the success of the sisters' work. The third group, the contemplatives, supports the sisters through prayer and penance. The contemplatives have three hours of prayer at home and one hour in church. These three groups exemplify "love in action," and share in the work of Mother Teresa and the Missionaries of Charity.

On December 10, 1979, Mother Teresa was awarded the Nobel Prize for her decades of work with the poorest and most destitute people of Calcutta. She was nominated by Robert S. McNamara, a Presbyterian layman and former head of the World Bank. He nominated Mother Teresa "because she advances peace in the most fundamental way possible: by her extraordinary reaffirmation of the inviolability of human dignity."[3] When she arrived in Oslo to accept the Prize, she was honored by thousands of nameless men, women, and children who turned out to welcome her in a torchlight procession. They presented her with $70,000, the sum of small donations which they called the "Poor People's Nobel Prize."[4]

When Mother Teresa received the ultimate accolade, the Nobel Prize for Peace, she accepted it "in the name of the poor." Since her work has been a living prayer, it is not surprising that she turned the award ceremony into a prayer. Breaking with tradition, she asked everyone in the University of Oslo hall— King Olav, the Nobel Prize Committee, diplomats, academics, members of the armed services, the immense press corps, and friends—to join her in saying the Peace Prayer of Saint Francis of Assisi. Eight hundred voices rose in unison:

> Lord make me an instrument of thy Peace;
> Where there is hatred, let me sow Love;
> Where there is injury, Pardon;
> Where there is doubt, Faith;
> Where there is despair, Hope;
> Where there is sadness, Joy;
> Where there is darkness, Light;
> O Divine Master,
> Grant that I may not seek to be consoled, as to console,
> To be understood, as to understand,
> To be loved, as to love;
> For it is in giving that we receive,
> It is in pardoning that we are pardoned,
> It is in dying that we are born to Eternal Life.

Communal prayer was not the only change in protocol. Ordinarily, Nobel recipients are honored with a ceremonial banquet, further emphasizing the prestigious occasion. Mother Teresa simply told the committee to "please cancel the banquet and give the money to me for the poor."[5] The committee complied, and the $6,000 donation to the poor of Calcutta enabled Mother Teresa to feed hundreds more for a year.

In recognizing Mother Teresa, the world's attention focused on the poorest of the poor, the dying, the disinherited of the Earth. For her, that was the benefit of the Nobel Prize for Peace.

When Mother Teresa was called to work with the poor, however, she had no well-trod path to follow or public accolades to support her work:

> I was going to Darjeeling to make my retreat. It was on that train that I heard the call to give up all and follow Him into the slums—to serve Him in the poorest of the poor. I knew it was His will and that I had to follow Him. There was no doubt that it was to be His work.
>
> The message was quite clear . . . . I was to leave the convent and work with the poor while living among them. It was an order. I knew where I belonged, but I did not know how to get there.[6]

Mother Teresa started her work on December 21, 1948, when, with a few abandoned children around her, she began a school "right on the ground." A lone nun in Moti Jihl, a bustee in Calcutta, she began a school on faith in answer to her call. Later, she moved into a single, sparsely furnished room: one chair, a packing case for a desk, and wooden boxes for seats.

On her first trip along the streets of Calcutta, a priest approached Mother Teresa to ask for a contribution to the Catholic Press. She had started with five rupees (less than one dollar), and had already given four to the poor. She hesitated, then gave the last rupee to the priest. Later in the afternoon, the same priest visited her with an envelope from a man who had heard of her projects and wanted to help. The envelope contained fifty rupees. Mother Teresa knew in that moment that God had blessed the work and would not abandon her.[7] Soon, other donations began to trickle in, and, when needed, Mother Teresa asked pharmacists for donations of medicine for the suffering poor. In one prominent Calcutta pharmacy, Mother Teresa presented her long list of requirements:

> The pharmacist glanced at the list, said he could not help them, and insisted on finishing a deskfull of work. So Gomes (an Indian who arranged accommodations for Mother Teresa) and Mother Teresa sat down to wait, and while the pharmacist worked, Teresa calmly said her rosary. When he came to the end of his work, he looked at the list again and said, "Here are the medicines you need. Have them with the firm's compliments."[8]

During 1949 Mother Teresa applied for Indian citizenship and became a part of the country and people she would serve. In March 1949, on the feast of Saint Joseph, a Bengali girl of nineteen knocked at Mother Teresa's door, saying she would follow the dedicated nun anywhere and suffer whatever she suffered. Mother Teresa said what she has told hundreds who have responded to the call to love and serve: "There's no salary. There may not be even enough to eat. Just more and more work, more and more sacrifices, more and more service."[9]

The Bengali sister and several other followers were forerunners of a new community called the Missionaries of Charity. In late 1949, the archbishop began steps to have Mother Teresa and her small group recognized as a congregation for his archdiocese. Within two years, there were 28 young women who came to join Mother Teresa. Today there are 3,000 nuns serving all over the world. On October 7, 1950, the Missionaries of Charity were accepted as a new congregation in the diocese of Calcutta. The degree of recognition read:

> To fulfill our mission of compassion and love to the poorest of the poor we go:
> —seeking out in towns and villages all over the world even amid squalid surroundings the poorest, the abandoned, the sick, the infirm, the leprosy patients, the dying, the desperate, the lost, the outcasts;
> —taking care of them,

—rendering help to them,
—visiting them assiduously,
—living Christ's love for them, and
—awakening their response to His great love.[10]

This was not social work or a humanitarian project. Rather, this was a call from God to express His love in the world.

The first group of twelve nuns took the vows of the new order—poverty, chastity, obedience, and charity. Sister Teresa became Mother Teresa, foundress of the Missionaries of Charity. Each sister wore a white cotton sari. "The sari with its blue band is the sign of Mary's modesty; the girdle made of rope is the sign of Mary's angelic purity; sandals are a sign of our own free choice; and the crucifix is a sign of love."[11]

A young girl who leaves her life behind to express "God's love in action" with the Missionaries of Charity must meet four conditions: "She must be healthy in mind and body, have the ability to learn, and have common sense and a cheerful disposition."[12] All conditions are necessary to live a life totally dedicated to love.

It is a spartan existence. The sisters are free of possessions to more closely identify with the poor people they serve. There are no clothes from their personal life, no watches, no rings, no spending money. Each sister has two saris, underclothes, bedding, and a tin bucket in which to wash clothes. She has prayer books, pen and pencil, and paper for work purposes. The Missionaries of Charity begin their days early with Mass, Holy Communion, and meditation:

> We begin the day at 4:30 in the morning, with prayer and meditation. (Our community is very closely woven together, so we do everything together: we pray together, we eat together, we work together.) We begin with Mass, holy communion, meditation.
>
> Then, since we each have only two saris, we have to wash one every day.
>
> By 7:30, some of the sisters go to the Home for the Dying, some go to work with lepers, some go to the little schools that we have in the slums, some go to prepare food, some go to families, some to teach catechism, and so on.

They spread all over the city. (In Calcutta alone, we have fifty-nine centers: the Home for the Dying is just one of them.) They spread all over the city with the rosary in hand. It is the way for us to pray with the rosary in the street; we do not go to the people without praying; the rosary has been our strength and our protection.

All over the world, we dress as I do and we always go in twos.

We come back at 12:30 and then we have lunch. Then we often have to do housework. Then for half an hour every sister goes to rest, because all the time they are on their feet. After lunch, we have examination of conscience and say the divine office and the stations of the cross.

By 2:00 we have spiritual reading for half an hour, then have a cup of tea.

By 3:00 the professed sisters go out again. Novices and postulants remain in the house. They have classes of theology and scripture and other things, like constitutions.

Between 6:15 and 6:30 everybody comes back home. From 6:30 to 7:30 we have adoration with the Blessed Sacrament exposed. To be able to have this hour of adoration, we have not had to cut down the work. We work ten hours, twelve hours without having to cut back our service to the poor.

At 7:30 we have dinner. After dinner, for about twenty minutes, we prepare for the work for next morning.

From 8:30 until 9:00, we have recreation. (Everybody talks at the top of her voice because all day we have been working.)

At 9:00 we go for night prayers and preparation of meditation for next morning.

Once a week, every week, we have a day of recollection, and that day, the first-year novices go out, because they are the ones who don't go every day. All the professed sisters stay in for the day of recollection. This is a very beautiful time when we can regain all our strength to fill up the emptiness again. That's why it is very beautiful!

That day we have our confessions and adoration.

The work that we Missionaries of Charity are doing is only a means to put our love for Christ in a loving, in a living action.[13]

Mother Teresa created this rigorous schedule and follows it with one exception. While everyone else is asleep, she works until midnight or after.

True self-transcendence results in a whole new experience of time. Unencumbered by hours and seasons, we love God in the simple things while living in the present moment. Self-projections into the future and retrospection into the past fade away. Instead, minutes of the day become like threads woven into a tapestry made visible by love. So, long after the voices of the day are silent, Mother Teresa works in the stillness of night, under the eye of God.

A new dawn finds her showering the poorest of the poor with loving kindness. It is not a love, however, that divides and separates like walls in a house of stone. "Who is worthy of love?" is a question which rejects others and chooses self. There can be no love where there is rejection. Love unifies; it is expressed in the work of Mother Teresa as she obeys an ever new call without end. It is a call to love one another as He, the Master of creation, loves us. God does not love one of his children and shun another anymore than the voice of the wind sings only to trees but not to flowers. God is like the sun which warms both those who face its light and those who stand in the shadows. Mother Teresa would say, "If we cannot love the one who is in front of us, we cannot do the larger work of loving the masses."

She exemplifies love-in-action. And, it is a gift of love that wherever there is dire need, Mother Teresa sends the sisters: to wealthy countries, Third World countries, to large, overcrowded cities, and to refugee camps. Wherever there is desperate hunger for food or love, Mother Teresa sends the Missionaries of Charity:

Let us not love in words but let us love until it hurts. It hurt Jesus to love us: he died for us. And today it is your turn and my turn to love one another as Jesus loved us. Do not be afraid to say yes to Jesus.[14]

She believes that the most bitter, ingrained poverty is the absence of love. People are starving for love and kindness; they die lonely, unloved, forgotten. Mother Teresa of Calcutta creates a footpath to these people, sending "hearts to love, hands to serve."

The House of Dying

Mother Teresa's work has been dictated by the need of suffering people. She had no preconceived plan. Each mission, every response was according to serious need and God's direction.

Though she first turned her energies to children, Mother Teresa could not ignore the destitute and dying she found in the streets: people alone in their death agony, people starving with raging illness, people infected with maggots in open wounds. The only way off the street for these helpless, rejected people was to die.

On one occasion, Mother Teresa picked up a woman half-eaten by rats and ants and took her to the nearest hospital, but they refused to admit her. Mother Teresa stood her ground and would not move until the woman was finally admitted.

She went from hospital to hospital carrying the destitute by whatever transportation she could find—taxi, rickshaw, even a wheelbarrow transported what was left of a human being. Time and time again she was the strength for the helpless, the voice for the voiceless.

Calcutta hospitals were too overcrowded and understaffed to care for so many street people. There was nothing left to do; people could not be discarded in the streets. If Mother Teresa could do nothing else, she would see that these pathetic, disease-ridden people would spend their last hours with dignity. "We cannot let a child of God die like an animal in the gutter," she said. She appealed to the Commissioner of Police and to the Health Officer of the Calcutta Corporation. Finally, a building near the Temple of Kali, Calcutta's most revered shrine, was offered for her use. In a week, the sisters had changed this former pilgrim's hostel into a home for the dying. Mother Teresa called it Nirmal Hriday—Place of the Pure Heart. It was named in honor of the Virgin Mary and opened on August 22, 1952, on the feast day dedicated to Mary's Immaculate Heart. Ambulances soon began to deliver to the Home for the Dying all those who were refused by city hospitals. It was the last stop before death for Calcutta's street people. The sisters washed and cleaned each patient. They looked beyond the stench, the sores, the maggots, and the pain and saw in each person "Jesus in His distressing disguise."

In Calcutta, Nirmal Hriday is called Kalighat, the name for the cremation place near the Kali Temple. For a time, temple priests opposed the work going on so near their shrine. After seeing how the sisters cleaned and cared for the abandoned dying, including one of their own priests, however, temple officials had a change of heart. This was a place of peace where people could die with love and dignity, surrounded by tenderness and constant care. For many, it was the first time in their lives that someone quenched their thirst for love:

> I have lived like an animal in the street, but I am going to die like an angel, loved and cared for, said a grateful man nearly eaten up with maggots. He died a beautiful, peaceful death.[15]

Nirmal Hriday was Mother Teresa's first large project. It has served as the final home to the castoff, the abandoned, the most destitute of the human family. Within the first five years, more than 8,000 of the dying were accepted at Kalighat. Eight thousand broken bodies received compassionate love with nothing asked in return. Calcutta was the birthplace of a home in which people died with dignity. Today, the Missionaries of Charity serve in over 145 homes for the dying, spanning the earth from Los Angeles to Delhi.

The Lepers

In 1957, five lepers, all fired from their jobs and rejected by their families, knocked on Mother Teresa's door. They were only five among 40,000 lepers in Calcutta. But to Mother Teresa it was a sign. It was now time to help those afflicted with leprosy. She began the work in a mobile van which evolved into a clinic on wheels. It initially traveled to four centers with a doctor, three sisters, and supplies of medicine and food. Some of the lepers were able to walk to the van; others had to be carried. The worst cases had stubs for hands and feet. Their fingers and toes had rotted away:

> The leprosy clinic was held out-of-doors at the end of a dead-end alley way. Treatment began at two o'clock in the afternoon and by three o'clock, Mother Teresa began counting the numbers of patients who had presented themselves. Because their dossiers were in a numbered file, she could tell that many were not on the line for treatment. We went searching the neighborhood for the missing lepers. Some we found laboriously making their way to the mobile clinic, bringing their boys and girls, already positive cases, with them. An old Muslim whose hands and feet were wasted, and whose legs could no longer support him, was being pulled slowly by his wife in a wooden cart, the size of a youngster's go-cart.
>
> We reached the sequestered spot where the leper families were congregated and here we found the people for whom Mother Teresa was searching.
>
> . . . Here in the corner of Dhappa, Mother Teresa had encountered what might be called a nest of lepers, a nucleus of infected families living off by themselves in several rows of low houses around an open space muddy with swamp water. They were cut off from normal living as the marks of disease were on almost all of them. We went from hut to hut and Mother Teresa talked with them, telling them to make their way to the van clinic . . . .
>
> Most of the men and women were sitting or lying on the tiny porches in the afternoon sun. Some were somnolent from hunger or from the debilitation of the disease; a few grimaced as though in pain.
>
> A prone woman in a red sari, grayed with dust, twisted in pain as Mother Teresa came over to her. She tried to sit up and then huddled down once more on the bed of sackcloth. Scantily dressed men drew pieces of cloth over them as Mother Teresa approached. A glazed orange sun lit up the afternoon scene, the mud houses, and the

scourged human forms lying or sitting on sackcloth on the verandas; and not far away the dark flocks of vultures wheeled and turned in incessant search for the rejected pieces of dead flesh.

When we returned to the mobile clinic later that afternoon, there was still a long lineup in the alley. The doctor and the two nursing Sisters, with Mother Teresa plunging in to help, were occupied until the short twilight was over at about six o'clock.[16]

In 1959, Mother Teresa gave out medicines and dressings from under a tree in a weeded clearing. She was in an industrial slum area near Calcutta, where raw sewage in open drains was a way of life. Lepers, venturing out from nearby colonies to beg and steal, discovered Mother Teresa at her tree-side clinic. Slowly, they came to her for treatment. She eventually moved from the tree to a van; later on she built a building on land the government donated. Over 15,000 outpatients a year came for diagnosis and medicines. As new medicines arrested, or, in some cases, cured the disease, Mother Teresa was faced with a new need: training and work for these people and a place for them to live. Lepers turned carpenters, painters, and gardeners made the leper station at Titagarh a self-supporting community.

The greatest suffering for lepers, however, was being shunned. Mother Teresa and the Missionaries of Charity gave them tender loving care and training for a new, more normal life. In those days many believed leprosy to be a curse of God. The Missionaries of Charity touched wounds of the body and of the spirit. At Christmas they hosted a Christmas party for the lepers of Calcutta. Mother Teresa remembers:

> I went to them and told them that God has a very special love for them, that they are very dear to Him, that what they have is not a sin.
>
> An old man who was completely disfigured, tried to come near to me and he said, "Repeat that once more. It did me good. I have always heard that nobody loves us. It is wonderful to know that God loves us. Please say that again!"[17]

To the disfigured lepers, she was a vision of love. To Mother Teresa, each leper was "Jesus in His distressing disguise."

The Children's Home

Mother Teresa says she learned how to love with great love from a little child in Calcutta:

> Once, there was no sugar and I do not know how that little Hindu child four years old heard in school that Mother Teresa had no sugar for her children.
>
> He went home and told his parents, "I will not eat sugar for 3 days: I will give my sugar to Mother Teresa." His parents had never been to our house before to give anything, but after 3 days they brought him. He was so small, and in his hand there was a bottle of sugar. How much can a 4 year old child eat? But the amount he could have eaten for 3 days, he brought. He could scarcely pronounce my name, but yet he gave and the love he put in the giving was beautiful.
>
> I learned from that little one that at the moment we give something to Him, it becomes infinite.
>
> A young boy we had picked up had lost his mother who had died in our Home for the Dying. She had been of a good family, but had come down in life.
>
> The boy grew up and wanted to become a priest. When he was asked, "Why do you want to become a priest?" he gave a very simple answer, "I want to do to other children what Mother Teresa has done for me: I want to love as she loved me, I want to serve as she served me."
>
> Today he is a priest and a wonderful lover of all those who have nothing, who have no one, who are wanted by no one, of people who have forgotten what human love is, what a human touch is, what even a smile is.
>
> I asked for holy priests to be like angels in our disturbed families, in our suffering families, because I think that the passion of Christ is being relived in our homes![18]

Once a man came to our house and he told me, "There is a Hindu family with about eight children who have not eaten for a long time."

So, I quickly took some rice for that evening and went to their family and I could see real hunger on the small faces of these children. Yet the mother had the courage to divide the rice into two portions and she went out.

When she came back, I asked her, "Where did you go? What did you do?" And she said, "They are hungry also!"

Who are they? A Muslim family next door with as many children. She knew that they were hungry. What struck me most was that she knew, and because she knew, she gave until it hurt.

This is something so beautiful! This is living love.[19]

Mother Teresa loves children. In Calcutta, she started a home for unwanted and crippled children, Nirmala Shishu Bhavan, The Children's Home for the Immaculate. It provides a children's ward for sick children, a service center to provide food to destitute families, and a clinic to treat women living in the general area. Shishu Bhavan is the only home for many of Calcutta's children: those born on the streets; those deserted by parents too diseased or blind to care for them; those whose parents have died. Stolen young children who have been raped or forced into prostitution are later dumped on the streets. Homeless and defenseless, these children have no place to go. Abandoned, sick, and uncared for, they are street children. The Sisters find them and bring them to Shishu Bhavan. These Missionaries of love help to heal the sores of the body and wounds of the heart. Those who become healthy are adopted. Mother Teresa says of unwanted children, "Bring them to me. I will take them." Whether it is an unborn child a mother does not want or one of the destitute living, "send them to me. We will find homes for them." For Mother Teresa, a child is a gift of God.

The "Gift of Love" AIDS Hospice

I never expected that I would open a Kalighat in New York. When I heard that people were dying of this disease, I knew we must do something. We care for the dying in Kalighat and that must be our work in New York, too . . . .

On Christmas Eve, 1985, we saw Mother Teresa help a small man up the steps into a hospice in New York's Greenwich Village. He had come to die. The hospice was called "Gift of Love" and was run by four Missionaries of Charity. It was for patients in the final stages of AIDS, the affliction whose inexorable course toward death could not be halted by any medical means.

The opening of an AIDS hospice was a triumph for Mother Teresa, since plans to open such a center in other localities had been rebuffed by residents.

This little man, Ramon Galvan, enjoyed the attention he received as Mother Teresa settled him in the lounge. He was greeted by the mayor of New York City, Edward Koch, Cardinal John O'Connor, and a group of dignitaries. He was the first of many prisoners with AIDS furloughed to the care of the Missionaries of Charity. Already over 150 victims of the disease had died behind prison walls.

Mother Teresa explained why she wanted the opening to be on Christmas Eve. "Then Jesus was born, so I wanted to help them to be born again in joy and love and peace. We are hoping that they will be able to live and die in peace by getting tender love and care, because each one of them is Jesus in a distressing disguise . . . ."

Sister Dolores, the superior of the hospice, gave the patients the same sensitive, tender care she had given when she worked at Kalighat. There was a tragic difference in that while more than half of the patients in Calcutta survived to take up life anew, the sentence on those entering the hospice was irrevocable. It was not long before Ramon Galvan died, passing his last days in Saint Clare's Hospital, which supported the hospice with expert medical services. The patients regularly released to the Missionaries of Charity knew gentle, loving care before death took them. When returned temporarily for hospital care, the patients asked to be allowed to "go home" to the hospice.

The opening of the AIDS hospice seemed to open many hearts.

"So many people have come forward," Mother Teresa told me. "It is beautiful. I have letters from people who are ready to give a house for the work. People are asking me to open a house in San Francisco. I hear that there are babies and little children who have the disease. I want to open a home for them."[20]

The AIDS hospice was not Mother Teresa's first mission in North America. In 1971, she opened the "Queen of Peace Soup Kitchen" in the South Bronx. The Missionaries of Charity, with help from volunteers and novices, run the soup kitchen and men's shelter in this high crime area of New York. The South Bronx destitute come to East 146th Street for soup, salad, day-old bread, donated buns and donuts, and fruits and vegetables. The hungry come in three feeding shifts. Most are between the ages of twenty and forty, tough street people without jobs. The Sisters pray, sing a song, and serve lunch; conversations are laced with laughter and words of brotherly love. It is a quiet, respectful scene. The Sisters reach people with kindness and their simple message about God.

Retirement

In 1990, Mother Teresa demonstrated once again her selfless charity. When health problems made it impossible to maintain her hectic travel schedule, she resigned as superior-general of the Missionaries of Charity. She stated that "the work and the cause of my mission is more important than any individual . . . my organization needs to be run efficiently."

Weeks after the announcement, the ailing nun arrived in Rumania at the bedside of AIDS babies. With the thawing of the cold war, walls between nations came down. Behind the walls of Rumania's hospitals, a large group of babies with AIDS struggled, alone in cribs and without adequate care and medical treatment. As she has done for forty years, Mother Teresa traveled to offer help to the tiny, suffering "poorest of the poor."

Mother Teresa's retirement plans were short lived. When the ballots for a successor were cast by 103 delegates representing the Missionaries of Charity around the world, Mother Teresa was re-elected. Until that moment, her plans to retire were unchanged. When she heard the results, she characteristically said, "If this is God's will, I will serve . . . ."

Mother Teresa will serve until she dies. The work is God's plan, His mystery. It is a work of grace. Mother Teresa is His instrument.

Early Years

The woman known worldwide as Mother Teresa was born in Skopje, Yugoslavia on August 26, 1910. The youngest of three children, she was baptized the day after her birth and given the names Agnes Gonxha Bojaxhiu. Her parents were from Albania, a country in southern Europe, in the Balkan Peninsula between Yugoslavia and Greece. At the time of Agnes Gonxha's birth, however, Albania was still part of the Ottoman Empire. Her parents moved to Skopje in the early nineteen hundreds where they enjoyed a comfortable lifestyle in a city that was a cultural crossroads of Turkish, Islamic, and Christian influences. As a child, Agnes Gonxha walked in the streets of a culturally diversified city, where she witnessed the sun set on all alike, regardless of differences in culture, religion, or dress.

In the years before her birth, however, seeds of strife were being sown in Europe, scattered by hate and greed and power. Citizens of neighboring countries lived in dreaded apprehension that the cold winds of war would blow through their countries, rattling doors and windows, threatening the peace with fearful sounds in the night. Agitations escalated, culminating in the first Albanian uprising in 1910 and the Balkan War in 1912. Finally, the boundaries of the map were marched over, as World War I broke out in Europe in 1914. Young Agnes Gonxha spent her early childhood in the shadow of war.

Her father, a successful merchant and entrepreneur who sympathized with Albanian nationalists, followed the commands of conscience and provided financial support and encouragement for the independence movement. Although he lived in Yugoslavia, Nikola Bojaxhiu's Albanian heritage had not vanished in memory. The house was often filled with patriot friends whose hearts also dreamed of independence. The whispers of a dream were realized when independence was achieved in November 1912, and Nikola hosted a long-awaited victory celebration.

Nikola Bojaxhiu was a conscientious provider for his family, who frequently traveled on business while his three children— Agnes Gonxha, Age, the oldest daughter, and Lazar, the only son—always eagerly awaited his homecoming. Although he was a severe disciplinarian, Nikola was also supportive of his children. He encouraged them to seek the depths of knowledge and to excel in school, to choose principles over possessions, generosity over selfishness. A compassionate man, he taught his children not to muffle their ears and harden their hearts to the sorrows and needs of others. He had compelling inner beliefs and sought to pass on these virtues to his children.

Drana, his wife, was a deeply religious woman who never turned away a needy, hungry soul. Agnes Gonxha grew up with a strong sense of values and often accompanied her mother on missions of mercy:

> Once a week they visited an elderly woman who had been abandoned by her son. They brought food and cleaned the house. Another woman who received regular visits was File, an alcoholic who was covered in sores and very ill. Twice a day Drana washed File and cared for her, and often Agnes helped her.[21]

Lessons of love in action came early for Agnes Gonxha. Drana often entered dirty surroundings to wash sick bodies and clean wounds. She gave of herself joyously and with gentle humility. Agnes Gonxha received her first missionary training while living in the heart of her family:

> Drana Bojaxhiu was certain that anything she gave to the poor, she was giving to God. She taught this to her children. "When you do good," she told them, "do it unobtrusively, as if you were tossing a pebble into the sea."[22]

Mother Teresa's memories of her mother reveal the spirit of Drana's generosity and compassion. She gave of herself and her possessions, not for reward or recognition, but because it was needed. She silently poured water on the scorching desert of a person in need. From generous hands and an open heart, God speaks. Drana was an instrument of giving, certain that her gift was to God Himself. Mother Teresa has recalled how Drana's generosity was expressed in her own home:

> Many of the poor in and around Skopje knew our house, and none left it empty-handed. We had guests at table every day. At first I used to ask, "Who are they?", and Mother would answer: "Some are relatives, but all of them are our people." When I was older, I realized that the strangers were poor people who had nothing and whom my mother was feeding.[23]

Drana possessed immense inner strength and commitment. Her heart was in her spiritual life, and she never separated her faith from her actions. Family life centered around the church, and prayer sustained them through joy and sorrow. Each evening the family gathered in the living room for prayers, usually reciting the rosary. In later years, Mother Teresa and the Missionaries of Charity sisters walked two-by-two to their work, reciting the rosary each step of the way.

When Agnes Gonxha was nine years old, her father died unexpectedly after attending a dinner meeting with fellow city councilors in Belgrade. He had returned home gravely ill and hemorrhaging and was rushed to the hospital for emergency surgery. But he could not be saved.

Large crowds attended the funeral. A much loved public figure and patron of charities, he was admired by members of all religions. Skopje had lost a prosperous, well-respected citizen.

These were days of devastating sorrow and loss for Drana. Overnight, the life of her family had dramatically changed. She had to find work to support her children. To make matters worse, the family's merchant income ended when Nikola's business partner seized the assets of their business. For awhile, there was nothing left but the house in which they lived.

Drana relied on her faith and strong character during these difficult days. Once beyond the initial grief, she created a sewing and handcrafted embroidery business. She accepted her situation, and refused to live in the twilight of memories. Drana had lost worldly possessions, but the house of her soul was rich in faith, kindness, love, and never-ending compassion for the poor. Agnes Gonxha witnessed a living example of selfless charity.

The life of a great worker for God is sculpted by such experiences. The way is prepared as God provides teachers and friends who influence the spiritual growth of His child. Agnes Gonxha's family was one of those profound "influences"; the Church was another.

The parish of the Sacred Heart was the center of religious life for Albanian Catholics in Skopje. It was also the center of Bojaxhiu family life. The archbishop and parish priests were regular visitors to their home. One priest in particular played a pivotal influence in Agnes Gonxha's spiritual life. Father Franco Jambrekovich's enthusiasm was for foreign missions. He encouraged parishioners to get involved at a practical level by giving money and offering prayer for the work among the poor and the lepers.

Although the family focused on politics when Nikola was alive, it was their enduring faith which sustained and nourished them after his death. The church became an even bigger part in Agnes Gonxha's life and Father Jambrekovich focused her attention on missionaries. Catholic magazines and newspapers which he distributed in the church contained regular reports on missionaries in Calcutta. The magazines were an inspiration to Agnes Gonxha, according to people who knew her, already giving character to a distant vocational call.

By the time she was twelve years old, Agnes Gonxha experienced the longing to belong completely to God. Her soul beckoned her to prayer often, especially on the annual parish pilgrimages to the Shrine of Our Lady of Letnice. Since she was a frail child subject to malaria and whooping cough, her mother arranged additional trips to the Shrine hoping to improve her health. It was a time of spiritual nourishment, long walks, and adequate rest. There was time for reflection and the solitude to wonder about her vocation.

The pastor of Sacred Heart introduced teenagers to the

Sodality of Blessed Virgin Mary, a Christian girls' society which sponsored parties, cultural meetings, walks, and other activities. He recited the words of Saint Ignatius Loyola in his *Spiritual Exercise* as a challenge to the young parishioners: "What have I done for Christ? What am I doing for Christ? What will I do for Christ?" One of the society's activities was to learn about the lives of saints and missionaries. When priests of the Society of Jesus left Yugoslavia for missions in Bengal in 1924, they wrote home describing their adventures. It served to increase Agnes Gonxha's zeal for missionary work.

Between the ages of twelve and eighteen years, Agnes Gonxha experienced uncertainty and questions about God's call. She wanted an inner certitude that the call was genuine, so that she could be directed toward His will. For awhile, she put vocational thoughts aside, and experienced normal, happy teenage years. Sooner or later, she reasoned, her future and her call from God would be clarified.

It was a full life, complete with a loving family, good friends, and church activities. Agnes Gonxha was a gifted student, at the top of her class academically. Her childhood dream was to be a teacher, so it was natural for her to tutor friends with their studies. Unprejudiced by nature, she was kind to everyone. Nothing stood in the way of friendship, not differences in religion, language, or nationality. Her heart did not know discrimination.

Growing up in an artistic family, Agnes' passion was poetry and music. She loved literature, read voraciously, and wrote poetry. The whole family sang, and she and her sister Age were involved in church choir. Frequently, Agnes Gonxha sang soprano solos and was called "nightingale" because of her lovely voice. She was active in all of the young Catholic activities— singing, acting, playing instruments—and was also known as an excellent organizer. She assumed organizational responsibilities and accomplished them skillfully. This talent would serve her well later as the Superior General of the Missionaries of Charity.

Agnes Gonxha nurtured dreams of a life in music or writing, but knew if she answered God's call those dreams would have to be sacrificed. There was no doubt, however, that she would willingly make the sacrifice. Obedience was second nature to Agnes Gonxha even as a child. Her brother remembered:

I never heard her refuse to do anything for our parents. Often Mother said to me, "Follow Agnes' example, even though she is younger than you."[24]

Though active and happy during those years, her vocational call was not forgotten. Questions surfaced, and she longed for an answer. Her mother, to whom she was especially close, sensed Agnes' inner spiritual restlessness:

Drana once contemplated her gifted daughter and re-marked, out of her hearing, that she would probably not have her company for very long; either she would lose her because of her fragile health, or Agnes would consecrate herself to God.[25]

Seeking God's will for her life, Agnes Gonxha asked her confessor for advice:

How can I know if God is calling me and for what He is calling me? He answered, "You will know by your happiness. If you are happy with the idea that God calls you to serve Him and your neighbor, this will be the proof of your vocation. Profound joy of the heart is like a magnet that indicates the path of life. One has to follow it, even though one enters into a way full of difficulties."[26]

By the time she was eighteen years of age, Agnes Gonxha could no longer ignore the call that so inflamed her heart. During the two years before she surrendered to God's call, Agnes Gonxha spent two months at Letnice and participated in a number of retreats. In the sanctuary of our Lady of Letnice, she heard the divine call. The wish "hidden in her heart" throughout her teenage years was ready to be fulfilled. All that was left to do was to tell her family and friends, and ask her advisers how best to arrange for going to India.

Her mother once said, "My daughter if you begin something, begin it wholeheartedly. Otherwise, don't begin it at all."[27] Once she heard her daughter's decision, Drana withdrew to her room and remained twenty-four hours behind closed doors. (In those days, when a daughter became a nun in an international order, it was a lifetime separation. There were no vacations or money for travel.) When Drana came out of her room, she gave Agnes Gonxha her blessings and said, "Put your hand in His—in His hand—and walk all the way with Him . . . . Be careful to be always of God and Christ, only."[28]

Lazar, Agnes Gonxha's brother, could not believe she would leave a good life for India, never to see them again. His question penetrated the only reservation she had about becoming a missionary nun. Her home was an exceptionally happy one. "We were a family full of joy and love, and we children were happy and contented."[29] It was in the heart of the family, however, that she also learned about the priorities of love:

> My mother was a holy woman.
> She imparted to all her children that love for God and that love for her neighbor.
> . . . She herself prepared us for our first communion, and so we learned to love God above all things from our mother.[30]

On September 25, 1928, family and friends gathered for an emotional farewell. As the train slowly pulled out of the station, Agnes Gonxha waved goodbye to her loved ones and to her personal life. In the silence of her heart, God had spoken. She had answered and surrendered her life to God.

> Total surrender consists in giving ourselves completely to God, because God has given Himself to us . . . . To surrender means to offer Him my free will, my reason, my own life in pure faith. My soul may be in darkness. Trial is the surest way of blind surrender.[31]

Now the training and preparation, the tests and struggles began. It was the dawn of a new day, the beginning of her life as a missionary nun.

Agnes Gonxha's journey to India and her life work was through the Loreto Sisters, an Irish branch of The Blessed Virgin Mary. In 1841, the Order established a foundation in Calcutta to provide schools and medical services. Agnes Gonxha's first stop enroute to India was Rathfarnham House, the Loreto Abbey in Dublin, Ireland. It was her first time in a religious house and her first preparation period for the work ahead. For several months she studied English and the history of the Loreto order. She also adopted the symbol of her new life: she wore a novice's habit and chose a new name. Agnes Gonxha became Sister Teresa of the Child Jesus.

Sister Teresa strongly identified with her namesake's love of missions and attitude toward the spiritual life. Saint Teresa preferred "the monotony of obscure sacrifice to all ecstasies." Jesus said, "unless you become as little children, you shall not enter the kingdom of heaven." Saint Teresa's "little way" to God was "the way of spiritual childhood, the way of trust and absolute self-surrender." The adoption of the Saint's name was an ideal choice.

In December 1928, Sister Teresa and Sister Mary Magdalene set sail on a long, wearing trip to India. Sister Teresa's pilgrimage of love brought her to Calcutta on January 6, 1929, and she did not leave the province for thirty-one years. Memorable months followed in which she received additional instruction, and on May 23, 1929, Sister Teresa became a novice. Her chosen name became permanent for life.

The novitiate is a two-year, intense training process in prayer and spiritual development:

> The most important thing is silence. Souls of prayer are souls of deep silence. We cannot place ourselves directly in God's presence without imposing upon ourselves interior and exterior silence. That is why we must accustom ourselves to stillness of the soul, of the eyes, of the tongue.
>
> God is the friend of silence. We need to find God, but we cannot find him in noise, in excitement. See how nature, the trees, the flowers, the grass grow in deep silence. See how the stars, the moon, and the sun move in silence.
>
> . . . Interior silence is very difficult, but we must make the effort to pray. In this silence we find a new energy and a real unity. God's energy becomes ours, allowing us to perform things well. There is unity of our thoughts with

His thoughts, unity of our prayers with His prayers, unity of our actions with His actions, of our life with His life.[32]

Such prayer and will to serve God does not occur overnight. The way is long; the path narrow. The novitiate is only the beginning of the disciplines and giving up oneself. It can be an extraordinarily difficult time of preparation and probation for religious life. Nothing in the novice's former personal life compares to this training period.

Sister Teresa took her temporary vows on May 24, 1931, and renewed them annually until her final vows six years later. She was immediately sent to teach school children in the Loreto convent school in Darjeeling, a city 450 miles north. She loved her teaching assignment and brought enormous energy to her work. At dinner time she read aloud, especially the lives of saints and mystics. The saints had inspired her as a teenager; she hoped their lives of courage would serve as an ideal for her students.

Sister Teresa had a deep spiritual compassion toward the suffering and poor of Darjeeling. They were never far removed from her heart, even though her days were occupied with prayer and classes. It was the poor that had drawn her to India; but the way to serve them had not yet been revealed.

When her time in Darjeeling was completed, Sister Teresa's superiors sent her to Calcutta. Nine years had passed since the farewell at the Skopje train station.

On May 14, 1937, she became a professed nun and took lifetime vows of poverty, obedience, and chastity. Sister Teresa never doubted her choice. Her path was the way of love and devoted service.

She continued teaching, mostly geography classes, in Saint Mary's school in Calcutta. After her final vows, she became Head of Saint Mary's. With joy and excitement, she wrote to her mother and described her new life. Drana's response was typical and timely:

Dear Child, do not forget that you went out to India for the sake of the poor. Do you remember our File? She was covered in sores, but what made her suffer much more was the knowledge that she was alone in the world. We did what we could for her. But the worst thing was not the sores, it was the fact that she had been forgotten by her family.[33]

Sister Teresa had not forgotten. She was painfully distressed at what she witnessed on the streets of Calcutta. The suffering and the poor were everywhere, dying lonely deaths in front of her. She walked through the streets and came face to face with crowds of homeless people. Her mother never protected her or shielded her eyes from the sight of human agony. Now as she walked among the lepers, the poor and the dying, Sister Teresa did not shut her eyes or heart. With compassion and a deep reverence for life, she witnessed these sad, miserable scraps of humanity. There were no throwaway human beings for this woman who lived by eternal values. Something within her stirred; she sensed a "still, small voice" calling her to serve the poorest of the poor. But how? The answer was years away.

For twenty years, Sister Teresa lived enclosed at the Loreto Convent. She was a teaching sister who loved her work and her students. During her tenure, she agreed to be Head of the Daughters of Saint Anne, a community of Indian nuns who wore blue saris and taught in Bengali schools. She also worked with the Sodality of the Blessed Virgin, the Catholic young people's group similar to the one she joined in Skopje. The group was strongly committed to missions and service. When the girls visited the poor and returned to talk about their experiences, Sister Teresa heard firsthand about Calcutta's devastating poverty.

Her own longing to serve the poor had not diminished with the years. She tried to bring the poor into the convent to receive an education, but the contrast between convent and family environments was too great. The poorest students returned to the streets, unable to adjust.

From her window in the convent, Sister Teresa silently watched. The teeming slums overflowed with people abased in poverty. Slowly, she came to the conclusion that if the poor would not come inside, she would have to go where the poor were—outside the convent walls.

On September 10, 1946, Sister Teresa went on her annual retreat. While traveling by train to Darjeeling, God called a second time. Throughout her retreat, she prayed and meditated about this "call within a call." Days in solitary communion with

God revealed what she must do: seek permission to leave her happy life in Loreto Convent and serve the poorest of the poor.

Her request, however, was not approved immediately by her superiors. The Archbishop deliberated on whether this was a genuine call of God. There were setbacks and disappointments which provided the opportunity for additional testing and purification. "Thy will be done" requires purity of heart, of mind, of motive. It asks uncompromising devotion to the exact call of God. Church officials asked her to consider working once again with the Daughters of Saint Anne who already worked among the poor. The Daughters, however, did not share the same vision. They returned to the convent at day's end. Sister Teresa wanted to *live* among the poor, share the misery of their lives, and provide help for them. Prayerfully, she considered what direction God wanted her to take. She was aware of Rome's view of new Orders: unnecessary duplication depletes spiritual and organizational resources. Sister Teresa did not pray for the easy way; instead she prayed in complete, absolute surrender to the will of God. She received her answer: no compromise. The "call within a call" dictated that she serve the poor by becoming one of them.

In early 1948, the Archbishop began the permission process required for Sister Teresa to leave the convent. In a letter of introduction, she explained her reasons: "God has called on me to leave everything and give myself up to Him in order to serve the poorest of the poor in the slums of the city."[34] Permission was granted on April 12, 1948, but inexplicably the letter of notification did not arrive until August 7, at the end of the school year. Leaving the convent was another of Sister Teresa's sacrifices to serve. It was an emotionally wrenching time, even more difficult than leaving her family. Her life and work at the convent "meant everything."

On August 16, 1948, she closed the door on convent life and began yet another period of training. She traveled 240 miles to the Medical Missionary Sisters at Patna. Sister Teresa received basic medical training and met Mother Superior Dengal, who provided sage advice. When she discussed future plans, Sister Teresa explained, "My Sisters and I will eat only rice and salt." Mother Dengal strongly objected, saying it was medically unsound to identify so closely with the poor by existing on an inadequate diet: "Do you want to help the poor and the sick, or do you want to die with them? Do you want your young nuns to lose their lives, or do you want them healthy and strong, so they can work for Christ?"[35]

Sister Teresa took the advice and the medical training and applied it when she returned to Calcutta in December 1948. The early days were "times of joy and happiness, but also of weariness, testing, and difficulties of various kinds." Sister Teresa relied solely on God. She had renounced everyone and everything for hard labor and utter exhaustion in His name, according to His will. She desired nothing for herself; her will was wed to His will. In the darkest of days, she prayed, "Oh, God, if I cannot help these people in their poverty and suffering, let me at least die with them, close to them, so that in that way I can show them your love."[36]

One solitary individual gave voice and action to God's love. She worked unceasingly as days and nights blended into one. So many suffering people, so few hours in a day; it was an overwhelming effort. Later when Sister Teresa became Mother Teresa, the first missionary sisters followed the same busy pace in limited space:

> An American cardinal came to visit us here at Creek Lane . . . . It was Cardinal Spellman, and Archbishop Perier sent him, I think. It must have been in 1952. We were very crowded but I brought him here to this room. He asked me where we lived. I told him, "Here in this room, Your Eminence. This is our refectory. We move the tables and benches to the side." He wanted to know where the rest of our convent was, where we could study. "We study here, too, Your Eminence," I said. Then I added, "And this is also our dormitory." When the Cardinal asked if we had a chapel, I brought him to this end of the room.
>
> "It is also our chapel, Your Eminence," I told him and I showed him the altar behind the partition. I don't know what he was thinking but he began to smile. He said mass for us.[37]

When the number of Sisters outgrew the allotted space, Mother Teresa added a House to the prayer list. There was no money and no plan—just prayer and trust in God to provide. A Muslim moving to Pakistan offered his house for sale. Father Henry made an offer substantially below the value of the land on which the house was built. Incredibly, the offer was accepted, and the transaction completed in only three days. When Mother Teresa was shown the house, she said, "Father, it is too big; what will we do with all that?" He replied, "Mother you will need it all. There will come a day when you will ask where you can put all your people."[38] And so there was. In the center of town, 54a Lower Circular Road, Calcutta is the Mother House of the Missionaries of Charity.

Over the years, Mother Teresa divested herself of everything—privacy, comfort, time, self-will—any hindrance to her inner life. In later years, she said:

> Our progress in holiness depends on God and on ourselves—on God's grace and on our will to be holy. We must have a real living determination to reach holiness. "I will be a saint" means I will despoil myself of all that is not God. I will strip my heart of all created things, I will live in poverty and detachment, I will renounce my will, my inclinations, my whims and fancies, and make myself a willing slave to the will of God . . . .
>
> Saint Augustine says: "Fill yourselves first and then only will you be able to give to others." If we really want God to fill us, we must empty ourselves through humility of all that is selfishness in us.[39]

"Filled with God," Mother Teresa has spent herself in joy and love for the poor. She has become "as clear as glass" in her emptiness, a light shining into a darkened world.

Contemplative in Action

"The more we empty ourselves, the more room we give God to fill us." Mother Teresa has been God's instrument for forty years. Her face and radiant smile are recognized even by children. Thousands simply call her "Mother." People who come into contact with her feel they have been in the presence of holiness. Mother Teresa would be the first to say, "Not I but Christ in me":

> Often you see small and big wires, new and old, cheap and expensive electric cables up—they alone are useless and until the current passes through them there will be no light. The wire is you and me. The current is God. We have the power to let the current pass through us and use us to produce the light of the world or we can refuse to be used and allow the darkness to spread.[40]

Mother Teresa is a contemplative in action. A contemplative is silently receptive to God's action in the soul; the whole inner life is centered on God alone. A soul longing for God experiences overwhelming love and heart-piercing emptiness while being readied for union directed by the mystery of grace:

> Christ created you because he wanted you. I know what you feel—terrible longing, with dark emptiness—and yet, he is the one in love with you.[41]

> Prayer enlarges the heart until it is capable of containing God's gift of Himself. Ask and seek and your heart will grow big enough to receive Him and keep Him as your own.[42]

To receive God, one must surrender self-will and begin dying to self. Mother Teresa speaks of the "little deaths" of the self-centered nature:

> . . . It is only by frequent deaths of ourselves and our self-centered desires that we can come to live more fully; for it is only by dying with you that we can rise with you.[43]

> The spirit pours love, peace, joy into our hearts proportionately to our emptying ourselves of self-indulgence, vanity, anger, and ambition and to our willingness to shoulder the cross of Jesus.[44]

A contemplative in action is totally consecrated to God and lives His holy inspiration in the world. The majesty of God's presence in the soul is overwhelming, humbling. Consequently, the profound love of God experienced in union with Him is turned outward into the world to carry out His divine purpose.

Mother Teresa surrendered to the call within a call and entered the world with abounding love and humility to "bear the cross of Jesus." All self-centered desires were completely submerged in love and service to God, with nothing asked for self. After years of selfless living, personal needs have been extinguished; her will is one with God's will.

The contemplative in action discovers God everywhere—in the universe, in work, in people, in every circumstance of life. All life is sacred, including rejected people. In union with God, Mother Teresa has become like a light which beams love to everyone in its path:

> God dwells in us. That's what gives Him a beautiful power. It doesn't matter where you are as long as you are clean of heart. He is there with you and within you twenty-four hours. That's why He says, "Love others like I love you."[45]

> Today, in the world, is an "open Calvary." People throughout the world may look different or have a different religion, education, or position, but they are all the same. They are people to be loved. They are all hungry for love.[46]

> Love must come from within—from our union with Christ—an outpouring of our love for God.[47]

This mystery of grace is available to everyone who seeks God. However, to live in the unitive state habitually requires special grace and strong determination. Few people, even the religious, commit themselves to such complete self-surrender.

> "Thou shalt love the Lord thy God with thy whole heart, with thy whole soul, and with thy whole mind." This is the commandment of the great God, and he cannot command the impossible. Love is a fruit in season at all

times, and within reach of every hand. Anyone may gather it and no limit is set. Everyone can reach this love through meditation, spirit of prayer and sacrifice, by an intense inner life.[48]

The sacrifices on the road to abiding love are great. Self-love must go the way of the cross. Everything is given up to belong deeply, completely to God. The contemplative in action embraces suffering as the cross God offers the soul:

What we allow God to use us for, that is important. Because we are religious and our vocation is not to work for the lepers or the dying, our vocation is to belong to Jesus. Because I belong to Him, the work is a means for me to put my love for Him into action. So it is not an end, it is a means. Because my vocation is to belong to God properly, love Him with undivided love and chastity, I take the vows. I see Christ in every person I touch because He has said, "I was hungry, I was thirsty, I was naked, I was sick, I was suffering, I was homeless and you took me . . . ."[49]

Our works of charity are only the fruit of God's love in us. That is why those who are united with Him love their neighbor most.[50]

Once you have got God within you, that's for life. There is no doubt. You can have other doubts, eh? But that particular one will never come again . . . . But I am convinced that it is He and not I. That it is His work, and not my work. I am only at His disposal. Without Him I can do nothing. But even God could do nothing for someone already full. You have to be completely empty to let Him in to do what He will. That's the most beautiful part of God, eh? Being almighty, and yet not forcing Himself on anyone.[51]

When asked if she had to use her own initiative, she said, "Of course. You have to do it as if everything depends on you—but leave the rest to God."

Those who live in a habitual state of union with God have less and less of themselves to give as years go by. They have *less self*, and *more of God*. Consequently, "they love their neighbor most."

Such selfless living does not deplete, but rather expands love. Prior to the unitive state, however, we can experience emotional burnout. Or, one may surrender self to the work rather than to God, thus depleting ourselves of energy and compassion. Mother Teresa is so emptied of self that she responds to suffering people with joy and kindness, though she may appear exhausted. She is continually peaceful and serene regardless of events in the outside world. A clear vessel, she is full of God's love. As a Christian contemplative in action, Mother Teresa connects Christ in the Eucharist with the broken bodies of suffering people. Christ sacrificed himself for humanity, so she makes lesser sacrifices in her love for Christ. For Mother Teresa, Christ is before us wherever we find suffering in the human family.

Mother Teresa has given so much of her self that there is no self left to give. She lives free of any self-centeredness. "The true inner life makes the active life burn forth and consume everything," she says.[52]

Even subtle, barely discernible desires have been purified and burned away. Mother Teresa spoke eloquently of the way of holiness and its requirements:

> I need to give up my own desires in the work of my perfection. Even if I feel as if I were a ship without a compass, I must give myself completely to Him. I must not attempt to control God's actions. I must not desire a clear perception of my advance along the road, nor know precisely where I am on the way of holiness. I ask Him to make a saint of me, yet I must leave to Him the choice of that saintliness itself and still more the choice of the means that lead to it.[53]

Those who work with God are a living light of truth. On one occasion, the "light" was actually recorded on film:

This Home for the Dying is dimly lit by small windows high up in the walls, and Ken was adamant that filming was quite impossible there. We had only one small light with us, and to get the place adequately lighted in the time at our disposal was quite impossible. It was decided that, nonetheless, Ken should have a go, but by way of insurance he took, as well, some film in an outside courtyard where some of the inmates were sitting in the sun. In the processed film, the part taken inside was bathed in a particularly beautiful soft light, whereas the part taken outside was rather dim and confused.

How to account for this? Ken has all along insisted that, technically speaking, the result is impossible. To prove the point, on his next filming expedition—to the Middle East—he used some of the same stock in a similarly poor light, with completely negative results. He offers no explanation, but just shrugs and agrees that it happened. I myself am absolutely convinced that the technically unaccountable light is, in fact, the Kindly Light Newman refers to in his well-known exquisite hymn . . . . Mother Teresa's Home for the Dying is overflowing with love, as one senses immediately on entering it. This love is luminous, like the haloes artists have seen and made visible round the heads of the saints. I find it not at all surprising that the luminosity should register on a photographic film. The supernatural is only an infinite projection of the natural, as the furthest horizon is an image of eternity.[54]

For Mother Teresa, who is "overflowing with love," what matters is that we transcend cultural and religious divisions and love God and each other:

Every human being comes from the hand of God and we all know what is the love of God for us. My religion is everything to me but for every individual, according to the grace God has given that soul. God has his own ways and means to work in the hearts of men and we do not know how close they are to Him but by their actions we will always know whether they are at his disposal or not. Whether you are a Hindu, a Moslem or a Christian, how you live your life is the proof that you are fully his or not. We must not condemn or judge or pass words that will hurt people. Maybe a person has never heard of Christianity. We do not know what way God is appearing to that soul and what way God is drawing that soul, and therefore who are we to condemn anybody?

It matters to the individual what Church he belongs to. If that individual thinks and believes that this is the only way to God for her or him, this is the way God comes into their life—his life. If he does not know any other way and if he has no doubt so that he does not need to search then this is his way to salvation. This is the way God comes into his life. But the moment a soul has the grace to know and to want to know more about God, more about faith, more about religion, then he has to search and if he does not search then he goes astray. God gives to every soul that he has created a chance to come face to face with him, to accept him or reject him . . . .

Some call Him Ishwar, some call Him Allah, some simply God, but we all have to acknowledge that it is He who made us for greater things: to love and to be loved. What matters is that we love. We cannot love without prayer and so whatever religion we are we must pray together.[55]

Mother Teresa's life has been an active prayer. She simply lives the Sermon on the Mount on a daily basis. When asked about the Missionaries of Charity's future after her death, she said, "Let me die first, then God will provide. He will find someone more helpless, more hopeless than I to do His work."[56]

Emptied of self and filled with the light of God, Mother Teresa has served as an "instrument of His peace" for forty years. The world has honored her with the Pope John XXIII Peace Prize (1971), the JFK International Award (1971), the Templeton Award for "Progress in Religion" (1973), The Albert Schweitzer International Prize (1975), The Presidential Medal of Freedom (1975), and the Nobel Peace Prize (1979), to name a few. To the public, she is a world figure, but she turns the spotlight of attention on God and the work among the poor.

She once visited an old man in Melbourne whom no one even knew existed:

I saw his room in a terrible state, and I wanted to clean his house and he kept on saying: "I'm alright!" But I repeated the same words: "You will be more alright if you will allow me to clean your place," and in the end he allowed me. There in that room there was a beautiful lamp covered with the dirt of many years, and I asked him, "Why do you not light your lamp?" Then I asked him, "Will you light the lamp if the Sisters come to see you?" And the other day he sent me word: "Tell my friend the light she has lit in my life is still burning."[57]

Mother Teresa serves as God's Lamplighter. The lights of love are still burning.

Irina Tweedie (1907-   )

Photograph by Nancy D. Potts, March 13, 1990

113

Chapter V

Irina Tweedie

What is the spiritual life? We, all of humanity, will go home one day. Only some of us want to go a little quicker, because we have no time, or we are more eager, or we want Truth more badly. But there is really nothing extraordinary about that. It is perfectly natural. It is our birthright, you and me and everybody else.

It's all so simple. It's the mind which makes it complicated. Why make it simple when it can be complicated? The wonders, the miracles, the phenomena, my goodness. It's the simple things—just be good, stand with both feet on the ground, just love your neighbors. That's far too dull. We would like something much more sensational.

Again and again he [her Teacher] said to us, "No hysterism [sic], no exaggeration, please. Both feet on the ground, but your head *must* uphold the vault of the sky that it shouldn't fall on others." Commonsense, commonsense, and even more commonsense.[1*]

*Footnotes 1-13, 44, 48-49, are from a personal interview conducted by the author with Irina Tweedie in London, England on March 13, 1990. Editing of her comments was kept to a minimum to maintain the purity of her remarks.

In her quest to God, Irina Tweedie left England in 1959 and the place of her memories to meet her Teacher in Aryanangar, a district in India. As the train pulled into the noisy Indian railway station, she stepped into scorching heat, hordes of flies, and crowds of squatting passengers waiting for soon-to-depart trains. At age fifty-two, Mrs. Tweedie was home. Her heart, joyous with its hunger and thirst, was flooded with the sweetness of home-coming. Her joy, however, soon evaporated into doubts, questions, confusion, and unimaginable suffering. Her Teacher was like yeast to bread. Due to him, everything hidden within the depths of her consciousness rose to the surface. She was forced to face that which she had shunned all her life.

Suffering reminds us of our slavery to the idols of our soul. Resentments, faults, vanities, beliefs, pride, the need to mentally understand, our view of how the world "should" be, all we possess within us is relinquished and given to the sacred fires of purification, until in the end, we sit on the ash heap with nothing. Such are the trials of love that reveal the tests which linger around the corner of our awareness. It is a painful process to be awakened to love. God breaks the heart of one who seeks Him, to then fill the empty vessel with love.

Irina Tweedie is a Sufi and a servant to humanity. She explains that Sufism is neither a religion nor a philosophy, but a way of life:

> It is very individual, very intimate, a very personal path to Truth. And God is Truth. That's really all there is to it. Anyone can be a Sufi—Christian Sufi, Hindu Sufi, Moslem Sufi. . . . You see every religion and every philosophy leads you to God. You can use the pathless path which is ours which is neither religion nor philosophy, or if you are a believer in any of the religions it will lead you there. There is a wonderful Sufi saying, "In the name of Him who has no name, but who will appear by whatever name you will call Him." If we believe in Jesus, He will come to us as Jesus as He did with all the great Christian saints. If you are Hindu, He will appear in a shape as Krishna or Rama. He will appear as the Muslim believer needs for Him to be. There is nothing else but God—every spider,

every pussycat, every atom has the Light in it. We are made in the image of God.

Sufism is not Islamic mysticism. It's very much older than that. Before the Vedas, there was a sect called "blanket wearers." They were the Brotherhood of Purity who traveled in countries in search of Truth. As desert wanderers, they rebelled against the luxury and corrupt power which began after the Prophet Mohammed's death. The great Sufi teachers founded schools and guided people in various practices. Their teaching stories were passed down from one generation to the next.

We are servants. We do not go into bliss; we work for humanity. This is the bodisattva motif in Buddhism. You turn your back to the Light and you face humanity and all its miseries. And you work. One of Buddha's disciples said, "Why should we be responsible for other human beings? There are so many children dying of hunger in Behar. (Behar is one of the northern provinces of India where there was constant famine when Lord Buddha was alive.) And if it is Karma to die of hunger, why should I help them?" And the Buddha answered, "How do you know if it is not their Karma to be helped by you?" It answers the questions perfectly correct. So when we see a need, we have to help.[2]

Sufism is a mystical path of love, a love affair between lover and Beloved in which Truth (God) is found within the heart. The Journey Home is our return to the Center, where He awaits us. These lovers of Truth became known as *Sufis* a few centuries after the death of the Prophet. The name *Sufi* has been given various interpretations: a reference to a white woolen garment *(Suf)*, wisdom *(Sophia)*, and purity of heart *(Safa)*.

The Sufi path in its essence is the uninterrupted succession of Teachers within a Sufi order. The chain of transmission is from heart to heart between the Teacher and the successor.

The Nagshbandi Sufis (named after Baha ad-din Nagshband who died in 1389) are known as silent Sufis because they practice the "silent meditation of the heart." God is silent emptiness, so they reach Him more easily in silence. The silent Sufis place great importance on dreams which they consider to be a form of guidance along the pathless path.

Dreamwork as practiced within Mrs. Tweedie's group, however, is not based on the Western analytic approach. Instead the focus is on spiritual content. Personal meanings are left for one to interpret on their own:

> Dreams are the equivalent to the ancient Sufi teaching stories. The Teacher would sit and tell a Sufi story, which sometimes contained reference to a scorpion or poisoned tail. Each student would think of its application in his or her life. But the dreams offer something infinitely more important than teaching stories because it's the unconscious of the human being telling its own story while the whole group listens to the words. Then it's interpreted and the whole group participates; so we are all learning. Of course, it's maximum satisfaction for the human being to receive guidance in that way. It's really very personal and very beautiful.
>
> In the unconscious we have wisdom, such unbelievable wisdom in us. The Upanishads say that we can't *learn* anything spiritual, we have to *uncover the light* in us. They use the simile of onion skins that cover our light (and must be peeled away). Then Jesus said we put our own light under a bushel. But, of course, we not only cover our light—put our light under the bushel—but we also put it under the bed, hide it away completely. Nobody knows how much we know, neither do we ourselves.[3]

In London, Irina Tweedie's group meets in silent meditation followed by dreamwork. In Sufi dreamwork, spiritual and psychological approaches are combined to help participants realize the guidance that comes from within them and to understand "the inner processes of the Path as they are imagined in dreams. People share their dreams with others, offering interpretation of the symbolism. The dream offers a message from the unconscious on how to behave and provides guidance as to where the person is right then in their development":[4]

Dreams definitely are guidance. If you're on the spiritual path, you will be guided on your path. If you're not at all interested in the spiritual path, you'll be guided another way. Dreams come in themes or groups. There are future dreams, warning dreams, prophetic dreams, all sorts of dreams. It's wonderful how the unconscious takes over and guides the human being along the spiritual path. And also it helps me. People come with all sorts of psychological problems and conflicts. Everyone is human. They ask for advice. Never do I give advice if not asked. But, one can make mistakes, can't one? So, lo and behold, after awhile, the dream will tell me that I've made a mistake, that it was bad advice. You have to swallow it, eat the humble pie and say, "Look, let's begin from square one. Your dreams told me that I was completely mistaken. That's not the way to take and that's not the way to do." Sometimes people come with very basic questions—shall I divorce? What shall I do with my child? We just sit as human beings and discuss it together.

In this Sufi path, we work as much as possible on the psychological level. If we have experiences from a different state or level of consciousness, they cannot be interpreted psychologically; they have to be interpreted intuitively. But as much as possible, we do it psychologically.[5]

The mystical journey of the silent Sufi is concerned with setting the student free from desires, purifying the will, and learning self-abandonment to God. Mrs. Tweedie describes the essence of what it means to surrender:

God, for a Sufi, is called Beloved. We must give all away in complete surrender. Everything, including yourself, is surrendered. You do not surrender to the Teacher, but to the light within yourself.

We always surrender to something. Even if it's your computer, you're a servant of it. If you cook an omelet, you're a servant in that moment to the omelet if you give it absolute attention, and absolute attention is surrender. If you don't surrender to the omelet, it will burn. We're constantly surrendering ourselves all day long to our boss, to the bass which we're trying to catch, to our cooking, to our husband, to our children, and our arrogant minds and our rebellious hearts say, "Why should I surrender to God?" We forget we are surrendering all the time to something. Aren't we fantastic, we human beings?[6]

It is difficult for Western men to surrender—there's so much emphasis on educating the mind and competition. A woman can reach Reality just by being a woman, but it's just as difficult. You must give men a lot of practices, but for women there's only one practice—let go of worldly things. By nature, women are attached to comfort, children, money, security, beauty. It's with enormous difficulty that we give up the past and future, give up security to become nothing.

If you are attached to anything, the dearest thing to you will be taken away, because God is a jealous lover—only He must have your heart alone. For example, I love beauty so much. But, I'm going blind now, so I won't be able to see beauty. That will go. Everyone who lives deeply in her spiritual life gives up what they love most. He wants His heart for Himself.[7]

Mrs. Tweedie maintains that spiritual development is a special study, one beyond the capacity of the mind to understand. In fact, she says the biggest obstacle on the spiritual path is the mind, and that we have to confuse the mind so that it gives up and spiritual truth comes through:

Truth is One, absolute and undivided—it can't be known from the level of the mind. The mind divides constantly. But if we only understand by division, then we only understand by comparison. Truth can't be compared or divided. It can only be known in deep meditation where there is no mind. We don't meditate, however, to attain something, but as a state of being. There's an old Chinese proverb which says, "When you begin meditation, you must first give up what meditation is."

It's interesting that the more we meditate, the more we profoundly understand that this life is only a pilgrimage home. . . . Once you realize it in meditation, not as an intellectual concept but as an experience, you can never, never despise another human being. You may offer benevolent or constructive criticism but never criticism behind someone's back. We all, even the most silly, the most objectionable, the most criminal human being has infinite possibilities of God. The eternal part is in every human being.

In meditation, we transcend the thinking faculty of the mind and reach different spaces where spiritual experiences are possible. If we meditate regularly and sincerely, our own darkness comes. It's a hard time the first couple of years—all our doubts and jealousies surface. We feel people are against us. We're rude in our interactions with others. It passes. Then we experience the yo-yo syndrome—on every level of meditation we experience it again and again: we either have a wonderful meditation or nothing. Everything is like nature—the rhythm of the tides; light and darkness; burning love for the Beloved, then nothing. We work hard in meditation to reach the Beloved, but outwardly we have nothing to show for it.[8]

In her lectures and interviews, Mrs. Tweedie explains the Sufi understanding of suffering, ethics, our responsibility in the world, death, and other themes common to everyone. The eternal questions "Who am I? Why am I here? Why was the world created with so much suffering?" find answers in the promise of the soul. Our mysterious longing is calling us to our spiritual home, to the spiritual plane from which we came and will return:

The spiritual path is difficult—it is walking home quicker. If you have a deep longing, you will follow the spiritual path. If the longing is covered by too many experiences of this life, then you probably won't follow the spiritual life. But our personality is constantly influenced by the light within us. We are eternal, immortal.

Suffering has a very redeeming quality. We human beings are made in such a way that if we are happy with the state of our life, we forget where we belong. We're deluded by the beauty of the world—we forget everything. Doesn't it say in the Lord's Prayer, "lead us not into temptation?" Of course, He does, and He does it with a smile and a dance. By creating this wonderful world, we forget everything. Each of us lives as if we'll live forever, forgetting that one day we die. And this I'm learning now, being old. My body reminds me that it's not going to last. There is this pain, that illness, there is my heart; I get breathless and so on. Now I begin to think about it. I never thought about it before. You take life for granted. Suffering is a very redeeming and purifying process. When we suffer, we remember God and we pray. We remember home.[9]

The silent Sufi's path is a very ethical one which emphasizes character development and service:

Improve yourself; you will improve the world. Live as Jesus taught us to live. . . . Ethics are very important. We must live according to our conscience and the way the world should be. Every religion and philosophy says the same thing; the rules are the same: Love your neighbor like you love yourself. Don't steal, don't murder. Simple ethics of our humanity. Now the people who aren't spiritual, even children, know what is right and what is wrong. It's the inner guidance within us. But sometimes we don't listen, because it's inconvenient. It's easier to be naughty than good—it's much more fun.

There's this lovely saying—"all good things in life are illegal or immoral or fattening." That's perfectly correct—no fun in life. A saint is a very dull thing because it's absolutely a different thing. I remember the woman through whom I met Guruji. She's "L" in the book [Daughter of Fire]. She had no interest in anything. At that time, I was still not understanding what spirituality is. Whatever I said to her, she said, "Oh, I'm not interested." I wanted to go to the party and to the opera. "I'm not interested," she said. Now I am the same. My greatest bliss is just to go somewhere where there's peace, where there's gladness, and where there's absolute security and stillness—within. It is very dull for others, not for me. So a saint or even a Yogi is a very dull thing, but a sinner is lovely.

In our ethics, everything goes to helping others. I live on my pension. Not one penny of my books, (now translated in seven languages), goes to me. It goes into a charitable trust to help others. You don't need much really. And since I was in India, I learned how little we need. We are so wasteful in the West. One can live with one little soup can which you put on the fire and cook in. We don't need much. In our Sufi path of Yoga, we are stealing if we have too much furniture or too many chairs because someone else can use them. We are stealing if we eat too much. Give it to hungry cats and dogs. Life is the same. We are to be harmless—not just killing, that's the fringe of harmless. We're not to harm ourselves, and we do constantly by creating habits. When we create habits, we put ourselves in prison. If we crave cigarettes or tea or caffeine, we're not free. We're responsible for self, our environment, our brothers and sisters, all are parts of humanity. Whatever is around us—environment, people, animals, if we can help, we will. We're not Lords of the World, however. We can't help everybody.

We're not perfect, just human. We work for humanity in this life of Yoga. Anyone who has touched even with a finger the hem of the garment of Truth must tell others who they are—they are wonderful beings, they're immortal. They're not children of sin but children of light. We live in ignorance of who we are.[10]

Since her return from India in 1966, after her Teacher's death, Mrs. Tweedie has given countless lectures in England, Europe, and the United States to university students and spiritual seekers, to young and old. Some people are mildly curious; others experience the deep longing for Truth. Always, she speaks of other paths, other religions with utmost respect:

All paths are leading you to the One, the summit, the apex of the mountain. You can approach it from the river, from the highway, from the waterway, from the plain, from the city, from anywhere. You know Mohammed had to speak in a different way to the warring Arabs, the Buddha to the sophisticated Hindu priests, and Jesus to the ignorant fishermen. But, what they said in the inner core of the teachings is the same. The formal teachings may be different, but the inner core is the same. How would it be Truth if it were otherwise? It's really as simple as that.[11]

Before I went to India, I wasn't a good Christian. I disowned Christianity and walked out of the Roman Catholic Church because I thought Christianity was limited. I wanted the Rootless Root, the Causeless Cause which I told my Teacher. Christianity isn't limited however, one must only understand it. It was my stupidity. Since I was with a Teacher who had nothing to do with Christianity, I hope I am a better Christian now. I hope, but it is also not important. The main thing is that you live as a decent human being. To which religion you belong is irrelevant. Now I find all religions really good. They have in their depth the same experiences and moral values; they're just different roads to God. I have no criticism anymore, just love. We are to live with selfless love.[12]

Today, one of the most frequently asked questions is whether or not a spiritual teacher is necessary. Mrs. Tweedie answers:

You don't need a teacher from India. There are great people everywhere, East and West. The outer teacher always points to the inner teacher. All a teacher does is point within. We don't need to learn anything spiritually—we have it all. Divinity is within us, only it's covered by so many things—our educational conditioning, dogmas, beliefs, heritage. We must undress ourselves inwardly like removing onion skins. Sufis say a teacher is necessary because we come to situations which bewilder us. A teacher can tell us what's happening, not to be frightened, that we're experiencing a simple mystical state which will pass, and it means this or that. It's nice to have someone

one step ahead of us. One who has already climbed the mountain can help another following in the footsteps.

Of course, the greatest teacher is life itself, but to realize this we must be high on the path. Otherwise everyone who is seventy or eighty would be wise, and they're not. The greatest mystery is life with its obstacles. All are necessary. And with each lesson is a different psychological reaction. When you're with a teacher, one has to face oneself and realize that with all the darkness within ourselves, we can't judge anyone else anymore. To know how to handle life's obstacles would be perfection, I think.

The teacher doesn't teach anything on the level of the mind. We are given experiences and teaching is reflected into the mind from a different level of consciousness. It's a transmission from heart to heart.

There are certain stages, however, where one is left entirely alone. It's a difficult path, and you have absolutely no help. You don't know which way to turn. It's very important that you learn to stand on your own.[13]

Mrs. Tweedie's Teacher sent her to teach in London in 1963. It was part of the tradition, so as not to become too dependent. She returned before Christmas in 1965 and remained until his death in July 1966. In a story about teaching, Mrs. Tweedie conveys the hard work and inner guidance that is the essence of the path. It is a story about a newcomer to one of her meditation classes who questions another student:

> "Is this old woman teaching?"
> "No."
> "Is she lecturing?"
> "No."
> "Does she give us practices?"
> "No, there are no practices given."
> "What are we supposed to do?"
> "We must do everything ourselves."

The man never came back to class again. Mrs. Tweedie teaches that there is an eternal aspect in every human being. But the road to the Beloved is through surrender and love and hard work.

The Early Years

Born in Russia in 1907, Irina Tweedie lived with her parents and two younger sisters in a middle-class family, complete with servants. By age thirteen, however, family and economic stability shattered when her parents and the three young children fled Russia during the Russian Revolution. Uprooted from her homeland and a life of relative ease, young Irina and her family suffered another blow enroute to Vienna—her mother died, compounding their sorrow and turmoil. The family had to rebuild their war-torn lives without her.

There was very little money. They simply "did the best they could," and tried to pick up the pieces of their lives. Her father found a position as a civil servant in Vienna, and eventually moved the family into a small house. The young Irina, however, attended school in a Catholic convent where she ambitiously tackled her studies and learned to speak German. Although an all-around good student, she disliked convent life with its strict routines and lack of privacy. Personal time was rare. When she went home on summer holiday, her father was frequently away, so she occupied the house alone, finally with time to herself.

Educated in Vienna and Paris, Mrs. Tweedie is a trained librarian by profession and fluently speaks several languages—Russian, German, Austrian, English, Italian—and a"bit of French." She learned Italian on a two-week holiday in Italy which stretched to four years. World War II broke out during her vacation, prohibiting her return home. She nearly starved to death, as did many others, during the long years of the dreary war.

Her sorrows continued when her first husband, an Englishman, died in the war. Later, she met a British naval officer stationed in Italy, whom she married, and they returned to England after the war. When he died in 1954, Irina Tweedie was devastated. Desperate, she considered suicide, anything to ease the searing pain. "I just wanted to sit and die."

After the funeral, the despair overwhelming, a friend coaxed her to the Theosophical Library, where Irina decided to read.

Perhaps it would help her to live again, or at least ease her into a future without her husband. But she was not certain it would relieve anything. She only knew she had to do something. The first book she read was about life after death, in which the author claimed there was no death, only a change in consciousness. Much later, she discovered this truth was "perfectly correct."

But now, she simply longed for a way of life which had some meaning and would enable her to go on without her husband. She traveled to India in 1961 to the Center of the Society at Adjar near Madras. Studying was not enough, however, so she asked a friend where to go in India. Once she arrived in the Himalayas, one step led to another, like a strand of thread leading her to a "strange destiny." When she met her Teacher, he said, "You should have come before."

Underneath the sorrow, poverty, wars, relocation, and convent training of her life experiences, Irina Tweedie always felt a deep, penetrating longing. She did not understand it, so attributed it to "Russian discontent." Later she understood its true meaning and that this deep desire was for Truth. When she met Bhai Sahib ("elder brother"), she had a definite feeling that he could help her with this "Truth" she had wanted all her life.

The Spiritual Journey

Irina Tweedie's Teacher told her to keep a diary of her spiritual training in this ancient Yogic tradition, the journey to the "heart of hearts":

> "Keep a diary," said my Teacher. "One day it will become a book. But you must write it in such a way that it should help others. People say such things did happen thousands of years ago—we read in books about it. This book will be proof that such things do happen today, as they happened yesterday and will happen tomorrow—to the right people, in the right time, and the right place."[14]

Her expectations of what the spiritual training would be, however, were far removed from the reality of what occurred:

When I went to India in 1961, I hoped to get instruction in Yoga, expected wonderful teachings; but what the Teacher mainly did was force me to face the darkness within myself, and it almost killed me. It was done very simply—by using violent reproof, even aggression. My mind was kept in a state of confusion, unable to function properly. I was beaten down in every sense until I had to come to terms with that in me which I had been rejecting all my life.

Somewhere in one of the Upanishads—I do not remember which one—there is a sentence which puts our quest for spirituality in a nutshell: "If you want Truth as badly as a drowning man wants air, you will realize it in a split-second." But who wants Truth as badly as that? It is the task of the Teacher to set the heart aflame with an unquenchable fire of longing; it is his duty to keep it burning until it is reduced to ashes. For only a heart which has burned itself empty is capable of love.[15]

The diary begins with Mrs. Tweedie meeting Bhai Sahib for the first time. She originally went to India, however, as a tourist, but she found her guru "by chance." When we are diligent with our spiritual practices, or disciplines, it is like lighting a lamp in a darkened world. Someone will see our light and come to help us, to point us within to our higher self. When Mrs. Tweedie met her Teacher, the lamp within her heart was burning brightly. When she looked at Bhai Sahib for the first time, she realized at once that she was in the presence of a "Great Man":

. . . Next moment he stood in front of me, quietly looking at me, with a smile. He had a kindly face and strange eyes—dark pools of stillness, with a sort of liquid light in them.

I had just time to notice that he was the only one to be wearing wide trousers and a very long *kurta* (a collarless, India-style shirt) of immaculate whiteness; the other two were clad in rather worn kurtas and *longhi* (a straight piece of, usually, cotton material, tied round the waist and reaching to the ankles).

My mind had hardly time to register this; and it was as if it turned a somersault. My heart stood still for a split-second. I caught my breath . . . wild cartwheels were turning inside my brain and then my mind went completely blank.

And then it was as if *something in me* had stood to attention and saluted. . . . I was in the presence of a Great Man. . . .[16]

On the second day of their meeting, Bhai Sahib wanted to know if she had any dependents or obligations for which she was responsible. Knowing that he knew there was nothing to bind her, she was curious about his question:

"Yes I know of course that you are free. But I wanted a confirmation from yourself. Sometimes in this physical world we have to behave and to speak as if we know nothing."

It seemed a strange answer but I did not ask further.

Looking at me thoughtfully he said: "It takes time to make a soul pregnant with God. But it can be done; IT WILL BE DONE. . . ."

This too seemed a strange statement. I kept very still. Gazing at him and wondering.[17]

While there was complete acceptance initially, Mrs. Tweedie experienced the usual doubts and questions about her Teacher:

Doubts kept creeping into my mind. Many doubts. Such ordinary surroundings. Such ordinary people around him. Is he a Great Man? There seems to be none of the glamour of a great guru about him as we are used to reading in books. He seems so simple, living a simple, ordinary life. Clearly, he takes his household duties seriously. I could see that he was the head of a large family—six children, and his brother and his family living also in the same house, all sharing the same courtyard. And I saw also other people there, a few other families. The place was full of comings and goings, all kinds of activities, not to count his disciples of whom there seemed to be many.[18]

She was filled with questions about the spiritual life, why a teacher was necessary, and the system of training which she was entering. Bhai Sahib explained:

"A guru is a short-cut, a short-cut and a sharp one. But not a guru; a friend, a Spiritual Guide. I have nothing to teach."

"What do you mean by a system?" He often used the expression in conversation. I was not quite sure if I understood its meaning.

"A system is a school of Yoga, or a path to Self-Realization; the meaning is the same. We are all called Saints but it is the same as Yogis; in Wisdom there is no difference. The colour of our line is golden yellow, and we are called the Golden Sufis or the Silent Sufis, because we practice silent meditation. We do not belong to any country or any civilization, but we work always according to the need of the people of the time. We belong to Raja Yoga, but not in the sense that it is practiced by the Vedantins. Raja means simply 'Kingly,' or 'Royal'—The Direct Road to Absolute Truth."[19]

Mrs. Tweedie's mind was stuffed with knowledge and curiosity. Now her Teacher told her that she must forget her knowledge before she could take another step. He emphasized that there would be numerous difficulties in the spiritual training, and she would be hurt in those areas where she was most afraid of being hurt. But no one was making her take these steps. It was of her own free will.

She continued to learn day by day. Every morning, Irina Tweedie went to her Teacher's house. He might say something to her or nothing, speak in English or totally ignore her presence and speak to others in Hindi. Sometimes he would sing:

If I knew how painful Love is,
I would have stood at the entrance of the Lane of Love;

I would have proclaimed with beat of the drum:
Keep, keep away, keep away!
It is not a thoroughfare, there is only one way in;
Once entered, I am helpless, I stay here;
But you who are outside, look out!
Think before entering how painful it is,
Full of sorrow, to walk the Lane of Love![20]

He looked radiant, singing this Persian song, beating the time on his thigh with the palm of his hand.

L. told me afterwards that Sufis rarely speak directly; they will tell a story, sing a song or tell a parable. It is their way of teaching. "He might, for instance, speak to me and mean you," she said. "One has to learn how to listen. A Teacher has no right to test a disciple, or subject him to any trouble, without a previous warning. The warning is never given directly. Often the disciple does not understand it or is made to forget. But the warning is always given, for Sufis believe in the free will of the individual. The human being must consent. His consenting gives the Teacher the right to act according to the needs of the disciple who, himself, by consenting, draws down the Grace."

It made me think. Are those songs for me or L.? The one about the painfulness of love. . . . I wonder.[21]

Mrs. Tweedie was full of prejudices and judgments, all of which surfaced during the course of her training. Alone in her room, surrounded by the sights and sounds of India, Mrs. Tweedie faced haunting shadows on the walls of her mind. Judgments, doubts, prejudices, and self-pity stalked the glow of awareness. It was darkness made visible, and it struck like lightning across the desert sky of night. During such times, we pray that our longing for God outweighs the throes of self-pity that tempt us. Melancholy is born of self-importance, yet only when we are nothing do we become everything. The spiritual journey is filled with such paradoxes and levels of understanding. None of this was lost on Mrs. Tweedie. Whether in Guruji's presence or wilting from heat while under a protective tree in his courtyard, she aggressively was made to face herself.

In the early stages of spiritual training, we unconsciously judge the unknown, seeking to limit the Divind to our comfort and security. As our growth matures, we learn that our opinions, rationalizations, and intellectual understanding cannot limit eternity. Truth is not our prisoner, like a bird in a cage. The bird belongs in the air, carried by wings of discrimination and detachment to greater heights. True freedom and clarity is mastery over passions, desires, and judgments which bind our heart in self-tied knots. Spiritual training unties the knots, revealing a heart inflamed by the love of God. Although this love is our birthright, it requires persistent training to unfold our divine heritage as well as the grace of One who wants us for Himself. And, somewhere along the Way, we realize that our heart cannot be quieted by anything less. Nothing of the material world can touch our heart's deepest desire for the Beloved. Mrs. Tweedie was well aware of this even as she suffered from the heat, weariness, and the judgments which she disparagingly cast upon India, Guruji, and the people who surrounded her Teacher:

> I asked L. how it is that Guru's premises are full of most objectionable people? She answered that this is the Sufi way. All those who are without work, who are rejected by society, the awkward, the too loud, too weak in mind, too sick in body, to these he will give refuge and hospitality. So many people live in his courtyard, and one or two thatched huts are even in the garden.
>
> "Poor wife of his! She must be a saint herself to put up with such conditions!"
>
> "Yes," said L. "It cannot be easy to be the wife of a Sufi Saint!"[22]

Mrs. Tweedie faced hidden aspects of herself, suffered the heat, and tolerated the trouble Guruji continually placed in her path. In the Sufi tradition, a Teacher is a bridge over which we cross to the Reality of Life. Our crossing is a trip to unknown depths, to a world we previously could only dream about. Through the use of stories, dreams, parables, and yogic powers, the Teacher stirs the natural rhythms of the heart, awakening the wonders and possibilities within us. A vast new world opens to us, where we find strength and the ability to love without the need for complete understanding.

In crossing the bridge, however, we discover that the path of the soul is a narrow road paved by sharp, jagged stones. Initially, we view our rocky course as one of unrelenting hardships. But, in retrospect, we realize that each cragged rock was a stepping stone which was an essential link in our development.

The teacher casts a watchful eye over us as we traverse this rocky landscape. One of the responsibilities of a qualified teacher is to offer protective vigilance over the excesses of imagination, illusion, emotional enthusiasms, and pseudo-mystical states. Guruji cut her to the quick when Mrs. Tweedie overestimated extra-sensory perceptions. It is dangerous to overestimate spiritual progress or equate phenomena with spiritual advancement. Nor do we rely on intellectual conception as an indicator of spiritual expansion. Each movement to a new threshold of consciousness releases energy which must be integrated. And, between states of personal consciousness and universal consciousness, we experience interludes of aloneness. These states must be recognized and understood for what they are. At other times, memories awaken, long hidden in the depths of consciousness. They, too, require reintegration as they reach new levels of awareness. Profound states of sorrow can occur during this journey of unfoldment, so intense that they have the potential to isolate us like a solitary boat in an ocean of loneliness. The teacher is a Wayshower on the path of spiritual development, to direct us through the wilderness of our changing states of consciousness.

As we progress, we live in the center of being, not dominated by mind and emotion. Life, like a flower, is directed by inner unfoldment rather than by outward circumstances. If we plant a flower, however, we must water it if it is to live its full potential as a flower. The teacher offers water as the plant struggles to grow; the sun, created by Love, sustains the life of the unfolding child of light.

Guruji was vigilant over Mrs. Tweedie's flowering soul, using yogic powers, psychological insight, dream interpretation, and reproof, when necessary, to further the course of surrender. Irina Tweedie suffered endless heartaches and worries during this process, but she continued to progress:

"What do you feel exactly?" he said suddenly, sharply, looking at me.

"Well, all the oceans and all the seas of the world seem to be concentrated in my head. Walking down the street I had just enough consciousness left to keep to the right side of the road and not to be run over by the traffic. Crossing the road I could not see where I was going. I thought it was dangerous. I could see only when I looked straight ahead; right and left seemed obliterated as in a mist.

"If I see an object, for instance this chair in front of me, between the image of the chair and the realization that it is a chair and not something else, there is an interval of a fraction of a second. I have to concentrate on each particular sensory object to be able to name it. Indeed Krishnamurti mentions in one of his works that we should abstain from naming the things around us so that the interval between seeing an object and naming it may become longer and longer and it may happen that one day, in that moment, illumination may come." He nodded.

"You spoke of a miracle a few days ago," he said slowly. "Have you still the courage to speak of miracles? The roar of all the oceans is in your head, or the mind is not there at all, or you don't sleep without being tired, while at my home your thinking process is slowed down so much that you 'sleep'; there is a peace not of this world in you which you cannot explain; or a longing so strong that life is not worth living; upheavals, premonitions; tell me, are these not miracles? Great and important miracles?"

His voice was soft and very gentle as if full of deep compassion. I lowered my eyes and felt small. Smaller than a grain of sand.[23]

During times when the mind could still think, Mrs. Tweedie wondered how love would be produced in her heart. Would it come gently like the golden silence of sunset, or more like a transparent river that sweeps over tree roots and stones to finally break free and flow into infinity? Would it be woven into every moment, or be like the music of love, so exquisite that it breaks the heart? By this time, Irina Tweedie knew the basic requirements of the spiritual life: what is expected, what the disciplines are, the necessity to train the body and senses, the role of a teacher. But how would love come to her? Her question echoed the clear, ringing voices of those in every century who want nothing in life but to become united with the Divine.

Later, the experiential mystery of love would reveal its secrets and how it unconditionally embraces all in its path. Such love extinguishes any desire to live just for ourselves. Life is for the good of everyone and no power on Earth can inhibit our ability to give and to serve humanity as an expression of our love for the Beloved. Bathed in love, we see old limits thrown off, and we have access to unlimited strength and wisdom. *The laws of life are experienced in their full purity: wisdom does not lie, love does not harm, power does not abuse.* Through the alchemy of love, sorrow becomes compassion, a balm for the wounded heart of all that lives. Long years of living united with God reveal the nuances of love.

But, when first love is near, the summit peak and the vast chasm are glimpsed and commingle in the same moment. Hope and optimism unite with restlessness and despair as we wonder how to bridge the gap. Life seems so full of contradictions. Then, it dawns on us: the journey is made, not under our own power, but through grace. The tiny flame of love in the soul is kindled by grace. It is grace that carries us beyond what can be accomplished by the will alone.

In cooperation with grace, love is born. And nothing can destroy this divine capacity of love—nothing in our past, nothing we have done or said, no thought which flits through the mind unseen like the wind. Love is its own reward. For Mrs. Tweedie, it was like a flower which trembled in the evening breeze:

> And so it came . . . it slipped itself into my heart, silently, imperceptibly, and I looked at it with wonder. It was still, small; a light-blue flame trembling softly, and it had the infinite sweetness of first love, like an offering of fragrant flowers made with gentle hands, the heart full of stillness and wonder and peace.
>
> "Love will be produced," you [Guruji] said. And since then I kept wondering how it will come to me. Will it be like the

voice from the Burning Bush, the Voice of God as Moses heard it? Will it be like a flash of lightning out of a blue sky making the world about me a blaze of glory? Or will it be, as I suggested, that you will produce Love in general, Love of everything, and the Teacher will be included in it? But I told her that it could not be so for me; to be able to surrender completely, to sweep away all resistance, it must be big, tremendous, complete; without reserve; without limit; the conditionless, absolute forgetting oneself.

But what I felt was not so. It was just a tender longing, so gentle, so full of infinite sweetness.

Like all laws governing this universe, love will follow the way of least resistance. In all my life I never knew the feeling of love flashing suddenly into my heart. It always came softly, timidly, like a small flower at the side of the road, so easily crushed by the boots of those who may pass by; growing slowly, steadily, increasing until it became vast, sweeping like a tidal wave, engulfing everything that stood in its way and at last filling all my life. So it was in the past and this time too; it is coming to me in the same way. I suppose because our hearts are made in a certain way we cannot help being what we are.[24]

Gradually, Mrs. Tweedie lost interest in everything—beautiful surroundings, interesting people, lectures, friends. Words became meaningless. Everything seemed nonexistent. Now she understood that "complete surrender" was only a step in the process of self-annihilation in the Teacher. And, that was only a step to the final stage—"Union with God, Truth." She felt the need for solitude as she experienced a greater and greater longing. The suffering continued and aspects within herself were magnified:

Day after day to sit in these squalid surroundings. Amongst the screaming noisy horde of the dirtiest children, all running about the place, roaming freely everywhere, is at times beyond endurance. Twice I cried in sheer despair. But the most frustrating fact is that I do not get a single question answered. As soon as I ask a question, everyone present begins to discuss it expressing their opinion, in which I am not the least interested, for I want *his* answer. But he will sit there listening to everybody, smiling politely, until in utter despair I say that it was I after all who had asked the question and wanted his answer and as I do not get it, only a lot of useless arguing from everybody else, I won't say anything anymore. He just turns to me and smiles in the most maddening way.

It is of no use to be resentful and fight against the circumstances and create a barrier. I will not change India, nor the people, nor his environment. It is much better to make up my mind to bear them patiently. So much more, because I had ample proof that in no matter what beautiful surroundings I am, I don't see them; I long instead to be in his presence. I saw it happen in Adyar.

"Criticize yourself, criticize yourself constantly and you will get somewhere."[25]

Mrs. Tweedie's former life was over, an empty shell where once there was life. Now she understood why it is impossible to go back once on the Spiritual Path. There is nothing to return to. . . .

Now, an atonement process began for all previously committed wrongs:

> "You must write down all the wrongs and evil deeds you have committed since your childhood. It will serve as a confession. A kind of *curriculum vitae* of your sins. Otherwise you may be called by God one day to account for it; but when the culprit confesses he becomes free. Everyone had to do it. L. had to do it too. You must do it if you want to be taken into the Arena. There is no other way. Confession must be; there must be no secrets before your Teacher."

I went cold. That was an unexpected blow. How can I remember all the wrongs of my life? What a dreadful task. But I understood the value of it. . . .

Went home and cried for a long time without being able to stop. It is a kind of traumatic state, crying sometimes without apparent reason; forgetting things, being assailed by dark, terrible fears. All abnormal reactions, obviously magnifying certain happenings which are insignificant and neglecting important duties. It does not look good; let's hope it will end without permanent damage to my mental state.[26]

A week later, Mrs. Tweedie noticed the inability of her mind to function in certain situations:

I noticed that my mind is only working in so far as my spiritual duties are concerned. For instance, I can write my diary; I remember fairly well all that he tells us; but I cannot do more than that; the brain is not good for anything else. And, what's more, nothing seems to matter any longer. Neither reading nor letter writing, nothing at all. All I want is to sit at his place, and even the silly, irritating chit-chat of the crowd around him seems to matter less and less. Everything seems to fall away from me as in a crazy dream when all the objects are crooked, vacillating and empty of content.[27]

Everything said or done becomes an element of the teaching. Once when she and her Teacher went for an evening walk, Mrs. Tweedie spoke of her love for the deep, red sky and the dramatic sunsets of India. Bhai Sahib said:

"How many things do you love?"
We sat down for a short while on a bench near the edge of the reservoir, the colours of the sky reflected in the water.
"Oh, so many." I replied. "The song of the birds at dawn, the flowers, mountains and sky, India, England, the forests burning with the colours of autumn, and people and. . . !"
"Your heart is like a hotel," he interrupted darkly. "One can love only One, you cannot love two masters; either you love the world or you love its Creator."
"Oh, Bhai Sahib," I sighed.[28]

Renouncing the world is not enough. It is the invisible things that must be surrendered—the will, the character, everything.

"Surrender is the most difficult thing in the world while you are doing it; and the easiest when it is done," he said. Complete surrender takes time, but it is the only way. "We all have to cross the stream alone."[29]

"There are two roads: the road of dhyana, the slow one; and the road of tyaga, of complete renunciation, of surrender. This is the direct road, the path of fire, the path of love."

"But will you not treat a woman differently from a man? A woman is more tender; the psychology of a woman and of a man is different!"

He shook his head. "The training is somewhat different. But it does not mean that because you are a woman you will get preferential treatment."

"But don't you see I am at odds against your Indian disciples?" I exclaimed. And he shook his head. "No, it is always difficult. For everybody. If it is not one thing, then it is another. Human beings are covered with so much conditioning."[30]

A reorientation was occurring, slowly, but distinguishable. The heart was still pained, but a stillness now resided:

When going to Pushpa's for lunch today, I was so acutely aware of the suffering of nature, of so many little things dying in the drought. The air boiling, the soil parched, Guruji's garden withered, leaves hanging from the branches, getting brittle and yellow.

Still, I was aware of a leaden peace; joyless, dark, but nonetheless, peace. There was much heartache, a permanent feature nowadays. Even the feeling of love is no more. Such is the maya. Nothing remains save the pain in the heart.[31]

Understanding began to seep into her awareness, as she slowly moved to ever-deeper levels of consciousness:

I was thinking, not without bitterness, why all the most disagreeable people are attracted here, and why on earth will they always sit near me, or be shown to sit next to me? Why must I suffer such additional difficulties when the physical conditions are already difficult enough and hard to bear. And suddenly the cognition came: he is training me to detach my mind at will from all that which I do not wish to notice. To conquer the small irritations. Immediately the full significance of it became clear; here is partly the answer to the fact that he can live with his family without ever being disturbed. He does not need to go into samadhi to escape the physical conditions; and he is teaching me to do the same.[32]

Not only can the mind be trained to conquer "small irritations" which plague us, but in deep meditation we can also look into the depths of the mind and see where our weaknesses are located, how they have affected us, and how long they have resided within us. The conditioned mind can be seen, and through deep concentration and oneness of desire, will, and attention, weaknesses are transformed into strengths. A chronically agitated mind is one in which thoughts stumble over one another, weakening not only the health of the body, but also inducing emotions such as fear, anxiety, frustration, and irritability. As the mind slows down, through meditation and concentration, thoughts slow down revealing that in the space between thoughts, love, patience, kindness, and goodwill live. A teacher can harness the mind, slowing it down like a master charioteer who can pull the reins to slow down runaway horses. Or, he can provide the experiences necessary to enable the student to learn detachment from all surroundings and irritations which seemingly steal away inner tranquility.

Insight now moved to another level of confusion for Mrs. Tweedie, as she wondered: What will happen when all beliefs are taken away? Does a human being not have to believe in something? Guruji laughed:

"So strong is this belief that you stick to it until now, in spite of everything . . . . It will take time. By and by, this will go too. . . ."

"But you take a belief away and you don't give another one!" I exclaimed, exasperated. "You don't even take the trouble to explain anything."

He got up from the *tachat* and stood leaning against the column. "If you let the belief go, then after a while you will discover something very different," he said quietly, looking afar with half-closed eyes. He stood very still and again this feeling of *meaning* came over me, so strong, so powerful. . . .[33]

Mrs. Tweedie began to realize that beliefs are not permanent; they are born and die all the time. What is created by the mind can be changed—that is the mind's nature. Tired, she left Guruji, went home, put up her rope bed (charpay) in the courtyard, and unexpectedly:

> . . . it was as if something snapped inside my head, and the whole of me was streaming out ceaselessly, without diminishing, on and on. There was no "me"—just flowing. Just being. A feeling of unending expansion, just streaming forth. . . . But all this I know only later, when I tried to remember it. When I first came back the first clear, physical sensation was of intense cold.
>
> It was shattering. But what was it? Was it prayer? Not in the ordinary sense. For a prayer there must be somebody to pray. But I was not. I did not exist.
>
> The door was open; the door to what? Whatever it was, it was wonderful. There must be an infinite sea of it. Like a terrific pull of one's whole being. Is this the "prayer of the heart"; is this "merging"? I don't know. Because when I am in it, there is no mind. I seem not to exist at all; and when the mind begins to know something about it, it is already past. But even the idea of praying to somebody or something seems pointless now. . . .
>
> . . . This is ABSOLUTE security, I said to myself. But to reach it, one has to traverse the no-man's land; one has to wade through the morass of insecurity, where there is no foothold of any kind and where one cannot even see the ground under one's feet. . . .

And with a sigh of relief, I fell asleep, blown out suddenly, like a candle by a gust of wind.[34]

Still, the struggles were not over, the questions persisted. Mrs. Tweedie asked her Teacher about one of her biggest worries:

"There is something that worries me a lot: I seem sometimes to hate everything and everybody. Hate them thoroughly and completely. Everyone seems to be irritating, ugly, even horrible. A constant irritation about practically everything surrounding me. I seem to have become barren and arid. Surely this is not an improvement?"

He smiled. "It is a stage one is passing. There was a time when I too hated everybody."

"But L. told me she feels universal love."

"This is something else. Once you love God, you love His Creation, and then you do not hate anymore."[35]

Eventually, she was sent back to England, penniless. All her money had been given to her Teacher, which he dispensed to those who were in need. Now, as part of her training, she had to leave her Teacher and India, with nothing but trust to accompany her. It was part of the training and her destiny. She wrote to him twice a week from London. When he wrote for her to return, she would remain with him until his death. But, by this time, she had no more questions:

I will not ask any more questions. Surrender is the acceptance of everything *without exception*. I ACCEPT. I will go to the end of the bitter road. Will sit, endlessly sit, and ask nothing any more. And now, because I accept it voluntarily, the mind will not give me trouble and restlessness any more. Not from this side anyway. Acceptance of "everything" means also acceptance of deliberate falsehood and cruelty, to which he still treats me freely.

And so, this morning I was alone with him and asked nothing. He looked friendly, as if to encourage me to speak. But I kept quiet.[36]

The tests were not over, however, only intensifying at other levels. The Sufi training includes tests of hunger, of her desire for the Beloved, of her ability to rise beyond her attachment to illusions. Mrs. Tweedie encountered them all prior to the death of Guruji's physical body. A couple of months after her vow not to ask any more questions, and with her Teacher very ill, Mrs. Tweedie commented:

> I said to him, "Our relationship to God is something entirely different from what we usually imagine it to be. We think that the relationship of God and Man is a duality. But it is not so. I have found that our relationship to God is something quite different. It is a merging, without words, without thought even; into 'something'. Something so tremendous, so endless, merging in Infinite Love, physical body and all, disappearing in it. And the physical body is under suffering; it is taut like a spring in this process of annihilation. This is our experience of God and it cannot be otherwise."
>
> "What you have said is absolutely correct," he nodded gravely.[37]

Then came the test of hunger. She had no rupees and no food. But Mrs. Tweedie did not complain. She did not even mention her hunger. Finally, he asked her how long it took for her to prepare her food:

> "Very little time." I answered.
> "Good. Go now!"
> I left slightly puzzled. He gave an opening in case I could not bear it. He tested me. Or was it pity? No, it was a test. If I had said that I had nothing to eat, then it would have meant that I had not accepted the situation. He would have offered some food immediately. But no, my Master; I offer it to you, the Test of Hunger; and I will go through with it whatever happens. I will not die. And if I do, in this condition, it would mean Salvation at once. . . . I will have won in any case. . . .

"Not in financial difficulty?" he asked.

It made me smile. "As you ask me directly, I must answer." And I told him that on Monday, ten days ago, I had only four rupees left. Had carried on for as long as they lasted; and then began to fast; water and some nimbu juice; and then only water. "But let me go on. It is no hardship. I have no sensation of hunger even. I had no intention of telling you if you had not asked."

"No, you should have told me; I forgot completely."

"I cannot believe it; and I don't believe it." I laughed. "If you are the man I know you to be, you must have known. There were little signs that you knew."

He did not reply directly, but said, "Go to my wife. She will give you something to eat and tomorrow I will give you ten rupees."[38]

The nature of a test is that it strikes us where we are most vulnerable. No idea, belief, cherished attachment, or emotional reaction (anger, resentment, hate, fear, anxiety, etc.) is sacred. The test will emphasize that which we must accept within ourselves and rise beyond. That is the way forward. Consequently, Mrs. Tweedie suffered many tests, always in an area dear to her heart. Once she came upon her worst trial:

Yesterday I wrote down the sentence: I will accept the unjust treatment. And the word unjust gave me a clue; injustice is the worst thing for me. That's why he is testing me with the emphasis on all kinds of unjust treatments. And I became full of peace . . . if I am able to accept it, a great step forward would be made. All became still in me. And the irritation, I noticed, was no more. . . .[39]

And then, Mrs. Tweedie's desire for the Beloved was tested:

The world became a very interesting place to live. I came to know the thoughts of people, the reasons why they came to Guruji. I used to tell one of his disciples who sat near me: this one comes because his child is ill; this other one because he has a court case and wants some help and advice; that man on the right is ill and hopes that Guruji will heal him, and so on. . . . Of course I was delighted. Bhai Sahib did not take any notice of me, was talking to others, and I sat there full of wonder and delight, observing everything around me.

Then, one day, when he turned to me and said something, I took the opportunity and told him how pleased I was that only after such a short time with him I was progressing so fast.

"Oh?" he lifted his eyebrows, *"and why so?"* I told him, describing in detail what I saw and telling him that I knew the reason why each one came to him.

He listened. His expression was that of slight irony; then he gave me a sideways look and turned away to speak to others.[40]

The ability to know the thoughts of people vanished, however, and after three days of waiting for it to return, she stormed:

"You took it away from me!"
*"Of course!"*he answered quickly. *"Just look at you! You were blown up like a balloon! Are you after Absolute Truth or are you after illusions? How will the self go if you continue like this?"*[41]

Until the last moments before his death, Bhai Sahib did the ordinary things of life. The final day, drizzling rain blanketed the city. When the sun appeared, a breathtaking double rainbow arched overhead:

Right across the sky towards the south-east were two magnificent rainbows; they seemed to span from one side of the horizon to another. One very clear and bright and the other above, paler, delicate, ethereal; but both complete, parallel to each other.

I did not notice anything unusual. It did not occur to me to look and see if all the colours were there. But Satendra said next morning that his father went into the room for a moment and said to his wife:

"See, the Great Painter, what wonderful colours he paints. . . . But the yellow colour is missing . . . ."

And in the night, when Satendra was massaging his feet, he suddenly sat up, his eyes blazing, and said, as if speaking to himself:

"The yellow colour was missing . . . my colour was gone. . . ."

Once more that day it was one of those exceptional sunsets and I continued to watch the colours change. Then I noticed something rare, never seen in my life before— small, perfectly circular clouds stood motionless, right above the bungalow, very low. They were of purest, tender amethyst, surrounded by the great flood of orange and pink from the setting sun. . . .

"Then suddenly the whole garden, nay, the whole world, seemed to glow with an incredible golden-pink light. . . . He was sitting there, the white garment glowing, his skin also; his disciples seated around him. . . .

". . . I did not know at that moment that the Greatest Painter painted the sky in Glory and bathed the garden in Golden Light because a Great Soul of a Golden Sufi was leaving this world forever.

"It was his last sunset. . . ."[42]

After his death, memories crowded in, and she remembered a tender scene between her Teacher and a village woman which captured the essence of this "Great Soul":

It was a day with a sparkle in the air, a kind of trembling luminosity, a limpid transparency which in Spanish is called "dia luminosa."

He was already seated outside. An Indian village woman was talking to him.

She was small, very thin, her face was wrinkled, shrunken, as if dried-up by the merciless sun, the hot wind of the plains.

From the little Hindi I knew I understood that she was telling him her troubles of which she had many. . . . An endless sorrowful litany of illnesses, misery, death of her husband, of most of her children, and now she was alone, useless, and nobody needed her, she had nothing to hope for, nothing to live for.

And she came out with a question which seemed to burn, scorching her trembling lips:

"Maharaj, why did God create this world so full of troubles? Why did He create me to endure all those sufferings?"

I saw him leaning forward, a shimmering light in his eyes, the light of compassion I knew and loved so well. Soft was his voice when he answered:

"Why has He created the world? That you should be in it! Why has He created you? He is alone; He needs you!"

Never will I forget the broad, blissful smile on the lined, emaciated face when she was walking away. She went happy in the knowledge that she was not alone, not really, for God needed her to keep Him company because He too was alone. . . .

And never will I forget the utter admiration I felt then; only a very Great Soul could have expressed so simply and convincingly one of the greatest Mysteries to a child-like mind of a village woman. . . .[43]

Still, after his death, in July 1966, Mrs. Tweedie was deeply resentful that her Teacher had not taught her anything. That was the great secret—there was nothing to teach. It was all heart to heart. In the midst of this sorrow, Mrs. Tweedie was filled with the revelation of love and security with the Divine. She thought she "was going mad":

The whole world was in absolute glory. There was such oneness with myself and the trees, the dirty children who throw stones, the mangy dogs and the fleas—all that was me. If I'd had any money, I would have given it all away. A professor suggested I go to the Gandhi ashram in the Himalayas. It was around August and Guruji died in July. I needed solitude to find myself, but self didn't exist anymore. . . . I stayed at the ashram until shortly before Christmas, then stayed in another ashram until spring, when I returned to England. I spent a great deal of time in solitude.[44]

Watching the sun rise I sat for a while outside. This
love. My God, what love! All the beauties of this wonderful nature around are very secondary, are just on the edge
of consciousness; but deep, deep within there is this love
and this is the ONLY REALITY—this love that digs deep
into the heart its blazing abyss, this love that enwraps and
exalts my whole being and the whole of creation as one.
We are one, how very true; if only we could realize it,
everything would be so very different. If only. . . . But how
steep is the path that leads to this realization to this supreme experience. We have to be emptied, made nothing,
to be filled with thy divine love, with the purity of thy
love, O God! Guruji, now I understand; I was emptied to
be filled; I was made naught to be *human*. A steam-roller
went over me and I was the better for it; but what managed to get up afterward was something very different
from the human being who faced you in 1961!

And in bed I was thinking that it does not matter if I
stay with closed eyes or go outside to watch the sun-
rise. . . . It is all in me . . . not outside me. I can be in a cave,
in a prison, in eternal darkness, and it would matter little,
if I had this glory within forever. . . .

Was reflecting that this feeling of divinity has no pride
in it; it is on the contrary a very humble feeling. It is: I am
nothing before Thee.[45]

Her diary ends as Mrs. Tweedie experiences the joyous,
boundless merging with the Eternal Undivided Whole. Never to
be alone anymore, she reached God in silence. It began with her
courage to face Truth and culminated in the "glorious state of
consciousness, wherein the divine heart within myself was the
Divine Heart within the cosmos."

After her stay in India for a brief period of adjustment, Mrs.
Tweedie returned to England to begin the work which her
Teacher had started. Guruji once said that Sufi methods of training were everchanging to meet the progressive development of
humanity. Consequently, for Mrs. Tweedie's students, dreams
are the modern Sufi teaching story, used in conjunction with
daily meditation. Each day, Irina Tweedie meets with her disciples for a couple of hours at which time they may ask questions

about dreams, the Sufi path to the Beloved, or anything else of concern. For instance, a question may arise about a recurring dream in which the devil symbolically appears. Rather than fearing the return of this symbolic night stalker, the student embraces the dream and walks through it. In so doing, she faces the hidden aspects of self represented by the devil, thus discovering unseen beauty in the process.

Once the afternoon meeting concludes, everyone goes their individual ways, until promptly at 7:00 p.m. when disciples and other students gather for the evening session. After forty-five minutes of meditation, students ask questions regarding dreams or their meditation. Mrs. Tweedie may offer a dream interpretation, as may anyone else, or she may simply say, "That's interesting."

Sufi teaching manuals distinguish between "true" and "false" dreams, the latter being without spiritual or psychological value. "True" dreams provide guidance and are interpreted. Since the Sufi path has extremely powerful inner experiences, dreams are viewed as important to the process. If the dream is purely of a personal nature and without spiritual significance, the student is encouraged to explore its meaning independently. Hence, "it's interesting." Complete silence may indicate that the timing for interpretation is wrong or the meaning is already apparent.

In her diary, Mrs. Tweedie records her own dreams, some of which are interpreted:

> DREAM: I was looking at myself in a mirror and saw that I was very thin; very pale, my hair in disorder.
> INTERPRETATION: It is a very good dream! Thin and thinner until nothing will remain.[46]

Toward the end of her training, Mrs. Tweedie records a dream with a prophetic quality. In her "future" dream, she "merges with the Teacher," which is an essential aspect of the Sufi path:

> DREAM: I was dressed in black for a lecture. I looked in the mirror and saw that I had a beard . . . a white beard around my face, as Muslims have. No other hair was on my cheeks, only the beard about three inches long, like a

white, soft halo around the lower part of my face. Strange, that I go on lecturing to large audiences all over the world and nobody laughed at me, nobody called me a woman with a beard. Nobody seems to notice it. . . . [47]

She did merge with the Teacher. Years later she addressed large audiences. And, occasionally, people in the audience were certain they "saw" her wearing a beard.

Most people attend the Sufi meetings at the invitation of other students, but only with the prior permission of Mrs. Tweedie. Each newcomer is given the standard guidelines to follow: leave your shoes at the door, listen (one must *learn* to listen), raise your hand if you have a question, and do not challenge the teachings. If the challenge rule, or any other rule, is broken, the student is confronted and, on occasion, asked to leave. Mrs. Tweedie talks about living in the full presence of God. She does so honestly and with integrity. Never are students pitted against each other, criticized behind their backs, or tricked into mistrusting other seekers. Each person is treated equally. Even one who is asked to leave may return fully accepted and forgiven if he or she seeks to return, the unlearned lesson now learned. The offense is never spoken of again.

Prior to Mrs. Tweedie's return to London, she had already begun living in the states of consciousness in which she belonged completely to Him. Though only at the beginning of this state, she now knew deeply that our smallest act, our most casual thought or word, sets forces in motion which have far-reaching effects. All that she once knew, she now realized experientially as an effect of Oneness. Before his death, Guruji prepared her for the next phase of her journey. As she left for England, she carried within her heart his words of what the future would hold: health problems, continued growth, a conscious connection with Guruji, a life of fire, and misunderstandings by others, among other things.

Examples of his preparation can be found near the end of her life as well as in the beginning of her work. Several years before her recent retirement, Mrs. Tweedie attended the Sufi conference in Germany at which she, and other Sufis, gave individual lectures. She charged no money for her talk; other speakers required "extravagant fees." Conference leaders criticized her for this; some called her a hoax and said she had never been to India, much less received training. The whole diary was fiction, they said, a figment of her imagination. Some months later, Mrs. Tweedie was introduced to a well-known swami in the United States, whose first words to her were, "I saw you!" Excited to meet her, the swami volunteered that he had seen her in India, sitting in the miserable heat under the tree recalled in her diary. When she inquired why he had not come into the courtyard to say 'hello,' the swami replied that he, and others in his group, were late for a meeting. Slowly, the swami's verification made the rounds, eventually reaching those Sufis whose criticisms initiated the original misunderstanding. The path is littered with projections and misunderstandings. Truth is beyond them all, however.[48]

At the beginning of her work, another preparation was realized. On the fourteenth day of October, soon after her Teacher died and she experienced oneness with the Heart of All, Mrs. Tweedie "reached a conscious connection" with Guruji, and training began on a different level. Guidance was always provided now, not for herself, but for others. She remembers those days as being full of projections from people:

> Whatever people needed came to them and help was provided. People said, "It was you, Mrs. Tweedie, who gave what was needed." I knew very well it wasn't me, but there was no use to deny it because people continually said "It was you." People want someone to be a very convenient hook for their projections. So, they all projected onto me. Oh the projections—it was hopeless. People didn't know what they meant. And, I don't know what I was for them—an elder sister, a guru, a mother—who knows what I was for them. But, by 1967 or 1968, I didn't receive answers when people were in distress. So, I had to make my own decisions. Now there is neither Teacher nor me. In deep meditation, I just learn. It's very, very simple. And there is no pride when I tell you this, because it's not me as a person. It's a very interesting metamorphosis, and what's interesting is that I didn't notice it. The process was like growing up. . . .

In the Yoga book, it is said, "First you realize the Self and then you realize God." You begin to feel this unbelievable peace "that passeth all understanding," to quote the Bible. The joy in life is incredible. There are miracles around you. Guruji said, "Just look around, the Grace of God is in every shape around." And so it is. . . .

I understand union as oneness with the Beloved. You merge into nothingness and there is nobody there. There is nobody who loves you so much and will never betray you—only the absolute Nothingness that is God.[49]

In her diary, Mrs. Tweedie records her spiritual transformation. It includes not only the peace and bliss, but also the doubts, agonies, resistances, movements to surrender, and finally an all-consuming love. It is an amazing journey of ego-dissolution and union with the Beloved. On the beginning page, she quotes an early Christian mystic:

> The Path of Love
> Is like a Bridge of Hair
> Across a Chasm of Fire[50]

She followed the path and crossed the fiery chasm.

Saint Teresa of Ávila (1515-1582)

Photograph of a picture painted in her lifetime by Brother Juan de la Miseria, sixteenth century Spain.

Chapter VI

Saint Teresa of Ávila

... Oh, how good the Lord is and how powerful! He gives not only counsel but relief. His words are deeds. As He strengthens our faith, see how our love grows!

This is certain, and I would often remember how when a storm arose on the sea, the Lord commanded the winds to be still. Then I would say to myself: 'Who is this whom all my faculties thus obey? Who is it that in a moment sheds light amidst such great darkness, who softens a heart that seemed to be of stone and sheds the water of gentle tears where for so long it had seemed to be dry? Who gives these desires? Who gives this courage? What have I been thinking of? What am I afraid of? What is this? I wish to serve this Lord, and have no other aim but to please Him. I seek no contentment, no rest, no other blessing but to do His will . . . .'[1]

Even saints begin with questions and contradictions, doubts and fears, and Saint Teresa was no exception. But, if her life story began in a crucible of pain, it ended fulfilled in her aspiration to see God "face to face."

Who was this woman who went into a rapture with a frying pan of eggs in her hand, spoiling the dinner she was preparing? Who was this woman who told her community of nuns that "God is not only found on your knees before the altar, but in the kitchen among the pots and pans?" Who was this woman who danced and played a well-worn tambourine, and sang a hilarious song asking God to rid the nuns' new woolen habits of an "impertinent little flock" of bugs? Who was this Carmelite nun who, in deteriorating health, crossed swollen streams only to lose all her supplies to raging waters? Then with tired impatience, she heard her Beloved say, "This is how I treat my real friends . . . ." "Then it's no wonder," she mumbled, "that your Lordship has so few!" Who was this *determined* woman who was in jeopardy every time her pen flowed with line-by-line descriptions of her prayer life? Who was Saint Teresa of Ávila, who waved away fear and wrote books and letters during a time when culture and the Church said women could not teach or comment on scripture? What kind of nun threw caution to the wind and wrote:

> [T]hose who want to journey on this road . . . must have a great and very resolute determination to persevere until reaching the end, come what may, happen what may, whatever work is involved, whatever criticism arises, whether they die on the road, or even if the whole world collapses. You will hear some people frequently making objections: "there are dangers"; "this one was deceived"; "another who prayed a great deal fell away"; "it is harmful to virtue"; "it is not for women for they will be susceptible to illusions"; "it is better they stick to their sewing"; "they don't need these delicacies"; "the Our Father and the Hail Mary are sufficient." . . . [D]on't pay any attention to the fears they raise or to the picture of the dangers they paint for you . . . . Sisters, give up these fears; never pay attention in like matters to the opinion of the crowd. Behold these are not the times to believe everyone; believe only those who you see are walking in conformity with Christ's life.[2]

In an era that preferred women of silence, who was this nun who, through her love of words written, spoken, and sung, called women—and men—to a life of contemplative prayer? And why have her words reached across centuries of time to echo her invitation anew?

Saint Teresa was a sixteenth century woman of vision whose heroic quest into the inner life of the soul brought her to the promised land of God. It was 1554 and she was thirty-nine years old. After thirty years of uphill struggles, she reached the summit of "experience of God." As a reformer, writer, and spiritual guide whose life exemplified full, loving union with God, Saint Teresa challenged her contemporaries to intimacy and divine friendship with "His Majesty" through prayer.

> Wouldn't it show great ignorance, my daughters, if someone when asked who he was didn't know, and didn't know his father or mother or from what country he came? Well now, if this would be so extremely stupid, we are incomparably more so when we do not strive to know who we are, but limit ourselves to considering only roughly these bodies. Because we have heard and because faith tells us so, we know we have souls. But we seldom consider the precious things that can be found in this soul, or who dwells within it, or its high value.[3]

Saint Teresa knew from experience with the Master Gardener of the soul what awaited those who followed the path of inevitable grace. But she was an author of another century, writing in brilliant metaphor to nuns of that period. To fully appreciate this fascinating first woman doctor of the Church, we must visit the stage of time in which her life was enacted.

Paint a picture of her times, and we discover heresy—obsessed Spain in the midst of an Inquisition while rumors circulated that a daughter-of-faith was having raptures. Had she been unable to persuade her spiritual directors that the raptures were God-inspired, Saint Teresa could have been burned at the stake, convicted of falling prey to the devil. She wrote her *Autobiography* to "explain" her experiences of mental, or contemplative, prayer to severe critics such as the Dominicans. The Inquisition was run by the Dominicans, most of whom were *letrados* ("learned ones"), who believed that the only knowledge of God in this life was through study. They were the theologians of the era, and they scorned mental prayer, flaming the fires of fear with accusations that it would lead to delusions. Yet, discursive prayer, in which the reason or imagination actively considers a biblical passage or the content of a vocal prayer, was impossible for Teresa. Like "restless moths" her imagination fluttered away her concentration. She learned that technique and forced methods unsuitable to temperament contributed to slow, erratic progress. For Saint Teresa, prayer was love and cultivating a friendship with God, not technique. So in her own language, rich with allegory, Teresa described her subtle inner life of prayer and its transformative power. Her simple imagery drew word pictures free from theological jargon. When describing a particular state of the soul, for example, she said, "It doesn't seem that the soul feels anything. I think it goes out like a little donkey that's grazing."[4] And, in describing the intellect in her practice, she laments, "This intellect is so wild that it doesn't seem to be anything else than a frantic madman no one can tie down."[5] In her own simple language, Saint Teresa answered her critics. It was not critics, however, who alarmed her the most. "Without doubt," she said, "I fear those who have such great fear of the devil more than I do the devil himself."[6]

Paint a picture of the times and we feel the strong winds of political and spiritual reform that swept sixteenth century Spain, fanned by a longing among people for a deeper, more mystical life of prayer. Newly formed printing presses offered people a drink from the river of knowledge. Translations from Italian, German, and Flemish schools, from the Fathers, Protestants, scholastics, and humanists crossed Spanish borders to quench the spiritual thirst of those drawn to prayer and the interior life. The Franciscans were especially moved by this "new" spirituality. Francisco de Osuna, a Franciscan, wrote a mental prayer manual called *The Third Spiritual Alphabet* which propelled twenty-three year old Teresa into the deep waters of consciousness and the contemplative life. Like a shepherd leading his flock to water, *literature* was a messenger of ideas directing those who were drawn to prayer by some irresistible longing.

Seeds of change, however, had been planted centuries earlier. In fourteenth and fifteenth century Spain, the reform of ecclesiastical structures was conducted under government control and influence. For 800 years, Spain had been tormented by internal wars, effectively cutting off the flowering of Catholic mysticism that took root in other European countries.

In 1492 the last Moorish stronghold was defeated, and Spanish authorities began a campaign to solidify Spain as a "Christian" nation. Jews were given a choice: convert or be expelled. These *conversos* (Jews who accepted Christian baptism) were treated with contempt by Spain's "old Christians." Considered possible heretics for secret practice of their ancestral Jewish religion, the "new Christians" were regarded with suspicion. The Spanish Inquisition was created in 1478 to Christianize the Jews, then was expanded to protect the orthodox Catholic faith. Wealth from newly discovered America funded a university at Alcola which became a treasure-house of humanist scholarship, particularly that of Erasmus. His emphasis on interior prayer and the direct experience of God swept Spain like seeds gathered up and scattered in a swirling wind.

From 1556 to1598, Catholic King Phillip II not only continued government control but also initiated drastic reforms. Having little faith in Rome or the pope's ability to oversee religion, King Phillip II embarked on a strict reform of religious orders based on Spanish belief and control. He used every means possible to protect the purity of the Catholic faith from the infiltration of Protestant heretics and the religious hysteria of the *alumbrados* ("illuminists") who advocated direct, ecstatic contact with God. If he could have shut the doors and windows of his country to all foreign influence, he would have.

Increasingly threatened by encroaching heresy and eager to extend his control, the "Catholic King" burdened the nation with oppression. To "protect the faith" Protestants were exiled from Vallodolid, Seville, and Murcia in 1559; publication of papal decrees was delayed or forbidden; books were banned; printing presses were controlled; orthodoxy specialists were appointed to scrutinize religious practices. Imprisonment or execution often awaited those who committed crimes against the faith. An ecclesiastical crisis engulfed Europe: a Protestant reformation that threatened the purity of Catholic tradition. Consequently, church officials strongly emphasized outward compliance with ecclesiastical ceremonies and rites to separate the faithful from the heretical.

Paint a picture of the times in which Teresa initiated her monastic reforms, and we see examiners of the Church suspiciously watching both clergy and laity. Enormous significance was placed on the Mass, sacraments, relics, genuflections (crossing oneself), and keeping the eyes open and lips moving while praying. Practitioners of mental prayer (the *espirituales*) whose lips were still and eyes closed were viewed with increasing distrust and apprehension.

As a practitioner of mental prayer, Teresa and her confessors lived under a wandering cloud of oppression in a climate of fear. Her soul, however, eagerly accepted the invitation of Love. For Teresa, prayer was not learning poetic words or offering eloquent discussions. Prayer was a return to the heart, to awaken to the profound depths and presence of God.

In her *Autobiography*, she subtly addressed the crossroads of spiritual prayer. Both in Christianity and in other religions, the fork in the road creates controversy. In sixteenth century Spain, the paths were represented by the *recogidos* and the *dejados*. Both methods, in contrast to the *letrados*, believed that a direct, unmediated experience of God through contemplative prayer was possible in this life. The *dejados'* practice involved interior passivity and inspiration. Exterior devotion was rejected. The *recogidos* pursued systematic methods of interior prayer in which the soul withdrew from the outside world and everything created to be penetrated by God. The latter were closer to orthodoxy and was the path traveled by Teresa. She recognized, however, that there were appropriate stages of spiritual development in which it was essential to abandon human efforts and "let go"—let God take over. Teresa was aware of both the dangers of undisciplined interior prayer and the transforming power of mental prayer when practiced appropriately.

She entered the inner sanctuary of her heart to what was already there—everything that has already been given to each one of us. This sixteenth century saint entered an intimate, mysterious "friendship" with God and realized the truth in the Book of Revelation: "I stand at the door and knock." The door opened and Teresa of Ávila experienced what is beyond thought or feeling or emotion. She received the Divine Embrace, and the soul was united and transformed in God. Her books provide a torchlight on a darkened path; behind her words is the voice of a master of the spiritual life.

But when she first began to experience the presence of God in the center of her soul, she was still unenlightened about the stages of prayer. "Supernatural" experiences, beyond her efforts to create or control, illumined and becalmed her heart. The delicate touch of her Lover's first embrace flooded her heart with joy, but it was followed by trepidation of what was to follow:

> His Majesty began to give me the prayer of quiet very habitually—and often, of union—which lasted a long while. Since at that time other women had fallen into serious illusions and deceptions caused by the devil, I began to be afraid.[7]

As her fears intensified, Saint Teresa sought consultations from spiritual advisors and began her long labors to explain supernatural experiences.

Who was this woman of vision? Paint a picture of her times, and we discover Spain refreshed and then threatened by a "new spirituality," followed by a Protestant Reformation. The Church, obsessed by purity, worried about the devil. Inquisitors tormented. A flash flood of prejudice swept through the country. Women were held in low esteem by the Church, considered weak in nature, unsuited for contemplation, teaching, preaching, or scripture interpretation. Paint a picture of the times, and we discover a woman who embarked on an adventure of the spirit. For Saint Teresa of Ávila, prayer was a birthright for *everyone*, an instrument of love, courage, risk-taking. When the work of God was involved, she cut through the red tape and stood her ground with governors and bishops, directors and patrons. Look closely at the picture and it reveals a woman of courage, writing, reforming, teaching, traveling, praying—paving the way for others. The picture is a story for our times; it is a story for all time.

The Voice of Reform

She was attractive, popular, and an engaging conversationalist. But it was not enough. She was intelligent and a natural leader in an era when women were considered more nervous than bright, prone to weakness rather than strength. She was witty and charming with an ear for gossip. But it was not enough for Teresa de Ahumada.

She longed for something more. When she entered the convent, it was more out of fear for her soul's salvation than from love. In her red dress, she marched right up to the monastery of the Incarnation and presented herself for admittance. There had to be something more than marriage with endless children and a young death. Her mother walked that path. Old before her time, she had ten children and thirty-three years. Then she died. But did Teresa become a nun just out of fear—fear of worldly influences, salvation, being governed by sixteenth century marital realities in which a wife had no voice in decisions, choice of friends, social activities, or her own life?

Decades later, with her chiseled face wrinkled from the tug of years, her dark, shiny hair turned to winter, Teresa wrote about her faded childhood memories. In the mirror of her mind was a reflection of a little girl who had dreams and imagination and the spirit of adventure. Inspired by books on the lives of saints, little Teresa decided to run away from home. An heroic destiny of martyrdom awaited her in the land of the Moors, she concluded, a destiny she would courageously accept. Her long, wistful moments of fantasy and plans were prematurely cut short, however. Little girls have parents who do not always share the same dreams. So, Teresa settled for playing a game of nuns and hermits with her brothers in their own backyard.

Her childhood dream proved to be the parent of the future. She became a nun, a reformer of the Carmelite Order, who traveled the inner world of the soul. Once she stepped out of the shadow of fear, she discovered who inspired her innocent childhood plans—God. And, instead of reading about saints, she became one.

Yesterday's dream found its future on November 2, 1535. In the silence of night, young Teresa once again planned to leave home. Cloaked in early morning darkness, she secretly readied herself to leave her father's house to enter the Carmelite monastery of the Incarnation outside the walls of Ávila. She was twenty-one years of age. Her whole life stretched out in front of her. Yet sorrow stood like a sentinel in her lonely, desolate heart.

The fires of love had not yet descended from heaven to replace the pain of leaving her family. Teresa only knew how to love the world, not the One who breathed life into it. Later, Love would find its dwelling place within her heart. But in its own time.

There were no tear-stained goodbyes when Teresa left home. No final embrace from her father as she entered convent life. No torn heart that his comfort mended. She left in secret, without her strict, but adoring, father's permission, and presented herself at the convent with a paper dowry in the form of a will signed by her brother Rodrigo. The will was a promise of inheritance. Rodrigo assumed he would amass a treasure of gold when he joined his brothers in the Indies. No goodbyes, a rather suspect dowry, unpredictable tears that surged, then passed; it seemed like so many seeds sown on rocks. "I remember," Teresa said, "that when I left my father's house it was with such heartbreak that death itself would not be worse; I left absolutely torn asunder."[8]

But with resolute will, Teresa entered the Incarnation "family" of 150 to 180 nuns crowded into an economically strained monastery. Whatever her father's real reasons for disapproval, he recognized his favorite daughter's unflinching determination and forgave her. One year after her entry into the Incarnation, he signed the dowry papers required for her to receive the habit of the Order of Our Lady. She professed a year later on November 3, 1537.

Life at the Convent of the Incarnation was overcrowded but comfortable for those who could afford it. Accommodations depended on money, social status, and benefactors. The poorest nuns slept in the dormitory; the richest enjoyed individual rooms. Since the Primitive Rule was amended in 1432 by Pope Eugenius, nuns no longer left their worldly possessions outside convent walls. Privileges, gifts, and money from relatives followed girls into the Incarnation as a way of life. So did servants and live-in relatives thereby taxing overcrowded conditions even more.

Teresa had a two-room suite, or cell, with a kitchen area, an oratory, and a view of the valley. When she founded her own foundations, however, Teresa frowned on elegant architecture, overcrowded conditions, and worldly riches. Her convents, founded in poverty where possible, relied on God to influence alms or donations. But if architectural elegance was a low priority, Teresa thought a garden with towering trees and a beautiful view was essential. Flowers with beautiful faces and birds perched on high branches were nature's offspring. The heart naturally opened in prayer to the Creator of such beauty. Gardens became her hermitages.

While she was in the Incarnation, Teresa threw herself whole-heartedly into her life as a nun, including those aspects of convent life which preyed on her "weaknesses." Somewhat an extrovert, she delighted in parlor conversations—stories filled with sentiment, gossip, laughter, romance, news, irony, history—all the shadings of a sixteenth century Spanish town. Attractive and engaging, Teresa spun her charm like a silkworm spins cloth. It must have been a sight to behold—a vivacious, expressive nun with large, dark eyes and full, slightly curved lips, spinning tales to delight and intrigue her audience of admirers.

Teresa loved, and knew how, to enchant people, to make them love her. Who knows what kind of vulnerability resided in one so young, whose mother died too soon leaving ten children? Teresa thrived on her popularity. Yet it was that need to be admired that snared her best efforts at detachment and true humility. When not enthralled by parlor conversations, she retired to the privacy of her quarters to indulge her passion for reading. Yet, God, ultimately, had His way with this soul; the early seeds planted in the heart were nurtured to fruition, but in His timing, under His direction.

Incarnation life was much more than overcrowded conditions and parlor games. Given the economic hardships brought about by so many nuns, servants, and live-in relatives, visitors were welcomed, even encouraged. They always brought something to contribute—food or money, some gift needed but unaffordable. But this was a House of God. Prayer and devotion were not subject to crowds and the whims of young girls. There were days of fasting and abstinence, chanting, intricate ceremonies, celebration of the Divine Office. The spirit of continual prayer was encouraged through periods of silence. Teresa received instructions in the Carmelite Order, its origins, and an understanding of the devotion to the Blessed Virgin, Elijah, and Elisha. But there was no instruction in contemplative prayer. No time was set aside to teach her how to pray, to be recollected.

Mental prayer, or contemplation, was not seen as the invisible link which joins one to God.

Packed into an overcrowded convent with the parlor atmosphere of a sorority house, Teresa attempted to advance in prayer. She tried to calm her mind. It repaid her efforts by racing like a fox eluding hunters. Her attempts at discursive prayer were a mockery. No nectar of the gods followed her recitations, no deeper levels of consciousness. What was wrong? A cry rose from her heart. Her weakness for trivial conversations and subtle attachments drove her to confessors for help. There were dangers stirring within her. But her confessors failed to see them. Instead, they reassured her, told her not to be overly concerned. Those, after all, were not *big* sins. Her troubled heart was a beggar in search of wise direction.

Frustrated, discouraged, Teresa became sick after her profession. Illness had stalked her life as a teenager; now it stole her away from the Incarnation. The nature of her illness was a mystery—vomiting, heart spasms, partial paralysis, cramps—but from no organic cause. Perhaps she strained herself in unguided ascetic practices. Perhaps an intense desire for rewards in the form of visions and locutions unduly pressured her nervous system. Perhaps she released forces which she did not know how to integrate. She stopped praying and went home where her father arranged for her to see a healer. On the way to the countryside for treatments, she stopped to rest at her Uncle Pedro's farm. A religious man, Pedro sensed the deep gloom of his niece and offered her books to read. *The Spiritual Alphabet* opened the windows to the light within Teresa. According to *Alphabet* guidelines, she prayed. Threads of gloom lessened their hold, then slowly fell away. One book brought her from the wilderness. One book raised her from despair. In one moment of time, the spirit, like a candle in the wind, moved and showered the night with light. Though weak physically, Teresa continued to make progress in prayer. And it made all the difference.

For months she remained at her sister's farm. The healer's treatment required strength, and Teresa was far too weak to withstand an aggressive, harsh cure. She rested. She prayed. She read. The changing seasons greeted the leaves and branches; shafts of sunlight reached for trees like outstretched hands. Slowly, Teresa regained her strength.

In the midst of it all, she counseled the local priest who was tormented by his liaison with a village widow. He still conducted Mass yet lived in a "bad moral state." His seven-year affair was so public that his reputation was little more than frayed cloth. Teresa "showed him more love" for God in an effort to help him regain his virtue. Long discussions about God and His ways impressed the soul of this wayward priest. He ended his affair, but transferred his love to Teresa. One year after their introduction, he died. Later, Teresa insisted that there was no harm in his affections for her. Nothing compromising happened. But she added, if they had not remained in God's presence, "serious offenses" could have occurred.

Though Teresa made rapid progress in prayer and experienced what she later called the Prayer of Quiet and Prayer of Union, her healer's severe three-month "cure" almost killed her. Finally, she slipped into a coma, not moving for four days. Everyone but her father gave her up for dead. He stopped anyone who tried to touch her, repeatedly mumbling, "The child isn't dead." Lost in a silent coma, unable to move or speak, it seemed that her life as a nun was over before it began. But after four days, Teresa labored and strained to open her eyes. Someone had prematurely placed burial wax on her eyelids! At the Incarnation, a freshly dug grave awaited her return. A weakened, shriveled bag of bones in such bitter torment that she had to be carried around in a sheet, Teresa returned to the convent infirmary to improve or die. An invalid and paralytic for three years, she eventually walked again. But the rest of her life was a miserable parade of illnesses.

While still in the infirmary, Teresa's prayer life soared to new heights. She was unable to move for eight months; could not crawl on hands and knees for two years. But her deepening prayer life gave her a new understanding of love. Like first-born shoots which pierced blackened soil, new virtues began to grow. No longer could she speak evil of anyone. Fault-finding had to be avoided. The golden rule penetrated the silent depths of her heart. But they were the first shoots of new growth, still too tender to withstand coming trials. Teresa, as usual, condemned herself for being terribly wicked. Her books are laced with passages of self-reproach. Naturally, as she recovered from illness, she sought solitude and confession. Sorrowful tears of repentance accompanied a renewed awakening to serve.

Her faithfulness and virtue inspired those around her—nuns, family, friends. If her recovery was deemed a miracle, so was the change in her father. Teresa gave him books on mental prayer during her illness (1537-1538), and the man who forbade her to enter a convent not only learned to pray, but also became a truly holy man.

Unbearable pain, paralysis, a near-death experience, and deepening prayer were not sufficient, however, to keep Teresa free from the intoxicating lure of the convent parlor. She emerged from her ordeal still vulnerable to petty conversations, gossip, and holding court in the parlor "sorority house." Her illness *had strengthened* her—she emerged with greater charm, humor, and vanity than ever before. One nameless parlor regular was so attentive that Teresa allowed his "friendship" to derail her spiritual practices. It was impossible to be centered in God and in parlor memories at the same time. Once again Teresa turned to her confessors:

> The whole trouble lay in not getting at the root of the occasions* and with my confessors who were of little help. For had they told me of the danger I was in and that I had the obligation to avoid those friendships, without a doubt I believe I would have remedied the matter.[9]

It startled Teresa that she so swiftly fell from heightened graces of God into casual pastimes. What about her new virtues? What about her deepening desire to serve His Majesty? She talked about mental prayer and lent her books to other nuns hungry for a deeper "friendship" with God. But she felt powerless to escape the "thousand vanities" that suffocated her joy and newborn virtues. No longer at home with God or the world, Teresa strayed from her practice of contemplative prayer and fell into an abyss of pain:

> It is one of the most painful lives, I think, that one can imagine; for neither did I enjoy God nor did I find

---

*Occasions of sin - a nun was to avoid both the actions and the situations which led to sin, including the state of one's mind.

happiness in the world. When I was experiencing the enjoyments of the world, I felt sorrow when I recalled what I owed to God. When I was with God, my attachment to the world disturbed me. This is a war so troublesome that I don't know how I was able to suffer it even a month, much less for so many years.[10]

This was the state of the soul of one who, as a little girl, heard that martyrs for Christ went straight to heaven. So she grabbed her brother to run away to Moorish killing fields to obtain martyrdom and a quick ticket to paradise. This was a woman of contradiction and paradox. A rich tapestry of traits lived between the horizons of her consciousness. She loved her friends deeply and affectionately, yet called friars "wolves" if they persecuted the reform. She was strong-willed but humble; intelligent but loved simple men and women the most; a natural leader but obedient to her supervisors. This was a woman concerned about honor, yet covered up her ignorance with other novices. She expressed a "horror for lies" but deceived herself and justified to her small group of disciples her lapses in mental prayer. The need for love and admiration overpowered her usual candor. She knew about her deceit—deep down she knew. She always knew when a cold wind blew through her soul.

But what she called "weakness" eventually became a link in the chain of wisdom. In *The Book of Her Life*, she made no excuses for herself, no justification for deceit. She did not hide behind a veil of silence. Teresa painted the hills and valleys of her life in broad, colorful brush strokes for all to see. We can look out the window to a clear view of the landscape of her soul and God's work in it.

At the time of her lapses in prayer, however, Teresa's life was a battlefield. Distracted and stuck in the quicksand of vanity, casual pastimes, and attachments, Teresa's consciousness began to slip away from its heightened friendship with God. Embarrassed and ashamed, she feared the depths of prayer and felt undeserving of God's friendship. Later she realized that the lax atmosphere of the Incarnation was harmful to her spiritual development. She was given too much freedom—her faults flourished in the false light of negligence.

Inching along the path of mediocrity, Teresa had a vision in which Christ appeared to her to open her blind eyes to the dangers she was courting:

> I saw Him with the eyes of my soul more clearly than I could have with the eyes of my body. And this vision left such an impression on me that, though more than twenty-six years have gone by, it seems to me it is still present.[11]

But "the devil" offered a word of advice—the vision was an illusion and her honor was not decreased, but increased, by her friendship with her parlor guest. Confusion gnawed at her confidence in the vision, but she could never truly shake the feeling that it came from God. Since she resisted its message and was fond of her friend, she hid the truth from herself—most of the time.

Then along came the toad. A fast-moving "nasty little creature" appeared in the middle of the day in an area where she had never seen toads. On no other occasion had a larger-than-normal toad darted into the path walked by her and her friend. It was a warning, Teresa decided, that represented God's concern over the direction of her spiritual life. The mysterious toad's "message" was not heeded, however. The path of distraction continued.

Even her relative, an older nun, tried to warn Teresa of the dangers she invited by her friendship with the gentleman visitor. But what did she know? Annoyed, Teresa dismissed her advice, convinced that the elder nun created scandal where none existed.

To further complicate matters, Teresa fell into a "common temptation of beginners." She tried to help her father in the very area that she had avoided for over a year. Finally, she revealed the truth but offered no immediate explanation for her lapses in prayer. Now advanced in prayer himself, her father attributed her falling away to the persistent illnesses she suffered. But Teresa realized that "prayer is an exercise of love," not dependent on circumstances for its practice.

That was the state of her soul. It drifted along from one "occasion of sin" to another until shortly after her father's death in late 1543. Persuaded by de Alsonso's confessor to take communion every fifteen days, Teresa began to pray again and make regular confessions. There were no immediate graces from God, but never again did she totally abandon prayer. Her life was still a burden, however, and her prayer time an often-dreaded interruption. "Very often," she said, "for some years I was more anxious that the hour I had determined to spend in prayer be over than I was to remain there."[12]

A revolution in love was already on the horizon of consciousness. Teresa was twenty-three when illness forced her to leave the Incarnation to seek a "cure" that almost killed her. Almost forty, she experienced her second conversion during the Lenten observance of 1554. Entering the oratory of the Incarnation, she was walking past an image of the "much-wounded Christ" recently borrowed by the nuns for the festival observance. Who knows why the image of the crucified Christ pierced Teresa's heart with the wounds of a hundred sorrows? Who knows why twenty years of uneven, but continual, growth with God now tore to the surface of consciousness, leaving Teresa awash with tears of repentance?

"Utterly distressed," Teresa fell to the floor, sobbing as her heart melted in shame. Begging Christ to "once and for all" strengthen her determination, she vowed not to rise from the spot until He heard her.

From that moment on, she eagerly turned to prayer. Old torments lost their hold on her heart—indifference evaporated, the parlor lost its allure. Warmth and compassion for the other sisters swept over her like a gentle breeze. And, as if timed to answer a silent question, someone gave her a copy of another book which penetrated the depths of her heart. In Saint Augustine's *Confessions*, she discovered a kindred spirit, someone else who had received God's graces, but who pulled back, not ready for the abundance generously given. She wept for days. This was her story revealed in the life of another. Augustine's prayer could easily have mirrored her own. "Give me chastity, Lord. Give me continence . . . . But not yet."[13]

Conversion is like the ripples of the sea. One after another of the ocean's rhythms rise up to float on the surface, then spend themselves stretching for the shore, only to be pulled back merged with the whole. The image of Christ, Saint Augustine, then a dream of Teresa and other souls in hell, each rippled through consciousness and spent itself in returning Teresa to God.

This period of Teresa's life was like a new dawn, sweet and clean and refreshed after the storms of night. The new day of the soul was soft and gentle, awakened to a new hopefulness. The dreaded "occasions" were replaced by "delights and favors" from God. Without seeking them, she experienced raptures where she was lifted up out of herself to rest in God's presence. Like a bride swept into the arms of her lover, Teresa experienced His presence everywhere, always. The longing of a lifetime, from childhood innocence to becoming a nun, was fulfilled in the divine attentions of this love. When questioned by her directors, who wanted to know how she knew of His presence, she explained, "In the dark, when someone is close by, you just know He's there . . . ." Experience reveals what reason cannot.

In her first rapture, Teresa heard the words, "No longer do I want you to converse with men, but with angels."[14] The woman who had a gift for friendship and conversation now realized that prayer was a deep, intimate friendship with God. "Mental prayer," she said, "is nothing else than an intimate sharing between friends; it means taking time frequently to be alone with Him who we know loves us."[15] The deep connection with another, the desire for intimate sharing that the parlor visits could never meet, was found in her friendship with God. Later she looked back on her struggles with the wisdom and clear sight of one who viewed the valley from the mountain peak:

> In every favor the Lord granted me, whether vision or revelation, my soul gained something . . . . The vision of Christ left upon me an impression of His most extraordinary beauty, and the impression remains today; one time is sufficient to make this imprint. I had a serious fault that did me much harm; it was that when I began to know that certain persons liked me, and I found them attractive, I became so attached that my memory was bound strongly by the thought of them . . . . This was something so harmful it was leading my soul seriously astray. After I beheld the extraordinary beauty of the Lord, I didn't see anyone who in comparison with Him seemed to attract me or occupy my thoughts. By turning my gaze just a little inward to

behold the image I have in my soul, I obtained such freedom in this respect that . . . it would be impossible for me . . . to be so occupied with the thought of anyone that I couldn't free myself from it by only a slight effort to remember this Lord.[16]

As the inner hunger for God increases and is fed, attachments gently fall away, often unnoticed like mist on a cloudy day. Teresa discovered that what usually trapped her soul—like a fly stuck in bee's honey—no longer had the power to hold her. She could free herself and fly on delicate wings of light to a higher state of consciousness.

But as visions and mystical phenomena continued to mark her life of prayer, confessors became concerned. Accusations of self-delusion flew around her. Some confessors rejected her experiences as devil's play. Others doubted their authenticity. Teresa suffered the barbs of criticism and was torn between her own intuition that the phenomena were of God and the pressure of skeptics. With well-grounded advice from learned counselors, she developed greater discernment into the working of God in her soul. But the accusations of demonic influence accompanied her all of her life.

It was under obligation to her confessor that Teresa wrote *The Book of Her Life* to explain the mystical graces God granted her. She was nearing fifty, and graces had been flowing through her soul for ten years. *Life* stood as a witness to God's transforming power, illuminating the interior path she followed in the midst of Church dogma, oppression, and Inquisition. But it also recorded her long, uphill struggles: the fears, temptations, weariness, desire for comfort, and experiences with spiritual directors.

The first two people that she consulted had two things to say to her—the experiences were from the devil, and never be alone lest she be deceived again. Taking their words to heart and afraid her soul was in jeopardy, she ceased being alone in her room. Weary and increasingly agitated, Teresa heard the Lord speak to her. "Do not fear, daughter; for I am, and I will not abandon you; do not fear."[17] "I was given calm," she said, "together with fortitude, courage, security, quietude, and light so that in one moment I saw my soul become another."[18] The words liberated her; she soundly dismissed fears of the devil as useless: "I pay no more attention to them than to flies."[19] She had suffered from the thorns of unillumined advice, but her fears of the devil were now dissolved.

Teresa trusted mystical phenomena to increase her love for God and to make human will more determined to serve Him. But she was adamant that self-delusion could occur and that mystical phenomena could not be equated with holiness, wisdom, or the contemplative life. Teresa was cautious. She determined what was genuine and what was not, and offered skilled analysis of exalted states. But even she could misinterpret God's instructions.

Unable to always explain her lofty states of consciousness, Teresa left it to God to describe, through her, the flowering graces of the soul. To have mystical graces is one thing; to understand them is something else, and to explain them is yet another skill. Her nuns often discovered Teresa's face radiantly aglow as her pen sped along with divinely inspired words. But her lofty states were often unwelcome guests, especially to Teresa. How could she explain a rapture which occurred while she was in the choir? Being lifted up into the air while she prayed, in full view of the other nuns, was an intrusion. Yet exalted states were often educational, as well as inspiring. In moments of rapture, she actually witnessed her thoughts and imagination as they rumbled along and infringed on her state of consciousness.

In the final chapters of *Life*, Teresa dramatically recorded the beginning of a new life. Enkindled in love, the soul was inwardly driven to serve. Her reform ideas, once only a seed in the heart, sprouted to maturity. Seeds, like love, can never be idle. They grow to find their place in the sun. Reform may begin as silently as a whisper. But its voice will be heard above the roar of all exterior sound. Teresa's reformist ideas found their voice in an afternoon conversation with nuns and laywomen who regularly met in her cell to discuss prayer.

The Reform of the Carmelite Order

On a September evening in 1560, Teresa and her close friends once again discussed their favorite topic—the religious life and their desire for more solitude. The Incarnation, with its large numbers and laissez-faire attitude toward visitors, gave the convent a social club atmosphere. But it was not just those people who streamed *into* the convent. Nuns found perfectly acceptable reasons to be *out* of the convent. A revolving door of activity made solitude impossible.

Then María de Ocampo, a young nun who was Saint Teresa's niece, lightheartedly mentioned a possible solution. They could create another kind of religious life, one modeled after their hermit forefathers on Mt. Carmel. Teresa's own restless thoughts found voice in her niece's casual remark. The wheels of her mind turned with ideas, until finally nothing could stop their flow. There was no going back. Teresa picked up the reins of reform and moved forward in 1562. The need for solitude had prompted the birth of a new monastic life.

It began with Teresa's reform of herself. She had already determined, after her conversion, to live as consistently as possible to the spirit of her Carmelite vocation. Now she devoted herself to helping other nuns do the same in a reformed monastic life.

The nucleus consisted of only a small group of people. Teresa always preferred quality to quantity. "One person of quality will do more than many who are lacking in it."[20] The "committed few" could move mountains and learn to love each other in the process.

One of the "committed few" was Doña Guiomar de Ulloa, a close friend in whom Teresa confided her problems and hopes. When she explained her dream of a small house for a monastery, Doña Guiomar offered to fund it. Other friends voiced enthusiastic support. Planned in secret, the Convent of Saint Joseph was a dream come true.

But it was born not without difficult labor pains. When the Council of Ávila heard of the idea, they opposed it; the city was short of money. Townspeople whispered and gossiped against Teresa. Doña Guiomar discovered she did not have the financial resources to build the monastery as promised. Incarnation nuns interpreted Teresa's actions as severe criticism of their own spiritual practices. And her confessor told her to forget the whole idea.

Teresa brooked no compromise, however. This new convent would tolerate no lax practices. Girls who entered left their family names at the door, worked behind enclosed walls, and learned to pray contemplatively. To make matters worse, as far as townspeople were concerned, Saint Joseph's was established in "absolute poverty" and only accepted thirteen girls. The city of Ávila was in an infuriated uproar. Convents at that time served the needs of dynastic families as well as nuns. One which accepted only thirteen girls upset the economic applecart. What about a place for unmarriageable girls? What about those who did not favor austerity? And if nuns prayed contemplatively, how were patrons to count the prayers they bought for relatives? Silence was unmeasureable. Only vocal prayers could be counted. Ávila watched in horror as their insurance policy for the afterlife—endowed prayers—slipped from their grasp.

So began the work of the reform, directed by God, under the leadership of Teresa. Finally, the convent planned-in-secret was a reality. At dawn on August 24, 1862, a shrill bell woke the neighborhood with the announcement of the first Discalced Carmelite Monastery.

Problems continued. People screamed at the nuns in an effort to run them out of their new home of prayer and solitude. The Lord responded to the latest turmoil with the words: "Don't you know I'm powerful; what are you afraid of?" He reassured Teresa that the work "would not be undone."[21] Later Teresa was summoned to the Incarnation and threatened with monastic imprisonment. In time the storm calmed and Teresa returned to her little dovecote, as she liked to call Saint Joseph's.

If monastic life was different, so was Teresa. Her raptures had ceased; she needed neither raptures nor security outside herself. The Source of love had taken her deeper than attachments to passing comforts and affections. Fueled with the love of union, Teresa turned her attention to service.

She also changed her name. When she entered the discalced ("shoe-less") life in 1562, Teresa did that which she asked of others. She left her family name at the door. When she took her profession as a nun, she kept her mother's name. But now Doña Teresa de Ahumada became Teresa of Jesus. Only during the twentieth century has she been called Teresa of Ávila, a name that originated from someone outside of Spain.

After twenty-nine years as a nun in the Incarnation, Teresa of Jesus left to fully express her love for God as a reformer, teacher, and writer. By the end of her life, she had established seventeen convents. A skilled business woman, she cut through the red tape of Rome, rubbed shoulders with all levels of society as she traveled through Spain, and, yet, managed to stay out of the grasp of the Inquisition. On footpaths called roads, Teresa criss-crossed Spain in covered donkey carts with wooden wheels. Ignorant guides led her from place to place; sometimes a dirty inn was her lodging for a night's rest. She closed her eyes to sleep, finally resting in the arms of heaven.

It is difficult to track the steps of "God's wandering lady" from this point. Turn the pages of her life, and we see fleeting glimpses of a whirlwind in motion. In the picture book of her times, snapshots come to life; first one, then another, and still another of a woman propelled by Love. Turn the page. Teresa has borrowed money to begin her first convent expedition in Medina (1567) where she initially met Friar John of the Cross. The man destined to be a saint, mystical poet, and Doctor of the Church, became the first Discalced Carmelite friar.

Turn the page. Teresa is in Malagon (1568) so ill that every bone in her body ached. Builders told her the work on the foundation, or convent, required another six months. Up at dawn, Teresa surveyed the work herself and declared it must be ready for the Feast of the Immaculate Conception—only twelve days away. She worked with the builders from morning until night or directed the efforts from a stone podium. Twelve days, she asserted. It had to be ready in twelve days. It was. Another house was ready where women could be "alone with God alone." But when Teresa discovered the grave needs of the townspeople, she could not turn away behind closed walls. Nuns financed a sewing workshop for girls and paid a priest to teach boys. "What other alms but this can we give?" she asked.

Turn the page again. Teresa is back on the road. Back to Saint Joseph's and to Valladolid (1568) and to meetings with John of the Cross. Teresa loved Friar John; she loved his immersion in the mystery of God.

Turn the page of the picture book and we see Teresa of Jesus crossing a stream or going up into the mountains. Her health continued to deteriorate. But she founded another convent—Toledo (1569), and then Pastrana (Guadalajara, 1569). While on a week-long visit to Madrid, Abbess Juana de la Cruz remarked:

"Praise God who has permitted us to see a saint whom we can imitate. She eats, sleeps and speaks like the rest of us, and is completely natural and unassuming."[23] In Pastrana a princess, who generously donated to the convent, moved in. Unable to cope with her husband's death, she took the habit but retained her same character. Expelled for her ways, she sought revenge: she made public Teresa's manuscript of her *Life*, denounced her to the Inquisition, took back her endowment contract and all donations, and attempted to give the nuns a good dose of humiliation. Teresa moved her nuns to Segovia in the midst of the princess' storms of personality.

Turn the page to Salamanca (1570) after a cold, wet journey. Students refused to hand over the building which was dedicated to the nuns' use. Finally, they withdrew, and Teresa and Sister María del Sacramento bedded down on straw and old blankets. Wind groaned through the crevices in the window. Sister María was afraid:

> "What are you looking at?" asked Teresa. "Can't you see that nobody can come in?"
>
> "Mother," she answered, "I was thinking what would you do here alone if I were to die now."
>
> "Sister, if that happens I'll think of something. Right now, just let me get some sleep."[23]

At Salamanca, Teresa began writing *The Book of Foundations* which she continued until a few days before her death. Persistent illness accompanied her expeditions, which she alluded to in *Foundations*:

> When describing these foundations I don't say anything of the hardships endured along the way: the cold, the heat and the snow. At times it snowed all day, sometimes we got lost, other times I was so ill and feverish. Praise God, my health is usually poor, but I've always been conscious that God was giving me strength.[24]

Salamanca was one problem after another. The house, located too close to the city reservoir, became unsuitable for health reasons. Then when it was declared unfit to house the Blessed Sacrament, Teresa decided to move. But first she had to attend to business in Alba, Medina, and Ávila. The return journey was another in a series of eventful trips—first the mule that carried the money got lost; then everyone was lost. Once the nuns of Salamanca moved into another house, problems began on a different scale. The house owner lost his temper; he wanted money sooner than stipulated in the contract. It took forty-four years for the house to be purchased and everyone settled. In the interim, the nuns were evicted twice.

But Salamanca was also a place of friendship and mystical graces. Teresa befriended one of the Jesuits in whom she confided openly about everything. Whole evenings were spent talking about God until the Father fell victim to the French Huguenots. Teresa deeply missed him: "God help me, I wish I wasn't so fond of God's servants; then I wouldn't miss them so much."[25]

The mystical graces of this period were rich, heavenly, and noticeable to others. Isabel de Jesus reported that Teresa was so enraptured by a couplet she overheard her sing that "she had to be carried back to her cell in a state of apparent unconsciousness." The couplet that Isabel sang was:

> Would that my eyes could see You,
> Kind Sweet Jesus
> Would that my eyes could see You,
> And I then died.[26]

Turn the page again and Teresa's words foreshadow late twentieth century feminism:

> When you walked on this earth, Lord, you did not despise women; rather, you always helped them and showed great compassion towards them. And you found as much love and more faith in them than you did in men. Among them was your Most Blessed Mother, and through her merits we merit what because of our offenses, we do not deserve. Is it not enough, Lord, that the world has intimidated us . . . so that we may not do anything

worthwhile for you in public or dare to speak some truths that we lament over in secret, without your also failing to hear so just a petition? I do not believe, Lord, that this could be true of your goodness and justice, for you are a just judge and not like those of the world. Since the world's judges are sons of Adam and all of them men, there is no virtue in women that they do not hold suspect.[27]

The quote was censored from the first edition of her book. Her "feminism" and constant determination flowed from the springs of divine union. Therefore, there was no burnout from the demands of work. But there was wisdom—the soul in unitive partnership with God is neither male nor female, but united to the Beloved. Full and overflowing, the soul gives itself away in service, directed by the hidden hand of God. Consequently, when people encouraged Teresa of Jesus to rest or quit, that she was too ill, the monasteries too much trouble, she smiled and simply replied, "That wouldn't be loving God, would it?"

Turn the page of her life to one bitterly cold December day when Teresa traveled by donkey to carry out orders from her superior. As always, the fire of love drove her forward, sometimes on donkey or mule or horse; other times in covered wagon, carriage, or coach. When not in a wagon, however, Teresa usually rode her mule and was exposed to the scorching heat of summer and the blustery winds and snow of winter. Nothing stopped her, especially not the weather.

Pictures of travel, one after another, reveal the determined spirit of one whose work was an expression of her love for God. Look inside her covered wagon and discover a roving convent on wheels. Teresa turned the wagon into a sanctuary complete with holy water, crucifix, a tiny bell to mark the convent schedule, even statues of Mary, Joseph, and the Infant Jesus. The community life of the convent traveled in a wagon whose creaking wheels crawled slowly forward.

Inside, nuns laughed and joked and prayed. Teresa wrote lighthearted verses and sang mirthful songs to pass the time. There were scheduled periods of solitude, but also moments when a small choir of voices rose in cascading sounds of praise. This was a mission of joy, undertaken to uphold a spiritual ideal.

Singing nuns in a convent wagon moved courageously forward to their destination.

Outside the wagon, muleteers and guides struggled to find the right roads, keep the mules in line, search for barges on which to cross nature's swollen rivers. Cantankerous guides and a cargo of nuns made an odd cast of characters to be thrown together for a mission for God. So what did the wagon guides think of this traveling Mother Foundress? Actually, they were charmed by this one who was so concerned about everyone's needs. When she talked about God, they stopped their shallow conversations and petty arguments to listen, to drink the pure nectar so generously offered. There were, of course, exceptions.

Once after a long journey in pouring rain, the moveable convent reached an inn after nightfall. It was a miserable conclusion to a stormy day, one which would test the patience of the most merciful heart. There was no food, nothing to light the lamps. Even the beds were drenched; nature reached through cracks in the roof with welcoming rain. Teresa surveyed the potential nightmare and sought to raise everyone's spirits: "Come now, take heart, these are days very meritorious for gaining heaven." But the mule driver, tired and rain-soaked, was uninspired: "I could have also gained heaven by staying home," he lamented.

Turn the page to a map of Spain, now dotted with Teresean foundations. The reform movement had spread, seemingly taking on a life of its own. Officials were nervous. Somehow Teresa's intrusive reforms had to be stopped. Meanwhile the Incarnation was destitute and her nuns were starving. Teresa was blamed, of course, for its near collapse. But from crisis was born a solution. In October 1572, she was called to be the new prioress of the Incarnation, a position she did not want but obediently accepted, until her term ended on October 6, 1574.

The Incarnation nuns, afraid that she would try to convert them, greeted Teresa with hostility. To ease their fears, she called them to the chapter room where her inspired action calmed their dispirited voices. Silence fell as she placed a statue of Our Lady on the prioress seat and dropped her keys beside her to indicate that she, not Teresa, would be prioress. Then Teresa slowly sat down beside the statue and quietly, gently reassured her new community of nuns:

Mothers and sisters, through obedience Our Lord has sent me to this house to perform this duty . . . . I come only to serve you and to please you in any way I can. I am a daughter of this house and the sister of each one of you. Don't be afraid of how I shall govern, because although I have lived and governed among reform nuns, by God's goodness I am well aware how those who are not should be governed.[28]

The new prioress governed well. Before long the Incarnation returned to strength and solvency. Moreover, Teresa saw to the religious needs of the nuns and brought Friar John of the Cross as confessor to the community. Teresa, however, was a virtual prisoner behind convent walls, unable to obtain permission from her superiors to leave. The nets of the Church had trapped her, made her submit to "house arrest" in obedience to authority. But just as her heart could never turn from Truth, her body could not indefinitely be held in the web of her superiors. Teresa appealed directly to King Phillip II who granted her travel request. The convent gate swung open and the wandering nun was on the road again, traveling from the Incarnation to her appointed rounds.

It was no easy matter to remain in good standing with the sixteenth century Catholic Church being a woman who endorsed contemplative prayer, a writer of mystical theology who traveled to set up reform carmels. To make matters worse, Teresa had visions, levitations, and healings in an era when committees decided if such supernatural graces were devil-inspired. Somehow Teresa did everything she was not supposed to do—and publicly—yet managed to accomplish her work unscathed.

The "whole reason" for her communities, she said, was for the practice of prayer and related spiritual disciplines. But it was never an end in itself. Once established in the heart of God, the nuns and friars were to express their flowering love in service. To serve, to minister was the natural outgrowth of a life of prayer.

To ensure the continuation of her reform efforts, Teresa took both practical and highly imaginative steps to prevent the claws of the Inquisition from reaching into her coveys of prayer. She planned and flawlessly executed her strategies for opening new foundations, discussing her plans with learned advisors, her confessor, and God. After consultations, Teresa initiated the recruitment and journey phases of her work. Above all, she was flexible, adjusting to changing financial resources, red tape, litigation, and unexpected hassles. Acutely aware that her letters could have fallen under the magnifying glass of zealous inquisitors, Teresa devised a code. This mule-riding, independent but obedient nun sent letters with pseudonyms like "Joseph" to indicate Christ; "Grand Angel" for the Grand Inquisitor; "Ravens" for the Jesuits; "Egyptians" and "Owls" to denote calced enemies of the reform; "Seneca" for John of the Cross; "Butterflies" and "Grasshoppers" for groups of discalced nuns; "Angels" and "Laurencia" to refer to herself.

Again turn the page of her life to see an outspoken Teresa who knew that some Catholic clergy and directors lived with an immoral tempest in their hearts. Ignorance and moral waywardness contributed to the rift in the Church, she believed. So she called for a reform of the heart—skilled directors and confessors who practiced contemplative prayer; preachers whose passion for Christ directed their words. This advice was from a sixteenth century *woman*. No wonder Rome, much less village and countryside, gossiped about Teresa.

If the tidal wave of monastic reform was not cause enough for "burned-at-the-stake" alarm, Teresa also engaged in a healing ministry. As an instrument for healing body and soul, she never asked for anything that was not "in conformity with His glory."[29] The fact that He worked through her, the more it "quickens my love and causes an increase in my desire to serve Him," she wrote to her confessor.[30]

On one occasion her prayers resulted in a blind friend obtaining his vision, even though Teresa was concerned her sins might prevent God from hearing her. Before "eight days passed," the man could see.[31] On another occasion, Teresa reported:

> . . . there was a person very sick with a painful illness
> . . . . What he suffered for two months was unbearable; the
> pain was lacerating. My confessor . . . went to see him; . . .
> and told me I should by all means go to see him . . . . I went
> and was moved to such pity for him that I began to beg the
> Lord insistently for his health. In this experience I saw

fully and clearly the favor He granted me; the next day this person was completely cured of that affliction.[32]

The healing power of prayer was especially apparent in cases where Teresa interceded for those in poor moral states. And, of course, she was particularly moved by priests and Religious who needed prayer. Often God gave her messages for these nuns and friars or revealed to her the state of their souls. Because she was keenly aware that superiors often abused their powers if they were not sufficiently humble, she often prayed for the souls of such superiors.

In one case, Teresa entered the oratory with "much anxiety" to pray for a superior's soul, offering all the good she had done in her life. While in prayer on his behalf, Teresa saw him:

> . . . ascend to heaven with the greatest happiness. He had been well advanced in years, but I saw him as only about thirty . . . and his countenance was resplendent. The vision passed quickly; but I was so extremely consoled that his death could never cause me anymore sorrow . . . .[33]

Teresa, like holy men and women of all ages, unselfishly used her spiritual authority for the good of others—to heal physical ailments and spiritual afflictions, to help individuals and whole communities. For instance, she once traveled through a village whose residents helplessly watched a drought dry up their crops. Worried and afraid, they appealed to Teresa for help. She, deeply moved by their distress, began to recite the Litany to the Saints. It rained immediately.

Her charity, however, extended beyond people and situations she met in her travels. In accordance with her Catholic faith, Teresa extended prayers to those who made transition from life in this dimension to reside in purgatory, or the place of purification, where gradual training in love occurs. Both in her miracles and discernment of those "spirits" who live in an unseen state of existence, Teresa humbly considered herself to be an instrument to "help souls."

The unitive state of consciousness propels us into an irrepressible life of service. Teresa—founder, teacher, prioress, healer—continually expressed the fires of love in an outward movement of charity. Regardless of the century in which we live, time cannot dictate or oppress the inner life of the spirit. The will and purpose of God is a torch in the heart that glows regardless of external circumstances or the times in which we live.

Turn the page of her life to see Teresa writing in covered wagons by dim light; in monasteries in the long hours after midnight. For the last twenty years of her life, she penned a series of spiritual classics, each based on her own experience. Love sought expression and could not be contained anymore than a tree born in shade could be cheated from the sun. Teresa was impelled by a spiritual force so engulfing that she wished both hands at once could record the overflow of supernatural insight. But this was not, as others have suggested, automatic writing. It was the inflow of inspiration as she lived in union with God, *one with* God.

At times, Teresa struggled with the composition of her writings. She knew her words made a difference; perhaps, they would spark a transformation in those who read about her experience with God. A satisfied writer, though she balked at the self-discipline required for good composition, Teresa laced her books with anecdotes, conversations, and what she gleaned from other literary sources. Writing was her way to talk to her sisters and disciples. These manuals of prayer taught them what they needed to know. Later—after her death—the written word would be the vehicle that carried the mission forward. Inscriptions left by a soul enflamed by love would carry women beyond gender "limitations" to enter, through contemplative prayer, the realms of the interior life.

Words, however, are a poor substitute for experience, and the language of the spirit does not readily translate into marks on a page. But like a full river that majestically winds and sings its way into the sea, an echo is left for those who have ears to hear. Teresa left a beautiful, heavenly echo of the passage through prayer to God.

By the end of her life, she wrote *The Book of Her Life; Spiritual Testimonies* and *Soliloquies* (her prayers and personal notes); *Constitutions* and *On Making the Visitation* (notes and legislation on the discalced reforms); *The Way of Perfection* (education about the religious life and how to obtain the perfection of love); *The*

Interior Castle (her spiritual and literary masterpiece); *Meditations on the Song of Songs* (along with *Interior*, emphasized the practice of prayer and movements of the contemplative life); and *The Book of Her Foundations* (history of the foundations). The poems and song lyrics composed about convent life are recorded in *Poetry, A Satirical Critique,* and *Response to a Spiritual Challenge.* All of these works from a woman who wrote only in obedience to her superiors and then only reluctantly. The echo has grown stronger and clearer with the passage of time.

Who was this woman of sixteenth century Spain whose friendship reached into all levels of society while Inquisitors stalked her every move? Turn the page of her life as she finishes the work of her foundations with the help of friends and in spite of condemnation.

The formation of Segovia (1574), Beas (1575), and Segovia (1575) caused one friar to remark: "The older she gets, the more she travels."[34] At the same time, her health steadily declined, and her adventures mounted to tragic, sometimes comic, proportions.

On the journey to Seville, the nuns stayed at a hermitage the first night and alternated between sleep on a cold, stone floor and praying. Day two: while a "depraved group of men drew knives and fought among themselves," the nuns stayed enclosed in their wagon to avoid a potentially nasty scene. Food was scarce, most days consisted of beans, bread, and cherries. The sisters felt fortunate if they could find "an egg for our Mother." Day three: the boatman cheated them. His boat would not hold all that he promised. A wagon broke loose and drifted downstream, nuns and provisions still aboard. While a few of the sisters fell to their knees crying out to God, the rest pulled on a rope, hoping to save them. They received a quick answer to their prayers—the wagon landed on a sandbank. Day four: Teresa was so ill that they stopped for her to rest at an inn. The "room" in which she rested was previously used as a pig shed:

> The little room was roofed like a shed and had no windows. If you opened the door the sun blazed in. The sun here is not like in Castille; it is much worse. They put me to bed, but I would have been better off on the floor for

> the bed was so uneven that I didn't know what way to lie;
> it was like a bed of sharp stones.[35]

She neglected to mention the bugs, the swearing people, the dancing, and the tambourines.

Upon arrival in Seville, it took considerable efforts and time for the archbishop to offer his respect and the food and money necessary for the work. In the midst of it all, a discontented nun told lies about Teresa and brought the wrath of Inquisitors upon her. They decided to hold an inquiry into her life and the practices of her nuns. Teresa only laughed: "I wish they burned us all at the stake for Christ. Where matters of faith are concerned they will find nothing wrong with us; we would prefer to die a thousand deaths," she told one Father.

Caravaca (1576) and Villanueva (1580) followed, but, in the midst of her travels, Teresa was ordered to cease all founding activity and retire to a monastery. She appealed to King Phillip II, who once again resolved the matter to Teresa's satisfaction. These were years of great turbulence for the living saint: John of the Cross was arrested and imprisoned in Ávila; *Life* was seized by the Inquisition for close inspection, later to be returned with a favorable recommendation; Teresa lost use of her left arm after she reinjured an old problem sustained from a fall down the stairs at Ávila; and problems continued among discalced and calced Carmelite orders and among friars.

In Palencia (1580), Teresa received the "Brief Separating Discalced from Calced," a document by which the Pope separated the two branches of the Carmelite order.

Soria (1581), Granada (1582)—the only foundation which Teresa sent her representatives, John of the Cross and Anne of Jesus, to oversee, and Burgos (1582) were the last of the reformed Carmelite foundations. By the time Teresa reached Burgos, she was frail and cold but driven onward by the fire of love. From her sickbed she directed all activities, her voice barely a whisper, with a painful sore throat. Burgos was problematic from beginning to end—illness, jealous disputes, confusion, negotiations, and floods.

As the sisters approached a river of raging flood waters, they drew back, alarmed at the prospects for crossing it. True to character, Teresa saw it as just another obstacle to overcome.

Before they crossed, the sisters had confession, asked the Mother prioress to bless them, and recited the Creed, just in case death was imminent. According to Teresa's nurse, "The Saint laughed at us and said: 'Come on, daughters what more could you ask for than to be martyrs here for the love of our Lord?' Then she said that she would go first. If she drowned we were to turn back. In the end it pleased God to deliver us from this danger."[36]

On September 29, 1582, Teresa, in bed in a drowsy agony, prepared to die. The sisters, remaining at her bedside, prayed and wept. Although her voice trembled and her pulse rate spiked to drastic highs and lows, Teresa dictated her last testament. Then, as they removed the Blessed Sacrament, she sat up in the bed and with a burst of energy joyfully said: "My Lord, it is time to be going. Very well, Your Will be done."[37] On October 4, 1582, she died with her head in the arms of her nurse, at the age of sixty-seven.

In 1584 Teresa's tomb was opened. The body was whole with no signs of physical disintegration. In fact, her body had the fresh, unravaged appearance of one who had just been buried.

Who was this woman of vision who inspired love in those around her, had a gift for friendship yet endured illness, disappointment, betrayal, and her own personality weaknesses? Who was this nun who had an intimate friendship with God but suffered the accusations of her own Church? Turn the pages of her life and we see a woman in union with God who followed the illumined path of the inner life yet struggled outside with everyone and everything, without the benefit of health or money. But nothing stopped her; hardship only served to increase her faith and love. As a city corregidor once remarked: "Mother Teresa must have in her bosom some authorization from the Royal Council of God, which makes us do whatever she wants whether we like it or not."[38]

In His name and under His direction, Saint Teresa of Jesus, accompanied by strong and faithful women, was a clear mirror that reflected the light of Love.

The Young Years

Teresa Sánchez de Ahumada y Cepeda was born during the reign of Catholic monarchs Ferdinand and Isabella in the small, walled Castillian town of Ávila on March 28, 1515. Ávila, at that time, was a Christian stronghold in the Moorish wars in the century in which the remote peninsula of Spain was the greatest power in Europe.

In 1485 Teresa's grandfather, Juan Sánchez of Toledo, had to publicly confess before the Inquisition to the "crime" of reversion. As a Jewish *converso* (Christianized Jew), he pleaded "guilty" to secretly practicing his ancestral religion.

For his crime, Juan Sánchez and his children endured public humiliation. They marched in procession through the streets of Toledo, wearing the dreaded *sanbenito*, a yellow garment marked with black crosses. To complete the disgrace, the family was forced to visit the hallowed grounds of all the city's cathedrals, not once, but every Friday for seven weeks while Toledo's Christian citizens threw stones, cursed, and spat upon them.

It took courage to walk through streets with an odor of death in the air. People were burned at the stake for embracing their Jewish faith; but not Juan Sánchez. He stood cloaked in a garment of disgrace before citizens who mocked his humanity and religion. Though not burned at the stake, he and his family suffered the wrath and scorn that intolerance inflicted on the innocent. Such wounds to the soul are long in healing.

His good name ruined and his children forced to drink the bitter dregs of prejudice, he left Toledo, changed his name to "Cepeda," and, eventually, settled in Ávila, a city proud of its heritage of religious tolerance. In an ironic twist of fate, his son Alonso, who was fourteen during the Toledo "crime," later cradled a daughter destined to become a future Catholic saint. Although her father and grandfather suffered the tragedies of prejudice, Teresa never showed a trace of prejudice; never believed in conversion through force.

In 1505, Don Alonso de Cepeda, a tax-gatherer, married; but his wife died two years later, leaving him with two sons. He had suffered through persecution; now he suffered through sorrow. Four years later, when he was about forty, he married beautiful, young Beatriz de Ahumada.

Teresa described her mother as beautiful, intelligent, quiet, an outright recluse who was "a great invalid." Weakened by all-too-frequent pregnancies, the first when she was barely thirteen, Doña Beatriz spent her time swept up in the romantic currents of chivalric novels. She shared the books with her children who, in the spirit of intrigue, *secretly* passed them along to each other. They had to be cautious. Don Alonso disapproved of their frivolous pleasure and forbade them to read romantic novels and racy poems.

Already an aspiring writer, Teresa's passion for tales of love and chivalry inspired her to attempt to write a book, with her brother Rodrigo, on the themes she liked to read. The manuscript never surfaced in popular print, but an early Jesuit biographer, Ribera, said there was "much that could be said for it."

Even as a child, Teresa possessed an undaunted spirit of adventure whether setting out to have her head cut off for Christ at age seven, playing hermit with other children, or fearlessly riding horseback. It was this same spirit, coupled with her "all or nothing" attitude, which led her into swollen rivers with a wagon load of nuns in tow. In the spirit of adventure, a veiled Teresa in nun's habit mounted her mule and rode in the shadow of snow-capped mountains to her distant destination. She did not quit—not as a child, not as a nun. She pursued her goals relentlessly. Not surprisingly, Teresa was considered "wilder than her brothers put together."[39]

Adolescence, however, was stormy. Her religious piety coexisted with normal teenage vanity. Teresa cultivated her good looks, succumbing early to makeup, pretty dresses, and jewelry: "I began to dress in finery and to desire to please and look pretty, taking great care of my hands and hair and about perfumes."[40] All her life she was considered to be unusually attractive—black eyes with dark, curly hair, expressive hands and a vivacious manner. Of medium height and more plump than thin, Teresa was nicely-shaped and a fanatic about cleanliness. She loved to dress well—even as a nun she originally wore velvet.

Later she looked back on these days and regretted her sliding piety and the "bad" influence of a friend:

> For great harm comes of bad company, since we are inclined by nature to follow the worse rather than the

better. So it was with me. I had a sister many years older than I, from whose modesty and goodness—of which she had plenty—I learnt nothing, whereas from a relative who often visited us I learned every kind of evil. Her conversation was so frivolous that my mother had tried her hardest to prevent her coming to the house . . . . I loved the company of this person. I often talked and gossiped with her, for she helped me to get all the amusements I was so fond of, and even introduced me to some others.

My father and sister were most upset by this friendship, and very often took me to task. But as they could not prevent this person from coming to the house their efforts were of no avail, for I was clever at doing what was wrong. [41]

Sorrow returned in November 1528. Doña Beatriz died, leaving Alonso with ten children. Teresa was fourteen years old. She was bright, beautiful, energetic, and grieving over a mother who died too soon. There were questions unanswered; questions not yet asked about life and love and vocation. She was only fourteen years old—the passage through adolescence had barely begun.

Then the storms set in. Frivolous friendships with teenage relatives sounded a note of alarm to Alonso. A romance flared up with an unidentified male cousin. Teresa was enchanted with love and thoughts of marriage. She came close to compromising her honor, though it is unknown how far the relationship went; Teresa was stingy with the details. But it went far enough that the family honor was at stake. In sixteenth century Spain honor was everything; appearances were all-important. To go too far meant her father and brothers would have had to defend her honor, to protect her good name. It required extreme measures, managed with discretion. Don Alonso packed her off to a strictly governed convent school four years before Teresa entered Carmel.

Our Lady of Grace prepared young girls for the future. There was no public education system in Spain at the time. Reading was a skill learned at home. "The future" was preparation for marriage—cooking, sewing, embroidery. There was, of course, basic religious instruction, which was how Teresa met Doña

María Briceño, a nun with a deep prayer life, who meant more to Teresa than all her former friends.

She was astonished at her own happiness; the thrill of romance and flattery lost their hold on Teresa's heart. The calm of the convent, its focus on God, the serious prayer life of Doña Briceño seemed to trigger a part of Teresa trying to make its presence known. She asked the nuns to pray for her as she struggled with the question of vocation. Pray for clarity, she asked, so the way would be clear. But it did not come—not then.

Instead she wondered: Was her vocation to be a nun? What would such a life be like? Finally, the strain of endless questions, the pros and cons of life as a nun, harmed her health. After a year and a half at the convent school, Don Alonso brought his ill daughter home. "Still I had no desire to be a nun," she said, "and I asked God not to give me this vocation; although I also feared marriage."[42]

It was not romance she feared but marriage. She saw her mother, old before her time, die too soon. In *The Way of Perfection*, Teresa addressed the sisters: "They say that for a woman to be a good wife toward her husband she must be sad when he is sad, and joyful when he is joyful, even though she may not be so. (See what subjection you have been freed from, Sisters!)" Marriage would gain her submission, not heaven. The logic was compelling.

Once her health improved, Teresa went to her married sister's house in Castellanor de la Cañada, but stopped to visit her hermit uncle, Don Pedro de Cepeda. Asked to read devotional books aloud to him, she complied even though she was disinterested. The reading sessions, however, revived memories of the little girl who wanted to be a martyr for Christ. Once again, she felt drawn to piety but not at the sacrifice of her "pleasures." Three months of indecision followed. Finally, the *Letters* of Saint Jerome inspired her with the courage necessary to make the decision.

Don Alonso said "no." The daughter he adored, who made him laugh and sometimes cry, wanted to join a convent. This time she ran away from home not to sacrifice her head for Christ, but to give her heart. She was young and witty and had a genius for storytelling. She was, quite simply, a complete original.

The Journey Through the Castle of Consciousness

The morning of Truth cast its holy light into the shadows of her soul, then pierced Teresa's heart with the extraordinary pain and delicate delights of love. The years of aching loneliness, unrequited by all lesser loves, was fulfilled in exquisite union, as the inner Lover made love with his bride, the soul.

In *Interior Castle*, Teresa wrote a love story—a holy story rich in biblical tradition and the sensual language of *Song of Songs* in which Christ (the lover or bridegroom) pursued the soul (the beloved or bride). Teresa did not back away from such allegories. She spun her words into pointed arrows of imagery that found their mark in the human breast, enkindling the flame of love in the heart of her readers. A "mad" love affair with God is fully described in *Castle*—the explosion of sensation, the painful longing, seduction, and tender love of divine union. She described it all in the erotic language sanctioned by scripture.

"Dirty minds," however, preferred that she select "another style" to make her point. Christian people were shocked, embarrassed by the language of divine union. Like "poisonous creatures [that] turn everything they eat into poison," she said, such people "create fears" about language that was created by the Holy Spirit to impress on the soul how much God really loves it.

Teresa also drew on the analogy of human marriage to symbolize that as the wife endures both the richest and poorest times with her husband, so do we, in relationship with Christ, embrace both love and suffering.

Her love story—of loving and being loved completely—was born of experience as she ascended to the heights of holiness to which the Gospel invites everyone. Teresa's own mystical marriage with Christ occurred in 1572 after she returned to the Incarnation as prioress.

After an occasion in which she told John of the Cross, her spiritual director, how much she loved to receive a large host at communion, he humbled her:

> [W]hen I was receiving Communion, Father John of the Cross who was giving me the Blessed Sacrament broke the host to provide for another sister. I thought there was no lack of hosts but that he wanted to mortify me . . . . His

Majesty said to me: "Don't fear, daughter, for no one will be a party to separating you from Me," making me thereby to understand that what just happened didn't matter. Then He appeared to me in an imaginative vision . . . and He gave me His right hand and said: "Behold this nail; it is a sign that you will be My bride from today on . . . . [F]rom now on not only will you look after My honor as being the honor of your Creator, King, and God, but you will look after it as My true bride. My honor is yours, and yours Mine."[44]

And the two became one; the promise of scripture was consummated in divine marriage as God drew the soul into the room where He alone dwells. The soul, now in marital bliss, was a lamp illumined by eternal light, never to grow faint; never to be snuffed out. A new road had opened to a state of expanded consciousness and compassion and wisdom.

Whereas Teresa's other periods of union were of shorter duration, this experience was permanent, an initiation into the mature spiritual life. A profound inner peace permeated her being—every atom seemed to resonate in peaceful harmony. Regardless of the tremendous upheavals that accompanied Teresa's outside, active life, she now lived in steady, permanent union with God. The peacefulness of spiritual matrimony sustained her from that moment forward.

There are no words to adequately describe union. The soul kisses God, and God caresses the soul, with a touch so tender that it is beyond human comparisons and explanations. Teresa, a woman of words written and spoken, found the experience indescribable, and only said: "The Lord wishes to reveal for that moment . . . the glory of heaven. One can say no more than that the . . . soul is made one with God."[45] Later she remarked that her soul experienced the meaning of Paul's words, "For me to live is Christ, and to die is gain."[46]

Life is born anew. But the person married to God is not immune to suffering; in fact, quite the contrary. The soul "imitate[s] Him in His greatest sufferings," yet has no fear or anxiety about life.[47] Even death would be only a "gentle rapture." But the soul which emerges from the center of the castle does have a love-driven desire to serve others and their highest good. Whatever befalls us, we count neither cost nor suffering but walk serenely forward with our constant companion and Friend. How could suffering possibly detour one bathed in the love of God?

> These effects are given by God when He brings the soul to Himself with the kiss sought by the bride . . . . Here an abundance of water is given to this deer that was wounded. Here one delights in God's tabernacle. Here the dove Noah sent out to see if the storm was over finds the olive branch as a sign of firm ground discovered amid the floods and tempests of this world.[48]

In the most deeply personal way, Teresa invited her nuns to travel to the center of their own souls to meet their Beloved Friend; then to be thrust outward in compassionate loving service. The journey through the castle of consciousness, however, is made not by the intellect trying to think but through contemplative prayer as it gently draws us inward. Establish a friendship with God, she counseled; prayer is cultivation of a holy friendship.

If we look closely at her life, we discover that it was the thread of *friendship* that ran through the fabric of Teresa's growth in prayer, giving unity to the multitude of experiences recorded in her books. Prayer, according to the Saint, is "an intimate sharing between friends" for which we take time "to be alone with Him who we know loves us."[49] Teresa cultivated her friendship with God, relying not on technique, but on love: "The important thing is not to think much but to love much; and so do that which best stirs you to love."[50] Consequently, Teresa felt it useful, especially for beginners, to use paintings, statues, and holy relics as a "means for enkindling love."

She was a *kataphatic* mystic, one who followed the way of affirmation and images; she experienced God as personal, immanent, a friend rather than unknowable. In contrast, John of the Cross experienced God as imageless, "dark," "empty" in the *apophatic* tradition in which it is impossible to comprehend God with the intellect. Both paths lead up the mountain of Truth; each leads to the summit of spiritual maturity.

There are many doors to Truth. God's presence and power will be known to us in the way most suitable to our nature and destiny. Ordinary people of every century have heard the word of God, sought Him in the center of their souls, and been transformed into messengers of peace, love, and justice. How? Through contemplative prayer, Teresa said.

In *The Way of Perfection* she warmly wrote to the sisters of the three ingredients that bring the peace essential for real prayer: "The first of these is love for one another; the second is detachment from all created things; the third is true humility, which, even though I speak of it last, is the main practice and embraces all the others."[51]

We must love one another, Teresa explained, to avoid irritations which can steal away our peace and complete focus on God. "There is nothing annoying that is not suffered easily by those who love one another."[52] So we must learn to love. Yet we cannot fall into the distraction of excessive love or "particular friendships," where "the silly things that come from such attachment are too numerous to be counted.[53] But Teresa goes on to paint a beautiful picture of spiritual friendship, that is, a relationship whose purpose is a deepening of the spirit:

> It will seem to you that such persons do not love or know anyone but God. I say yes, they do love, with a much greater and more generous love . . . . In short, it is love.[54]

In a lighthearted but intimate, firm but humorous tone, Teresa launched into the need for detachment. Undue attachment to relatives, for example, can cause agitations which hamper the freedom of the spirit. But so can attachment to oneself, even to physical aches and pains:

> Hardly does our head begin to ache than we stop going to choir, which won't kill us either. We stay away one day because our head ached, another because it was just now aching, and three more so that it won't ache again.[55]

Nothing—not even physical symptoms—turn our attention away from God. In her usual candor, Teresa held up a mirror to reflect her own behavior: "In my case He granted me a great mercy in my being sick; for since I would have looked after my comfort anyway, He desired that there be a reason for my doing so."[56]

A strong student of human nature, Teresa well understood the wolves of pleasure which can devour strength and dissolve will. But she shied away from severe bodily penances, believing mature detachment is a gradual process brought about by "not giving in to our will and appetites, even in little things, until the body is completely surrendered to the spirit." Then Teresa issued a firm warning: "You will say that these are natural little things to which we need pay no attention. Don't fool yourselves, they increase like foam."[57]

Finally, she turned her attention to the third essential ingredient to prayer—humility. She drew from personal experience when she emphasized the temptation and dangers in making excuses for oneself, even if wrongly accused. While John of the Cross was her confessor, he remarked, "You have a fine way of excusing yourself!" Teresa remembered his teasing wisdom. The heart is an altar of prayer in a chamber of light; there is no room for pride and excuses in a soul seeking immersion in God.

The *Way of Perfection* winds up a staircase denoting the stages of prayer, then explains mental prayer through Teresa's commentary on the Lord's Prayer—a prayer she asked her nuns to recite to themselves at least once an hour. While *Life* was written to satisfy her critics, *Way* was an informal dialogue written for the members of her convents to teach them how to pray.

Interior Castle, on the other hand, was for anyone who wished to practice mental prayer. The *Castle* was written in 1577, fifteen years after her first two books. She was sixty-two and *La Madre Fundadora* to all of Spain, including King Phillip II. "Teach us to pray," they said. Seekers of every century have uttered the same plea.

The Castle of Prayer

What is contemplative prayer and why is it necessary to know its stages of development? The soul is a garden, Teresa explained, full of weeds in barren soil. "His Majesty" pulls up the weeds and plants good seeds; it is our job to water them. How much water? At what times? What is required for the garden to become a living paradise?

Teresa discussed four ways to water the newly planted seeds, with each way representing a level of prayer. By combining the "four waters" in *Life* with the seven mansions in *Castle*, the map of contemplative prayer is drawn, its stages highlighted in bold relief. But first it is necessary to understand prayer and the importance of its stages.

For the Saint, prayer was the mutual presence of two in love, an indwelling of the Beloved. This is not a new idea; in 1 John 4:16 we read, "God is love; and he who dwells in love abides in God." This was the focal point of prayer for Teresa—enter a place of silence to turn our gaze inward to find Him deep within ourselves. It was an experiential mystery awaiting our discovery in the center of our soul.

Teresa wrote about the indwelling mystery when she explained how "a feeling of the presence of God would come upon me unexpectedly so that I could in no way doubt He was within me or I totally in Him."[58] It was not a vision, however; nothing seen or heard or felt as an emotional sensation. To know and love God in this way is beyond the senses, although Teresa used sense imagery of warmth and fragrance, sight and sound to convey the fact of God's presence. Senses and emotions do not directly affect contemplation, but a deep experience of God can overflow, like water, into the emotional life.

Repeatedly Teresa referred to contemplative prayer as supernatural or infused, poured in by God, often unexpectedly:

> Often when a person is quite unprepared for such a thing, and is not even thinking of God, he is awakened by His Majesty, as though by a rushing comet or a thunderclap. Although no sound is heard, the soul is very well aware that it has been called by God.[59]

It was like being caught on fire with no perception of what caused the fire to ignite.

Even though the grace of contemplative prayer is a gift, unable to be forced, we must prepare to receive this divine gift, not only through desire, but also by taking concrete action. "In reality," wrote Teresa, "the soul in that state [of union] does no more than the wax when a seal is impressed upon it—that is, it is soft—and it does not even soften itself so as to be prepared; it merely remains quiet and consenting."[60]

It cannot be forced yet cannot be escaped. Like a strong wind engulfing a branch, the divine sweetness surrounded Teresa, enveloping her in the delights of love. Prayer, however, is not separated from the rest of our life. As contemplation deepens, it is reflected in our humility, patience, and love for neighbor, among others. *If the virtues are not growing neither is our prayer life.* Quite simply, this divine love which sweeps through the soul affects both our interior aspirations and our exterior actions.

But it is not a boring, static love; quite the contrary. God's work of love in the soul is a divine work of art expressed in various degrees of intensity, experiences of peace and pain, dry yearnings, delicate and deepening love, ecstatic absorptions, light and insight. The burning fire of love wounds the soul, then consumes it in a dying love for God.

The ebb and flow of love begins gently, however, and is punctured by distractions and periods of dryness. Teresa gave less attention to the purifying "dark nights" of John of the Cross, and what she does say is primarily concerned with the second or passive night. But she experienced times of dryness and purification when faith seemed dead and the soul was numbed in its love. Teresa knew the vast desert terrain of the soul and advised her nuns not to quit but *continue their pursuit of God.* To whine about purification and the loss of *feelings* of devotion denoted a lack of courage as far as she was concerned. Those who fail to reach the end of the road want no hardships; "they cannot bear it." Do not whine: surrender to God's work in the soul. Do not force prayer at the wrong time, she said. It can smother the newly developing dry love: "For even though a soul breaks its head in arranging the wood and blowing on the fire, it seems that everything it does only smothers the fire more."[61] Hence the need to understand the stages of prayer and what is required during each phase.

What is contemplation? It is an experience of God's presence, whether in loving peacefulness or a dry reaching out for Him. The beginning of infused contemplation is a refreshing peace that cannot be analyzed. It comes not from our efforts to quiet ourselves or from the absence of worry or from techniques or methods. Initially it is so delicate as to hardly be noticed, but it leads to contact with the indwelling God.

Progressively love deepens as we grow, as do periods of delight and dryness, and infusions of loving fire become stronger. In advanced contemplation, God occupies the inner faculties of will, then the imagination and intellect. Because initially only the will is "captured," distractions continue to accompany prayer. Later on, however, they cease during deep absorptions. This ever-deepening communion is accompanied by a progressive growth in virtue and holiness: humility, purity, love, patience. Genuine prayer is evidenced in the life of one who loves God—"By their fruits you shall know them."

Why is it important to understand the stages of prayer? According to Teresa, she described the "end of the battle" so that people were aware of their destiny, that prayer is for everyone. Secondly, we are less anxious if we understand the normalcy of the purifications and difficulties we encounter along the way. Encouragement is a breath of fresh air, an oasis in the desert of the soul. Further, we must recognize that the delicate beginnings of infused prayer is the place for "drinking at the spring," lest we lose the "blessings" of our communion with God.[62] Otherwise we may remain overly attached to vocal, or discursive, methods when the soul is ready to drink from deeper levels. Teresa's fourth reason is that we pray differently during different stages of prayer:

> I should like to explain this experience because we are dealing with beginners; and when the Lord begins to grant these favors, the soul itself doesn't understand them nor does it know what to do with itself. For if the Lord leads it along the path of fear, as He did me, it is a great trial if there is no one to understand it. To see itself described brings it intense joy, and then it sees clearly the path it is

walking on. It is a great good to know what one must do in order to advance in any of these stages.[63]

The journey is a long one; to see that we are nearing our destination is encouragement to the pilgrim of faith. Light splashed on the road of contemplation illumines the signposts along the way to help us get our bearings. With renewed hope and clearer vision, we courageously face the hurdles of the journey rather than loiter in their shadows.

Teresa's final reason for explaining the stages of prayer evolved from her own fears. She wanted her readers to be prepared to differentiate between genuine gifts from God and self-deception. The road of contemplative splendor and fulfillment is lined with the debris of illusion. Teresa wanted people to see the potential hazards yet fully embrace their destiny of prayer.

In *Interior Castle*, or *Las Morados* ("The Mansions") as it is known in Spain, Teresa masterfully traced the soul's progress from the First Mansions to the Seventh, where the soul was transformed into the Bride of the Spiritual Marriage. In obedience to her superior, Teresa penned word pictures of a sacred pilgrimage, but not without her humble objections:

> Why do they want me to write things? Let learned men, who have studied, do the writing; I am a stupid creature and don't know what I am saying. There are more than enough books written on prayer already. For the love of God, let me get on with my spinning and go to choir and do my religious duties like other sisters. I am not meant for writing; I have neither the health nor the wits for it.[64]

Life was in the clutching hands of Inquisitors; the sisters were hungry for guidance on mental prayer. So Teresa's superior instructed her to write "a fresh book and expound the teaching in a general way, without saying to whom the things that you describe have happened."[65]

The origin of *Interior Castle* would have been lost to us if Teresa had not been stuck in a snowbound inn. Frozen and tired, she and three nuns trudged through falling snow to the sheltering warmth of the inn, where she discovered her friend and former confessor, Fray Diego de Yepes already in residence. She was thrilled to see him, and the two spent their first evening in intimate conversation about their Divine Master. Snow continued to fall, however, building impassable snowdrifts. No one could leave the inn. Against the backdrop of another silent wintry night, Teresa told Fray Diego a remarkable story of how *Castle* came to be written. The next morning, however, she blushed at how freely she had spoken, explaining that love made her lose her sense of proportion. Fray Diego, upon hearing her concern, promised not to repeat what she had said during her lifetime.

In a letter written about nine years later, he shared with Fray Luis de Léon the story of Teresa's vision from God:

> He showed her a most beautiful crystal globe, made in the shape of a castle, and containing seven mansions, in the seventh and innermost of which was the King of Glory, in the greatest splendour, illumining and beautifying them all. The nearer one got to the centre, the stronger was the light; outside the palace limits everything was foul, dark and infected with toads, vipers and other venomous creatures.
>
> While she was wondering at this beauty, which by God's grace can dwell in the human soul, the light suddenly vanished. Although the King of Glory did not leave the mansions, the crystal globe was plunged into darkness, became as black as coal and emitted an insufferable odor, and the venomous creatures outside the palace boundaries were permitted to enter the castle.[66]

So began *Interior Castle*, a masterpiece of mystical theology which explains the slow progression of contemplative prayer. Listen closely. The sound of castle gates opening is Love beckoning the soul inward. But let the pictures tell the story—word pictures born of a vision.

The First Mansions

We consider our very souls to be like a castle made of a single diamond or of very clear crystal, in which there are many rooms, just as in Heaven there are many mansions.

This castle has many dwelling places, some above, others below, others at each side; and in the centre and midst of them all is the chiefest mansion where the most secret things pass between God and the soul.

The door of entry to this castle is prayer and reflection.[67]

We are speaking to souls that, in the end, enter the castle. These are very much absorbed in worldly affairs; but their desires are good; sometimes, though infrequently, they commend themselves to Our Lord; and they think about the state of their souls, though not very carefully. Full of a thousand preoccupations as they are, they pray only a few times a month, and as a rule they are thinking all the time of their preoccupations, for they are very much attached to them, and where their treasure is, there is their heart also. From time to time, however, they shake their minds free of them and it is a great thing that they should know themselves well enough to realize that they are not going the right way to reach the castle door. Eventually, they enter the first rooms on the lowest floor, but so many reptiles get in with them that they are unable to appreciate the beauty of the castle or to find peace within it. Still, they have done a good deal by entering at all.[68]

The first mansions begin with a description of the dignity and brilliance of the human soul, which is made in the image of God. Although the soul in the first mansions is in a state of grace, it is still caught in a web of attachments, smothered by pleasures, honors, riches, business, relatives. Intimacy with God is suffocated by our abundant selfishness. The Saint emphasizes the morass of petty faults that bog us down yet describes people in these mansions as being good, performing noble works, not wishing to offend God. Free from serious sin but submerged in worldly things, the soul has a tenuous relationship with the King in the castle and can only barely see His light.

What is the beginner to do? What steps to take? To go into the second mansions, we "put aside all unnecessary affairs and business." We give up our earthly ambitions, turn from a preoccupation with the world to face the One in the center of the castle.

In *Life*, Teresa used the image of watering the garden of the soul to represent four stages of growth in prayer. The "first water" requires enormous effort. As we draw water up from a well using only a bucket, our arms ache from lifting; the strained back begs for relief. It is an apt metaphor to describe the arduous struggle of the soul in the first mansions.

To the soul encased in the world, Teresa offers sage advice on prayer, self-knowledge, and humility. While she did not emphasize methods of discursive meditation, she recognized their benefits for beginners. But it was love, not reasoning, that was primary in the life of prayer, she counseled. To increase love, Teresa recommended reverent reflection on God's ways. She saw His fingerprints everywhere—on birds, lilies, rocks, pastures, mountains, flowers. Even a worm or bee caused her to rejoice in being a bride of One so wise and powerful.

But reflection on the wonders of nature was not enough either. Teresa meditated on the mysteries of the supernatural and recommended the Gospels as the purest source for reflection and recollection.

People who step into the rooms of the first mansions need a long training in discipline and humility. Teresa believed that self-knowledge was incumbent on the soul regardless of how high it flew in advanced contemplation. Doubts arise from lack of self-knowledge; we gather a distorted view of our own nature. Yet we never succeed in knowing ourselves unless we seek to know God:

> . . . However exalted the soul may be, self-knowledge is incumbent upon it, and this it will never be able to neglect even should it so desire. Humility must always be doing its work like a bee making its honey in the hive: without humility all will be lost. Still we should remember that the bee is constantly flying about from flower to

flower, and in the same way, believe me, the soul must sometimes emerge from self-knowledge and soar aloft in meditation upon the greatness and the majesty of its God. Doing this will help it to realize its own baseness better than thinking of its own nature, and it will be freer from the reptiles which enter the first rooms.[69]

The reptiles are the beasts, wild animals, snakes, and assorted creatures which force us to close our eyes to everything but ourselves. The castle is beautiful, but we are too busy being bitten by "reptiles" to see its light.

The first mansions, often identified with discursive meditation, are a treatise on attachments and distractions. Teresa ends with a reminder that true perfection is love of God and of our neighbor. This mutual love is so important that she warns her readers that if we look for faults in others, we may lose our own peace and disturb that of others.

The Second Mansions

This stage pertains to those who have already begun to practice prayer and have understood how important it is not to stay in the first dwelling place.

The Lord desires intensely that we love Him and seek His company. So much so that from time to time He calls us to draw near to Him.

The call comes through words spoken by other good people, as through sermons, or through what is read in books, or through the many things that are heard and by which God calls, or by illnesses and trials, or in enjoying the beauty of creation, or also through a truth that he teaches during the brief moments we spend in prayer.

However lukewarm these moments be, God esteems them highly.[70]

These are the Mansions of Prayer and Practice where the soul, no longer "deaf and dumb" in the first mansions, begins to receive the message. Still engaged in worldly pastimes, the soul is unable to turn completely to God but does hear Him through sermons, sickness, prayer, reading.

The soul has entered a battleground, a tug-of-war between earthly pleasures and the divine call. It is a heart-splitting state of existence in which we cling to family, friends, esteem in the world, and fear of penance yet are unable to turn away from God. Assaulted by unreasonable fears, we chart a course to return to the first mansions. But growth has overtaken us; it is too late. A haunting conviction that only God is permanent and sure has eclipsed our assurance in the world's message. After nightmares of ambivalence, the will takes a deep breath and decides to press onward; a seed of love now planted but unseen:

> The will is inclined to love after seeing such countless signs of love; it would want to repay something; it especially keeps in mind how this true lover never leaves it; accompanying it and giving it life and being.
> Then the intellect helps it to realize that it couldn't find a better friend, even if it were to live for many years.[71]

Virtues are still "young" in the second mansions; they "have not yet learned to walk—in fact, they have only just been born." For prayer to grow, the soul must now strive to live the message of the Gospels and walk in humility, love, patience, and obedience.

What does Teresa advise? What would help the soul in the house of prayer and practice? Her advice is fivefold: avoid close association with those who are not at least in the early mansions; especially seek those who have advanced to the mansions "nearer the center" because they raise the soul higher. Second, embrace the hardships of the Cross—including dryness in prayer—with gratitude, not resignation. Third, seek to bring the will in conformity with divine will. Fourth, do not lose heart when we fall but continue our efforts to progress, and God will bring good from our "failure." Finally, Teresa reminds those in the second mansions to maintain their commitment and fidelity to prayer: "The door by which we can enter this castle is prayer." There is no other way:

There is no other remedy for this evil of giving up prayer than to begin again; otherwise the soul will gradually lose more each day, and, please God, it will understand this fact.

Well, now it is foolish to think that we will enter heaven without entering into ourselves, coming to know our weakness and what we owe God, and begging for God's mercy.

So end the second mansions and the trials of the soul as it awakens to the divine call. [72]

The Third Mansions

While the second mansions are identified with affective-discursive prayer, the third mansions of Exemplary Life are concerned with active, simple prayer and continued interior trials.

I believe that through the goodness of God there are many of these souls in the world. They long not to offend God, even guarding themselves against venial sins; they love doing penance; they spend hours in recollection; they use their time well; they practice works of charity toward their neighbors; and they are very careful in their speech and dress and in the government of their household if they have one.[73]

The Saint calls the first three mansions a burden on the spirit, "like a great load of earth." Few spiritual joys accompany the soul through the third mansions. Instead we perform acts of charity, acquire discretion, and live with higher standards of virtue. We can, however, still fall back. The soul has not made a total self-surrender; it is not yet inspired by infused love. Progress is a slow crawl up a mountain in a cloud of aridity with only an occasional, fleeting glimpse of the mansions beyond.

How long is love still governed by reason? How long does the soul live without spiritual joy? At the beginning of the fourth mansions, Teresa remarks that:

It seems that, in order to reach these mansions, one must have lived for a long time in the others; as a rule one must have been in those which we have just described, but there is no infallible rule about it, as you must often have heard, for the Lord gives when He wills and as He wills and to whom He wills, and, as the gifts are His own, this is doing no injustice to anyone.[74]

Teresa warns not to overextend our expectations by comparing ourselves to the saints. Instead, we show our love through our good works even though what God needs from us is not service but resoluteness of will. Rather than begging Him for gifts and favors, we give back to He who has given us being.

Once again, Teresa emphasizes humility and cautions us not to brood over our aridity. Accept dry periods and tests as mirrors to our own shortcomings. We may even discover hidden pockets of grief over our attachment to earthly things or trifling ways in which we pretend to be virtuous. All tests only serve to further humility, the true ointment for our wounds.

The third mansions are filled with the winds and snows of the journey. It is our task not to succumb to the changing weather of the soul but to walk with good speed, meeting each obstacle with humility. Leave the fears which relentlessly overtake us in His hands; go on without delay. We cannot afford to serve at a snail's pace.

At this stage it is useful to have a teacher, someone who knows us so that we may learn to know ourselves. The teacher penetrates the heart's secrets and encourages us to fly to unknown heights of holiness. By seeing in another what we thought was impossible, the fledgling bird ventures to fly on new wings of courage and love.

How do we pray in the third mansions? Prayer is still somewhat discursive, but Teresa recommends focusing on the indwelling presence to *prepare* for the Prayer of Quiet. In today's language, we simplify our active efforts of prayer and begin use of centering prayer.

By the conclusion of the third mansions, Teresa reminds us again to tend to our own nest of shortcomings; leave other people's alone. Be careful, she warns, of our attempts to get others to travel the road we walk. We may not be ready to be a wayshower to the spiritual path. Are we certain that we even know what it is? God will take care of His own, nestling them under His wings of love. In humility and hope, we walk onward.

The Fourth Mansions

The fourth mansions are crowded with people who enter the beginnings of infused prayer. At this stage of development "the natural is united with the supernatural"; human and divine modes of praying coexist in the same rooms. The soul can pass quickly from ordinary prayer to infused prayer, but it has not yet received the highest degrees of infused contemplation. Because great problems can arise in this stage and relapses are still possible, Teresa writes expansively of the soul in the fourth mansions.

This is the house of transition where we receive less from our own efforts and more from supernatural graces. Mystical tides flow into the soul gently, almost imperceptibly. Consequently, if we are not well-instructed, we can miss or stifle what is being given in these delicate infusions.

Since we are now moving closer to where the King dwells, Teresa offers a prayer to beg Him to speak for her from this point forward. A touch by the supernatural is of such exquisite beauty that she felt incapable of describing the experience. "Please speak for me," she prays so that people will understand the mansions.

Enter in reverence the rooms which eyes cannot see, ears cannot hear. In these mansions, we shall discover the true value of prayer; our will becomes united with God's will; the spark hidden in the ashes is stirred, not by our efforts, but by His. Enter the fourth mansions in reverence—be receptive to the Spirit at work.

But what about the reptiles that have stalked our every move and nipped at the heels of our consciousness? Into these mansions the poisonous, biting creatures seldom enter, but if one slithers in, it is quite harmless. In fact the soul is strengthened when confronted by the temptation of an unexpected guest.

Teresa sets the stage for a discussion on infused prayer by saying, "Worldly joys have their source in our own nature and end in God whereas spiritual consolations have their source in

God, but we experience them in a natural way and enjoy them . . . much more."[75] Experiences we acquire through meditation proceed from our own nature just as our heart spills over with joy when we see someone we love, inherit a fortune, or see someone alive that we heard was dead. To awaken the will, Teresa advises that we add to our devout feelings acts of love, in which we praise and rejoice in God's goodness and desire Him. Be stirred to love, she says. Desire strong determination to please God—it is a sign of Love.

In the fourth mansions, graces ("spiritual consolations") are identified with the Prayer of Quiet or "second water" in *Life*. Teresa's water image distinguishes between discursive prayer (meditation) in which a basin is filled with water through human effort, and infused contemplation in which the basin is fed directly from the spring, or God. In meditation "spiritual sweetness" reaches us by thoughts. We almost continually work with the intellect and meditate on created things which fatigue our understanding. But the water does reach the basin—it comes in a noisy splashing, however, rather than a delicate peace.

Into the second basin pours a heavenly water from our very depths. It flows with great peace and quietness, penetrating the entire soul with the waters of divine wisdom. We will be tempted to seek a drink from the ever-flowing fountain of God. But we must not do so. We are asked to walk the road of love in humility, without self-interest, not to squeeze heavenly delights from our meditation to refresh us on our journey. The soul does not seek the gift of spiritual delights, but remains receptive to that which in His mercy God grants us.

Infused contemplation is a gift from the One who knows what is best for us. It is a loving awareness of God in which there are no images or visions, no ideas or concepts. The soul may be in loving attention or dry with desire or thirsting for love. But whatever the form of loving awareness, it cannot be forced, read, or reasoned into being. Whether infusions are gentle and brief or the burning, absorbing, and prolonged experiences of advanced states, they are a gift of grace.

In the fourth mansions, Teresa distinguishes between two kinds of prayer: recollection and the Prayer of Quiet. In recollection we desire to be alone with the Alone. Previously, the senses and faculties left the castle for days or years to consort with strangers. Realizing what they had lost, the castle inhabitants (senses and faculties) returned, but their habits were too strong for them to re-enter the castle. So they walked around the grounds, until finally the King recognized their good will and desired to bring them home to Him:

> So like a good Shepherd, with a call so gentle that even they can hardly recognize it, He teaches them to know His voice and not to go away and get lost but to return to their Mansion; and so powerful is this Shepherd's call that they give up the things outside the castle which led them astray, and once again enter it.[76]

In recollection, the senses and external things lose control while the soul regains control. We seek God within ourselves but not from reasoning or picturing Him within the soul. While an excellent meditation method based on the truth that He is within us, "the picture" is under direction of our will. Recollection is not like a "hedgehog or tortoise" which can withdraw into itself whenever it chooses. It occurs when God grants it; our will cannot create or sustain it.

This delicate recollection quite naturally brings the soul to the shores of the Prayer of Quiet where one can enjoy the interior awareness of God in differing degrees at different times. Distractions are still possible, however, for the memory and intellect may be still but not "lost." They are not absorbed in God. It is the *will* that is occupied with God; the key to the fourth mansions is the *will*.

In mansions four through seven, Teresa emphasizes the transformative aspects of infused prayer. In the Prayer of Quiet the virtues grow stronger . . . love for God has less self-interest . . . an "interior dilation" or inner freedom of the soul brings less constraint in serving God . . . fear of hell disappears . . . a craving for worldly things diminishes . . . God gives a strong desire to grow in prayer . . . there is a deeper resolve not to abandon prayer regardless of trials . . . a need for prayerful solitude increases . . . hopeless fears disappear . . . realization of our miseries increases as we know God better . . . bonds are broken which hinder progress . . . humility, patience, and love increase imperceptibly.

The soul has not, however, received the highest gifts of the Spirit. Relapse is still possible if we return to mediocrity and neglect.

What guidance does Teresa offer to souls in the fourth mansions? Be receptive to the Prayer of Quiet, she advises, but do not presume to initiate or intensify it. People "are tempted to imagine that they can prolong it and they may even try not to breathe. This is ridiculous: we can no more control this prayer than we can make the day break, or stop night from falling; it is supernatural (infused) and something we cannot acquire."[77] We cannot cling to delights or pour a cup of joy into our own souls; to try is self-defeating:

> This prayer, then, is a little spark of the Lord's true love which He begins to enkindle in the soul; and He desires that the soul grow in the understanding of what this love accompanied by delight is. For anyone who has experience, it is impossible not to understand soon that this little spark cannot be acquired. Yet, this nature of ours is so eager for delights that it tries everything; but it is quickly left cold because however much it may desire to light the fire and obtain this delight, it doesn't seem to be doing anything else than throwing water on it and killing it.[78]

Yet be receptive, Teresa advises, like a baby who effortlessly receives milk from its mother's breast. The soul, without analysis or reflection, should "drink the milk which His Majesty puts into its mouth and enjoy its sweetness . . . ."[79]

This does not mean, however, that we totally renounce discursive mental prayer or vocal prayer. When God wishes us to cease our human method of praying, He will lead us into absorption into Himself. Until then the soul is both active and receptive: "If we are not quite sure that the King has heard us, or sees us," says Teresa, "we must not stay where we are like ninnies, for there still remains a great deal for the soul to do when it has stilled the understanding; if it did nothing more it would experience much greater aridity and the imagination would grow more restless because of the effort caused it by cessation from thought."[80]

In the fourth mansions, the soul is blessed by the touch of the supernatural, though it may be a faint and fragile caress. Do not race through vocal prayers or void the mind. Be gentle, quiet, "noiseless"; use a centering prayer, if necessary, in these transitional mansions:

> The most we should do is occasionally, and quite gently, to utter a single word, like a person giving a little puff to a candle, when he sees it has almost gone out, so as to make it burn again; though, if it were fully alight, I suppose the only result of blowing it would be to put it out. I think the puff should be a gentle one because, if we begin to tax our brains by making up long speeches, the will may become active again.[81]

Finally, Teresa lists three conditions for growth in the fourth mansions: never give up the habit of prayer, continue detachment from self-centeredness, seek solitude within the Beloved.

These are the fourth mansions where we leave the soul in God's hands to do that which He wants with it. With the greatest disinterest possible in our own benefit, we surrender our will to His will. We come to Him like the poor before a great emperor, then lower our eyes and wait with humility. Mindful of God's honor, we forget our own profit and comfort, prestige and delight.

In this stage of prayer, the soul is not yet grown but is like a suckling baby. If we slide away from habitual prayer during times when we lack self-knowledge or the soul is dry and thirsty, we are like the baby who has just begun to "suck the breast." To be withdrawn from the mother is to die.

Remember we are in God's presence. To think and act less does more as He draws us inward; vocal prayers give way to silent contemplation. Remember that to love is to strive to please Him in everything. Be still in gentle peace, dear soul. Let love awaken and deepen in a crucible of prayer.

The Fifth Mansions

You will have heard of the wonderful way in which silk is made—a way which no one could invent but God—and how it comes from a kind of seed which looks like tiny peppercorns [mustard seeds]. When the warm weather comes, and the mulberry trees begin to show leaf, this seed starts to take life; until it has this sustenance, on which it feeds, it is as dead. The silkworms feed on the mulberry leaves until they are full grown, when people put down twigs, upon which, with their tiny mouths, they start spinning silk, making themselves very tight little cocoons, in which they bury themselves. Then, finally, the worm which was large and ugly, comes right out of the cocoon a beautiful white butterfly.

The silkworm is like the soul . . . through the heat which comes from the Holy Spirit, it begins to utilize the general help which God gives to us all and to make use of remedies He left in His Church—such as frequent confessions, good books and sermons for these are the remedies for a soul dead in negligences and sins and frequently plunged into temptation. The soul begins to live and nourishes itself on this food, and on good meditations, until it is full grown—and this is what concerns me now; the rest is of little importance.

When it [silkworm] is full grown . . . it starts to spin its silk and to build the house in which it is to die. This house is Christ . . . .

. . . You see what we can do with God's favor. May His Majesty Himself be our Mansion as He is in this Prayer of Union which . . . we ourselves spin. When I say He will be our Mansion, and we construct it . . . and hide ourselves in it, I seem to be suggesting that we can subtract from God, or add to Him. But of course we cannot possibly do that! We can neither subtract from, nor add to, God, but we can subtract from, and add to, ourselves, just as these little silkworms do . . . . And God will take this tiny achievement of ours . . . unite it with His greatness and give it such worth that its reward will be the Lord Himself.

. . . Let us hasten . . . to spin this cocoon. Let us renounce our self-love and self-will, and our attachment to earthly things. Let us practice penance, prayer, mortification, obedience, and all the other good works that you know . . . . Let the silkworm die—let it die, as in fact it does when it has completed the work which it was created to do. Then we shall see God and ourselves . . . hidden in His greatness as is this little worm in its cocoon . . . . I am referring to the way . . . He allows Himself to be apprehended in this kind of union.

What becomes of this silkworm . . . when it is in this state of prayer, and quite dead to the world, it comes out a little white butterfly . . . that a soul should come out like this after being hidden . . . and so closely united with Him, for so short a time—never, I think, for as long as half an hour! . . . the soul does not know itself. For think of the difference between an ugly worm and a white butterfly. [The soul] finds itself so anxious to praise the Lord that it would gladly be consumed and die a thousand deaths for His sake. It finds itself longing to suffer great trials and unable to do otherwise. It has the most vehement desires for penance, for solitude, and for all to know God.

To see, then, the restlessness of this little butterfly—though it has never been quieter or calmer in its life! Here is something to praise God for . . . it knows not where to settle and make its abode. By comparison with the abode it has had, everything it sees on earth leaves it dissatisfied, especially when God has again and again given it this wine which almost every time has brought it some new blessing. It sets no store by the things it did when it was a worm—that is, by its gradual weaving of the cocoon. It has wings now: how can it be content to crawl along slowly when it is able to fly?[82]*

In her most celebrated metaphor, Teresa describes how the soul can prepare to receive what, in essence, is a heightened gift of God. Then she goes on to explain the psychological effects of

*Saint Teresa introduces the silkworm (or caterpillar) and butterfly in the fifth mansions rather than the seventh mansions of transforming union (see *Women of Vision, Women of Peace,* Chapter Two).

this new degree of infused contemplation, in which, for the *first time*, the faculties are "asleep." Although the state lasts only a few minutes, the soul is completely possessed by God. Not only is the will taken up in God, as in the fourth mansions, but also the imagination, memory, and intellect. The soul is asleep to things of the world and to itself. Distractions cease during the time of full absorption; all of our inner energies are in union with the indwelling Beloved. The faculties are not so absorbed, however, as not to function; they are just completely occupied with God.

> The consolation, the sweetness, and the delight are incomparably greater than that experienced in the previous prayer [fourth mansions] . . . . This prayer is a glorious foolishness, a heavenly madness . . . . Often I had been as though bewildered and inebriated in this love . . . . The soul would desire to cry out praises, and it is beside itself . . . it cannot bear so much joy . . . it would want to be all tongues so as to praise the Lord.[83]

The Beloved is now everything to the soul. The deep absorption, though brief, is a never-forgotten experience so intense that the exact circumstances in which it occurred are remembered years later. In fact, the Saint says that if certitude of the divine presence is not there, then it was not a union of the whole soul with God. It is an indelible marking which time cannot fade.

This state of the soul has been described as the courting state of Spiritual Betrothal, the Prayer of Union (incipient union), and the "third water." In Teresa's water metaphor, a river or spring sweeps into our garden, and we direct its flow. The Lord Himself is the gardener of a soul totally and completely given over to Him. As the soul is strengthened by the fruit it receives, it becomes strong and well-nourished, until, with God's permission, it distributes its abundance to others. The "third water" is a joyous stage; a "sleep" of the faculties in which "the water of grace rises up the throat of this soul."[84]

The divine invasion of the fourth mansions has now grown into progressively greater love and detachment from self-centeredness. As the soul is less cluttered by finite things and more aware that it can find no rest in creatures, it becomes more other-centered and concerned with the good of the whole.

In the fourth mansions, we felt drowsy—neither asleep nor awake. Lizards from the imagination (thoughts) crawled into our rooms but did no harm, especially if we ignored them. In the fifth mansions, the agile lizards of distraction cannot enter.

The soul enjoys profound calm in this state but not continual joy and rest. Even severe trials emerge from such deep roots that they ultimately bring contentment and serenity. The little butterfly, however, has its cross to bear even though it flies on delicate wings of light.

The small, white butterfly has emerged from its cocoon a stranger to the things of the outside world. But where can the tiny little creature go? Only God can bring it to rest within Himself; the little one cannot return to Him of its own desire. The butterfly consoles itself that to live in exile is God's will. Even this assurance, however, is insufficient.

While the soul does act in conformity with the will of God, it sheds sorrowful tears at being unable to do more, but it simply has not yet been given the capacity. So many offend God, so many do not know or care about Him. But this is not the deepest grief that "tears the soul to pieces." What "grinds it to powder" is that we cannot serve God well enough. It is not a passing grief or one born in meditation. *This grief is infused.*

Just yesterday, it seems, we were concerned only with ourselves; now, we have been closely joined to God, if only for a little while. Teresa reminds us, however, that if we do not continue in self-knowledge and service to God, we will stray from the road to heaven. Divine favors alone are not sufficient. God intends for the soul to live a virtuous life in the service of others, that they may catch fire from its fire.

Teresa's second warning is directed to those who lead a prayerful life and do not offend God: be careful of worms. They are unrecognized until, "like the worm which gnawed through Jonas' ivy," they have gnawed through our virtues. Self-love, self-esteem, judging our neighbors (even in small things), a lack of charity towards others, and not loving our neighbors as ourselves prevent us from attaining a *complete union* with the will of God. We may not be certain if we love God, Teresa explains, but we recognize when we love our neighbor. It so pleases Him that we love His children that He will increase, "in a thousand ways," our love for Him. Perfect love, she reminds us, has "its roots in the love of God."

Her final warnings are that we are judged by actions not big plans; that when we ask to be humbled by God, take care not to hide tiny faults; and that *devotion and gratifying experiences without love of neighbor is a clear indication we have not reached union.*

These are the rooms in the fifth mansions to which "many are called, few are chosen." It is a courtship between the soul and God, in which He draws her to Him for a short meeting and they are united. In secret the soul knows Him in a way that would take "a thousand years by means of the senses and faculties." The soul is fired with love, but if she centers her affections on anything but Him, she loses everything. Be careful to follow the will of God or self-love can seep in, darken our understanding, and weaken our will. Why now? Why would the soul withdraw from such Love to indulge her own wishes, or become lost in the cares of the world? Undermining comes little by little, in shades of gray. But why would God permit such sliding? "Possibly," Teresa replies, "so that He may observe the behaviour of the soul which He wishes to set up as a light to others; for, if it is going to be a failure, it is better that it should be so at the outset than when it can do many souls harm."[85]

So end the fifth mansions. We rest in God's hand—the depths are yet ahead.

The Sixth Mansions

In the fifth mansions, the engagement of the soul to its future Spouse brought deepening prayer, absorption, and incipient ecstasy. But there is so much more; love knows not its own depth until penetrated by the Beloved. In the sixth mansions, lover and Beloved grow in intimacy as more time is spent together. The soul longs to be alone in this state while, at the same time, tries to renounce all that disturbs its solitude. It is not, however, time for the marriage. Instead, with greater intimacy comes increasing favors, afflictions, and preparation for the seventh and final stage.

In the sixth mansions, the longest of Teresa's chapters, the soul's romance has advanced from the courtship of the fifth mansions to Spiritual Betrothal in which the garden of the soul is watered by God Himself. In the "fourth waters," a "heavenly water (rainfall) soaks and saturates this entire garden."[86] With a deepening immersion in God comes an overflow of grace, or in today's language, "extraordinary" mystical phenomena. Saint Teresa describes several types of infused graces: rapture, ecstasy, transport, flight of the spirit, wounding, impulses, the betrothal, and occasionally, levitation. The first four previously mentioned states differ only accidentally. In *Interior Castle* the Saint equates transport with flight of the spirit; rapture is synonymous with ecstasy:

> Now let us return to raptures and speak of what is more common in them . . . the body was left so light that all its weight was gone, and sometimes this feeling reached such a point that I almost didn't know how to put my feet on the ground. Now when the body is in rapture it is as though dead, frequently being unable to do anything of itself. It remains in the position it was when seized by the rapture, whether standing or sitting, or whether with the hands opened or closed. Although once in a while the senses fail . . . this occurs rarely and for only a short time. But ordinarily the soul is disoriented. Even though it can't do anything of itself with regard to exterior things, it doesn't fail to understand and hear as though it were listening to something coming from far off. I do not say that it hears and understands when it is at the height of the rapture (. . . when faculties are lost to other things because of their intense union with God), for then, in my opinion, it neither sees, nor hears, nor feels.[87]

While rapture, Teresa says, comes upon one gradually, transport comes suddenly:

> The soul really seems to have left the body; on the other hand, it is clear that the person is not dead, though for a few moments he cannot be sure if the soul is in the body or no. He feels as if he has been in another world . . . and has been shown a fresh light there, so much unlike

any to be found in this life that if he had been imagining it
. . . all his life long, it would have been impossible for him
to obtain any idea of them . . . as quickly as a bullet leaves
a gun when the trigger is pulled, there begins within the
soul a flight . . . . Great things are revealed to it.[88]

Teresa goes on to describe *impulse* as a state of the soul in
which it "dies with the longing to die" as a "forceful blow of love
prostrates it [the soul]." An impulse comes upon the soul suddenly; nothing can comfort or ease the torment of being separated from God. The "forceful blow" leaves the soul unable to
walk but in possession of the ability to see and speak. As a result
of such powerful impulses, Teresa had "an extremely tender
desire to serve God, along with tearful wishes to leave this exile."[89]

In the *wounding* "an arrow is thrust into the heart or into the
soul itself," but it is a delectable wound, a delightful pain to
further purify the soul for the seventh mansions:

While the soul is in this condition, and interiorly burning, it often happens that a fleeting thought . . . wounds it
[the soul] with an arrow of fire. I do not mean that there
actually is such an arrow; but, whatever it is, it obviously
could not have come from our own nature . . . . It passes as
quickly as a flash of lightning and leaves everything in our
nature that is earthly reduced to powder . . . . It instanta-
neously enchains the faculties . . . . The soul burns so
fiercely . . . I do not believe it would feel anything if it were
cut into little pieces . . . . She is parched with thirst [for
God] . . . .[90]

Sublime communications to the soul occur during the sixth
mansions, but spiritual marriage—complete union with God—is
still ahead, in the seventh mansions. Before the consummation of
transforming love occurs, however, the soul endures endless
afflictions.

The trials of the sixth mansions may be *exterior*—undeserved
praise, misunderstanding and criticism by strangers and especially by friends, backbiting; bodily sickness; misrepresentation,

persecution, gossip; inexperienced, fearful or overly cautious spiritual direction. There are also interior trials in the sixth mansions. Spiritual torment occurs in the form of extreme desolation, aridity, and depression comparable to the "tortures of hell." Yet there is no desire to be free of this "delicate and penetrating" pain except by entering spiritual marriage in the seventh mansions.

The trials of the soul are what enable the dove (soul) to fly higher. In this "tempest of darkness and confusion," the soul waits until a word or chance happening drapes calm over it. Then its burdens vanish, "so that it seems as if it has never been clouded over, but is full of sunshine and far happier than it was before."

During such times of darkness, grace is hidden; no spark is visible. Even love for God is buried too deeply to remember. Mental prayer is impossible—the faculties are incapable of it. Solitude is a dry desert. Other people's company, once enjoyed, is also a torture. The soul feels trapped—there is no way to conceal such deep distress but no way to discuss the inexpressible. What name can be given to spiritual trials and afflictions? The desert tortures intensify before entry into the seventh mansions. Crucified between heaven and hell, the soul seems to receive no help from either direction.

What is the best remedy for these "spiritual afflictions and sufferings?" External works of charity coupled with hope in God's mercy. Accept the aridity, Teresa says, purification of the soul is needed. In actuality, this state is a gift: "The soul comes out of the crucible like gold, more refined and purified, so as to see the Lord within itself . . . . "[91]

It is well to remember that each of the mansions has as many as a million rooms. In *Interior Castle* Teresa is writing about her own life—"composing a life"—but it is not intended to limit the grace of God or the ways in which He works in individual souls. Teresa invites everyone to enter the Interior Castle. Infused contemplation is available to everyone, generally speaking, who has the inner resolve to follow the Way of Perfection. But Teresa never intended for her path to be followed step by step, although her map of the progress of prayer is consistent with other maps, with the notable exception of differences in detail and emphasis.

It bears repeating that God brings each soul to the summit of spiritual maturity in ways suitable for His purpose and the soul's destiny. Peak experiences—effects of God—are not sought but occur according to His grace. Teresa esteemed such experiences for increasing her love for God. But even mystical phenomena are outgrown as the soul advances in prayer. Father Julian of Ávila once asked Teresa why he no longer saw her in ecstasy. She replied that in the beginning the supernatural graces "were strange to her and caused her great amazement [which] resulted in her being carried away and unconscious in the excessive pleasure that her soul experienced within her. Now, as she was more experienced, she enjoyed it more and it made less noise, because she was more used to the great experiences God gave her."[92]

The secret of Teresa's life was not in peak experiences but in being *God-centered* and desiring to truly live the Gospel message. Jesus Christ was her "very good friend" who had "weakness and trials" and understood the human condition. She immersed herself in His mysteries and sacrifice, apprehending them not with the understanding but with the soul. Teresa's Christ was the man in the Gospel stories who walked along the shores of Galilee, taught his disciples in secret, understood the hunger and thirst of mankind. In His "most Sacred Humanity" He walked the path of love, forgiveness, poverty, suffering, humility, and compassion. The humanity of Christ was essential to Teresa's prayer life. His mysteries often stoked the fire of love in her soul; His example she felt called to follow. She did, however, live in the "company of both His Divine and His human nature."

The risen Christ, who dwelled in the heart of her own Interior Castle, was experienced in friendship, in the Eucharist, in vision and voice. Frequently without books during the book-banning Inquisition, she learned from "a living book"—Christ. Extraordinary mysteries about Truth were "impressed" upon her during times of "very loving communication" with God. The core of the Christian mysteries were revealed to her, igniting her love and understanding.

These are the sixth mansions. The safest way to enter these rooms is to want only what God wants; to place ourselves in His hands so that the Greater Will be done in us. The soul, with genuine humility, walks the way of truth, madly in love, with its consciousness and words completely centered on the Beloved.

True humility is gained in the sixth mansions as exalted states of prayer, like a bright sun, shine on dust in the corners of consciousness, revealing our slightest weakness.

Addressing her sisters, Teresa ends with a quote from Saint Matthew (20:22): "Can you drink the chalice (that I shall drink)?" Her answer: "We can."

The Seventh Mansions

It has been a long journey, but now, at last, God brings the soul into His own dwelling to consummate the Spiritual Marriage. What is this Love that awakened the soul from life's slumber to suffer a passionate longing for her Beloved? What is this secret hidden in the seventh mansions? It has always been there, but now God draws the soul to Himself—not by rapture—but by an intellectual vision to reveal the Most Holy Trinity:

First of all the spirit becomes enkindled and is illumined, as it were, by a cloud of greatest brightness. It sees these three Persons, individually, and yet, by a wonderful kind of knowledge which is given to it, the soul realizes that most certainly and truly all these three Persons are one Substance and one Power and one Knowledge and one God alone; so that what we hold by faith the soul may be said here to grasp by sight, although nothing is seen by the eyes, either of the body or of the soul for it is no imaginary vision. Here all three Persons communicate Themselves to the soul and explain to it those words which the Gospel attributes to the Lord—namely, that He and the Father and the Holy Spirit will come to dwell with the soul which loves Him and keeps His commandments.[93]*

Spiritual marriage was a "secret" union which began when Jesus appeared to Teresa in the center of her soul in an intellectual vision "just as He appeared to the Apostles" after the Resurrection. Taking place "behind closed doors," wedded union is a magnificent splendor of love without limit, a heaven in the soul that is sublime and joyous. Words, however, cannot do it justice.

*Saint John of the Cross does not mention a trinitarian vision at the entry of transforming union. Both Carmelites, however, make no distinction between what today we call "ordinary" and "extraordinary" phenomena, though both advise us to seek the highest contemplation, not visions.

But Teresa tried, using simple images to explain the indescribable: The soul remains in the center like two lighted candles
which join flames and become one. Or falling rain becomes
merged in a river; joined waters cannot be separated. Or light
from two windows enters a room, their brightness blended into
one light. "The essential part of her soul," she said, "seemed
never to move from that dwelling place . . . they have become
like two who cannot be separated from one another."[94] A gentle,
deep, passive awareness of the Trinity's presence never ceased.

The soul in Spiritual Marriage, however, is not so absorbed
that it cannot attend to anything else. On the contrary, the hall-
mark of the seventh mansions is service, in companionship with
God. The active and contemplative life—represented symbolically by the coming together of Martha and Mary—are indistin-
guishable. This, according to Teresa, is the whole purpose of
prayer—the birth of good works.

Actually, the unitive state of consciousness propels us to
serve. The soul could not do otherwise. The outward movement
of energy is state specific, an effect of Spiritual Marriage. It is not
tied to a specific mission, but to a state of consciousness.

What are the effects of this Spiritual Marriage? The state is
notable for "forgetfulness of self; a desire to suffer; deep joy in
persecution; a desire to serve; great detachment; and no fear of
the devil's deceits."[95] There are no more raptures, "save very
occasionally" in the sixth mansions as God and His unitive partner settle into a deeper dimension of living.

"Endowed with life by God" the soul awakens to a new
consciousness and a new compassion. In the silent temple of
God, it is peaceful and stable. Fear is absent. Before God revealed
the secrets of the seventh mansions, the poor little butterfly was
worried and frightened. Too afraid to stay, she flew away. Now
that she has found her rest in Christ, weakness has vanished.
Strong and "fit to serve," the soul is a new creation, living a new
life:

> I assure you, sisters, that they have no lack of crosses,
> [in the seventh mansions] but these do not unsettle them
> or deprive them of their peace. The few storms pass
> quickly, like waves of the sea, and fair weather returns,

and then the Presence of the Lord which they have within makes them forget everything.[96]

In the solitude of contemplation, Teresa entered the dwelling place of her Beloved. But it never meant estrangement or withdrawal from other seekers along the way. About friends, Teresa says:

> People will tell you that you do not need friends on this journey, that God is enough. But to be with God's friends is a good way to keep close to God in this life. You will always draw great benefit from them.
> This is to love:
> bear with a fault and not be astonished,
> relieve others of their labor and take upon yourself tasks to be done;
> be cheerful when others have need of it;
> be grateful for your strength when others have need of it;
> show tenderness in love and sympathize with the weakness of others.
> Friends of God love others for more, with a truer, more ardent and a more helpful love. They are always prepared to give much more readily than to receive even to their Creator. [97]

Teresa painted a beautiful picture of friendship. Framed in wisdom, her picture is rare, based on a love rooted in deeper qualities than need or possessiveness. It is spiritual friendship in which one has an intense longing that their friends be immersed in God. It was only to such "spiritual persons" that Teresa could be close. Once she was told to converse not with men but with angels, she discovered that she could no longer be indiscriminately affectionate:

> ... for I have never again been able to tie myself to any friendship or to find consolation in or bear particular love for any other persons than those I understand love Him and strive to serve Him; nor is it in my power to do so, nor does it matter whether they are friends or relatives. If I'm

not aware that the person seeks to love and serve God or to speak about prayer, it is a painful cross for me to deal with him.[98]

The degree of immersion determined the degree of loving friendship, and genuine friendship to Teresa was eternal. But it was also truthful. To one of her nuns, she said, "God grant that you are telling the truth: I should be delighted if you were, but you are a fox, and I expect there is a subterfuge about it somewhere."[99]

As a friend, Teresa was affectionate and natural. The wit and humor once used to charm her admirers in the convent parlor were now effectively used to help her spiritual friends keep their feet on the ground. But no longer was there gossip or idle words. No longer did she use people to get her own needs satisfied. Divine love intensifies human love creating a non-exclusive, pure, freely expressed affection.

The Saint was fiercely loyal. In a letter to a friend she writes, "The love I have for you in the Lord . . . produces a natural weakness in me and makes me resentful that everybody should not realize what they owe to you, and how you have laboured, and I am unable to stand hearing a word against you."[100]

There are few friendships like what the Saint described: selfless, unchanging in illness or old age, permanent closeness, nonpossessive, interested only in the workings of God. In today's language, it would be a friendship born as an expression of our love for God, unconditionally loving, desiring whatever is for the highest good of another. A holy friendship, capable of such depth is not likely in beginners of the spiritual life. Spiritual maturity seasons love.

Whenever one found such a friend, however, Teresa advised her nuns to make every effort to further such a relationship. Such a friend could not be loved too much.

Teresa's journey in prayer led her into the castle deep, where she lived in union with her Beloved Friend. As her pen flowed over the last pages of *Interior Castle*, she ended as she began with love and humility:

> What I conclude with is that we shouldn't build castles in the air. The Lord doesn't look so much at the greatness

of our works as at the love with which they are done.

If you find something good in the way I have explained this to you, believe that indeed God said it so as to make you happy. The bad you might find is said by me.

May God our Lord be forever praised and blessed.

AMEN[101]

Afterword

We began with a question: "What transformed these women into examples of selfless charity?" What abruptly, without warning, changed their interior and exterior lives beyond anything previously known or experienced?

Through an act of grace, God invaded the deepest level of consciousness and slowly brought each soul to spiritual maturity. The transformation process is a long journey directed by the Divine in which the soul is purified, tested, trained, and prepared to fulfill her original design as God's unitive partner.

The process requires a complete emptying of self, an unmasking of all illusions and attachments. The soul dies to a personal existence, yet soars to new heights of intelligence, strength, creativity, and freedom. But she does not fit society's expectations or embrace the world's immature values. Even if she tries to explain her life of charity and love for God, she is misunderstood and often condemned. Others cannot see the mountain's summit of spiritual maturity from their own vantage point on the journey.

God's unitive partner is filled with wisdom, love, and peace at a deeper level than the mental, intellectual, or emotional planes of existence. The soul experiences deep joy, but it is not emotional joy. It does not involve the senses, emotions, or things of the world.

The soul in full, supernatural union with God uses up all subtle threads of self-consciousness until, finally, no duality exists between she and God. A complete, permanent integration occurs at a time governed by His wisdom.

This is a journey of the human spirit that is beyond mental comprehension. It must be lived and then viewed in retrospect.

May those in the process of climbing the mountain of Truth be inspired by the lives of spiritual pilgrims who live at the summit in a mature state of consciousness.

> That prayer has great power
> Which a person makes with all his might.
> It makes a sour heart sweet,
> A sad heart merry,
> A poor heart rich,
> A foolish heart wise,
> A timid heart brave,
> A sick heart well,
> A blind heart full of sight,
> A cold heart ardent.
> It draws down the great God into the little heart,
> It drives the hungry soul up into the fullness of God.
> It brings together two lovers,
> God and the soul,
> In a wondrous place where they speak much of love.

Mechthild of Magdeburg
The Flowing Light of the Divine Godhead (5.130)

Notes

Introduction

1. Richard Maurice Bucke, M.D., *Cosmic Consciousness: A Study in the Evolution of the Human Mind* (New York: E.P. Dutton, 1901 or 1969), 383-384.

Chapter I. Growing Up Spiritually

1. St. John of the Cross, *The Collected Works of St. John of the Cross*. Translated by Kieran Kavanaugh, O.C.D. and Otilio Rodriguez, O.C.D. (Washington, D.C.: ICS Publications, 1979), 117.
2. Ibid., 119.

Chapter II. Spiritual Maturity: The Unitive Life

1. Elizabeth Burrows, Interview (Seattle, Washington, 1989).
2. Robert J. Smith, *Ancestor Worship in Contemporary Japan* (Stanford, California, 1974), 60.
3. Bernadette Roberts, *The Path to No-Self: Life at the Center* (Boston: Shambhala, 1985), 27-29.
4. Eileen Egan, *Such A Vision of the Street: Mother Teresa* (New York: Doubleday, Image Books, 1986), 308.
5. Roberts, *The Path to No-Self*, 121.

Chapter III. Peace Pilgrim

1. Peace Pilgrim, *Peace Pilgrim: Her Life and Work in Her Own Words.* Compiled by some of her friends (Santa Fe: An Ocean Tree Book, 1983), vi.
2. Ibid., 27.
3. Ibid., 29.
4. Ibid., 32.
5. Ibid., 37.
6. Ibid., 130.
7. Ibid., 40-41.
8. Ibid., 25.
9. *Letter to the President, Vice-President, and Congressional Leaders* (Hemet, California: Friends of Peace Pilgrim - photocopy).
10. Ibid.
11. Peace Pilgrim, 41.
12. Ann and John Rush, interview by author, tape recording, Hemet, California, 20 July 1989.
13. Rush, interview, 89.
14. Ibid.
15. Peace Pilgrim, 1-2.
16. Rush, interview, 89.
17. Ibid.
18. Ibid.
19. Peace Pilgrim, 7-8.
20. Ibid., 139.
21. Ibid., 8-9.
22. Ibid., 7-20.
23. Ibid., 21-22.
24. Ibid., 86.
25. Ibid., 74.
26. Ibid., 22-23.
27. Ibid., 24.

Chapter IV. Mother Teresa

1. Mother Teresa, *My Life for the Poor: Mother Teresa of Calcutta.* Edited by José Luis González-Balado and Janet N. Playfoot (New York: Ballantine Books, 1985), 10-11.
2. "Find Your Own Calcutta," *Woman's Day* (December 19, 1989), 86.

3. Eileen Egan, *Such A Vision of the Street: Mother Teresa - The Spirit and the Work* (New York: Doubleday, Image Books, 1986), 401.

4. Eknath Easwaran, *Supreme Ambition* (Petaluma, California: Nilgiri Press, 1982), 60.

5. Ibid., 61.

6. Egan, *Such A Vision*, 29.

7. Mother Teresa, *My Life*, 9.

8. David Porter, *Mother Teresa: The Early Years* (New York: Harper and Row Publishers, Inc., 1976), 69.

9. Easwaran, *Supreme Ambition*, 63.

10. Egan, *Such A Vision*, 48-49.

11. Mother Teresa, *The Love of Christ*. Edited by Georges Goree and Jean Barbier (San Francisco: Harper and Row Publishers, Inc., 1982), 107.

12. Mother Teresa, *My Life*, 17.

13. Ibid., 43-44.

14. Ibid., 40.

15. Egan, *Such A Vision*, 487.

16. Ibid., 92-94.

17. Mother Teresa, *My Life*, 88.

18. Ibid., 82-83.

19. Ibid., 80.

20. Egan, *Such A Vision*, 429-430.

21. Porter, *Mother Teresa*, 14.

22. Ibid., 13.

23. Ibid.

24. Ibid., 24-25.

25. Ibid.

26. Mother Teresa, *My Life*, 2.

27. Porter, *Mother Teresa*, 28.

28. Mother Teresa, *My Life*, 1.

29. Porter, *Mother Teresa*, 15.

30. Mother Teresa, *My Life*, 4.

31. Mother Teresa, *Love of Christ*, 102-103.

32. Ibid., 8-9.

33. Porter, *Mother Teresa*, 52.

34. Ibid., 61.

35. Ibid., 63.

36. Ibid., 66-67.

37. Egan, *Such A Vision*, 107.

38. Ibid., 78.

39. Mother Teresa, *Life in the Spirit: Reflections, Meditations, Prayers*. Edited by Kathryn Spink (San Francisco: Harper and Row Publishers, Inc., 1983), 24.

40. Ibid., 7.

41. Mother Teresa, *A Gift for God: Prayers and Meditations* (San Francisco: Harper and Row Publishers, Inc., 1975), 17.

42. Mother Teresa, *Life in the Spirit*, 17.

43. Mother Teresa, *A Gift for God*, 73-74.

44. Mother Teresa, *Life in the Spirit*, 62.

45. Desmond Doig, *Mother Teresa: Her People and Her Work* (New York: Harper and Row Publishers, Inc., 1976), 136.

46. Mother Teresa, *Prayer Times With Mother Teresa: A New Adventure in Prayer Involving Scriptures, Mother Teresa, and You*. Edited by Eileen Egan and Kathleen Egan, O.S.B. (New York: Doubleday, Image Books, 1985), 25.

47. Mother Teresa, *Life in the Spirit*, 37.

48. Mother Teresa, *A Gift for God*, 67.

49. Doig, *Mother Teresa*, 158.

50. Mother Teresa, *Love of Christ*, 26.

51. Doig, *Mother Teresa*, 24.

52. Mother Teresa, *Love of Christ*, 110.

53. Ibid., 104.

54. Malcolm Muggeridge, *Something Beautiful for God: Mother Teresa of Calcutta* (San Francisco: Harper and Row Publishers, Inc., 1971), 43-44.

55. Mother Teresa, *Life in the Spirit*, 81-82.

56. Egan, *Such A Vision*, 444.

57. Mother Teresa, *Life in the Spirit*, 40.

Chapter V. Irina Tweedie

1. Irina Tweedie, interview by author, tape recording, London, England, 13 March 1990.

2. Ibid.

3. Ibid.

4. Ibid.

5. Ibid.

6. Ibid.

7. Ibid.

8. Ibid.

9. Ibid.

10. Ibid.

11. Ibid.

12. Ibid.

13. Ibid.

14. Irina Tweedie, *Daughter of Fire: A Diary of a Spiritual Training with a Sufi Master* (Nevada City, California: Blue Dolphin Publishing, 1986), ix.

15. Irina Tweedie, *The Chasm of Fire: A Woman's Experience of Liberation Through the Teachings of a Sufi Master* (Dorset, England: Element Books, 1979), 7.

16. Irina Tweedie, *Daughter of Fire*, 5-6.

17. Ibid., 14.

18. Irina Tweedie, *Chasm of Fire*, 15.

19. Irina Tweedie, *Daughter of Fire*, 19-20.

20. Irina Tweedie, *Chasm of Fire*, 32-33.

21. Ibid., 33.

22. Ibid., 38.

23. Ibid., 41.

24. Ibid., 45-46.

25. Ibid., 53.

26. Ibid., 63-64.

27. Ibid., 66.

28. Irina Tweedie, *Daughter of Fire*, 146.

29. Ibid., 221-222.

30. Irina Tweedie, *Chasm of Fire*, 110.

31. Ibid., 111.

32. Ibid., 115.

33. Ibid., 129-130.

34. Ibid., 130-131.

35. Ibid., 143.

36. Ibid., 175.

37. Ibid., 179.

38. Ibid., 186.

39. Irina Tweedie, *Daughter of Fire*, 722.

40. Ibid., 772-773.

41. Ibid.

42. Irina Tweedie, *Chasm of Fire*, 193-194.

43. Irina Tweedie, *Daugher of Fire*, 800.
44. Tweedie, interview, 90.
45. Ibid., 804.
46. Llewellyn Vaughan-Lee, *The Lover and The Serpent: Dreamwork Within a Sufi Tradition* (Dorset, England: Element Books, 1990), 6.
47. Ibid., 7.
48. Tweedie, interview, 90.
49. Ibid.
50. Irina Tweedie, *Daughter of Fire*, v.

Chapter VI: Saint Teresa of Ávila

1. Saint Teresa of Ávila, *The Life of Saint Teresa of Ávila by Herself*. Translated by J.M. Cohen (New York: Penguin Books, 1957), 181.
2. St. Teresa of Ávila, *The Collected Works of St. Teresa of Ávila*, Vol. 2. Translated by Kieran Kavanaugh, O.C.D. and Otilio Rodriguez, O.C.D. (Washington, D.C.: ICS Publications, 1980), 117-121.
3. Saint Teresa of Ávila. *Interior Castle: St. Teresa of Ávila*. Translated and edited by E. Allison Peers (New York: Doubleday, Image Books, 1989), 29.
4. Saint Teresa of Ávila. *Saint Teresa of Ávila Collected Works*, Vol. 1. Translated by Kieran Kavanaugh, O.C.D. and Otilio Rodriguez, O.C.D. (Washington, D.C.: ICS Publications, 1976), 223.
5. Ibid., 262.
6. Ibid., 260.
7. Ibid., 201.
8. PP. Tomas Alvarez, CD. and Fernando Domingo, CD. *Saint Teresa of Ávila: A Spiritual Adventure* (Washington, D.C.: ICS Publications, 1982), 3.
9. Kieran Kavanaugh, O.C.D. and Otilio Rodriguez, O.C.D., *The Collected Works*, Vol. 1, 78-79.
10. Ibid., 94-95.
11. Ibid., 85-86.
12 Ibid., 97-98.
13. The Confessions of St. Augustine, 8:7.
14. Kieran Kavanaugh, O.C.D. and Otilio Rodriguez, O.C.D., *The Collected Works*, Vol. 1, 211.
15. Ibid., 96.

16. Ibid., 324.

17. Ibid., 221.

18. Ibid.

19. Ibid., 222.

20. Kieran Kavanaugh, O.C.D. and Otilio Rodriguez, O.C.D., *The Collected Works*, Vol. 2, 49.

21. Kieran Kavanaugh, O.C.D. and Otilio Rodriguez, O.C.D., *The Collected Works*, Vol. 1, 317.

22. PP. Tomas Alvarez, CD. and Fernando Domingo, CD., *Saint Teresa of Ávila: A Spiritual Adventure*, 56.

23. Ibid., 62.

24. Saint Teresa of Ávila. *The Collected Works of St. Teresa of Ávila*, Vol. 3. Translated by Kieran Kavanaugh, O.C.D. and Otilio Rodriguez, O.C.D. (Washington, D.C.: ICS Publications, 1985), 186.

25. PP. Tomas Alvarez, CD. and Fernando Domingo, CD., *Saint Teresa of Ávila: A Spiritual Adventure*, 66.

26. Ibid., 67.

27. Kieran Kavanaugh, O.C.D., and Otilio Rodriguez, O.C.D., *The Collected Works*, Vol. 2, 50-51.

28. PP. Tomas Alvarez, CD. and Fernando Domingo, CD., *Saint Teresa of Ávila: A Spiritual Adventure*, 83.

29. Kieran Kavanaugh, O.C.D., and Otilio Rodriguez, O.C.D., *The Collected Works*, Vol. 1, 342.

30. Ibid., 344.

31. Ibid., 342.

32. Ibid., 343.

33. Ibid., 340.

34. PP. Tomas Alvarez, CD. and Fernando Domingo, CD., *Saint Teresa of Ávila: A Spiritual Adventure*, 103.

35. Kieran Kavanaugh, O.C.D., and Otilio Rodriguez, O.C.D., *The Collected Works*, Vol. 3, 224-225.

36. PP. Tomas Alvarez, CD. and Fernando Domingo, CD., *Saint Teresa of Ávila: Spiritual Adventure*, 111-112.

37. Ibid., 168.

38. Ibid., 136.

39. Auclair, Marcelle, *Teresa of Ávila*. (New York: Doubleday, Image Books, 1961), 23.

40. Kieran Kavanaugh, O.C.D., and Otilio Rodriguez, O.C.D., *The Collected Works*, Vol. 1, 57.

41. Saint Teresa of Ávila, *The Life of Saint Teresa of Ávila by Herself.* Translated by J.M. Cohen, 27.

42. Kieran Kavanaugh, O.C.D., and Otilio Rodriguez, O.C.D., *The Collected Works*, Vol. 1, 61.

43. Ibid., 402.

44. Ibid.

45. Kieran Kavanaugh, O.C.D., and Otilio Rodriguez, O.C.D., *The Collected Works*, Vol. 2, 433-434.

46. Ibid., 434; cf. Phil., 1:21.

47. Ibid., 445-447.

48. Ibid., 442-443.

49. Kieran Kavanaugh, O.C.D., and Otilio Rodriguez, O.C.D., *The Collected Works*, Vol. 1, 96.

50. Kieran Kavanaugh, O.C.D., and Otilio Rodriguez, O.C.D., *The Collected Works*, Vol. 2, 319.

51. Ibid., 54.

52. Ibid., 54-55.

53. Ibid., 64.

54. Ibid., 78.

55. Ibid.

56. Ibid.

57. Ibid., 84.

58. Kieran Kavanaugh, O.C.D., and Otilio Rodriguez, O.C.D., *The Collected Works*, Vol. 1, 105.

59. Saint Teresa of Ávila, *Interior Castle*. Translated and edited by E. Allison Peers (New York: Doubleday, Image Books, 1989), 135.

60. Ibid., 109.

61. Kieran Kavanaugh, O.C.D., and Otilio Rodriguez, O.C.D., *The Collected Works*, Vol. 1, 327.

62. Kieran Kavanaugh, O.C.D., and Otilio Rodriguez, O.C.D., *The Collected Works*, Vol. 2, 106-113.

63. Kieran Kavanaugh, O.C.D., and Otilio Rodriguez, O.C.D., *The Collected Works*, Vol. 3, 136.

64. E. Allison Peers, *Interior Castle: St. Teresa of Ávila*, 9.

65. Ibid., 9.

66. Ibid., 8.

67. Ibid., 28-33.

68. Ibid., 28-43.

69. Ibid., 37-38.

70. Camille Campbell, *Meditations with Teresa of Ávila* (Santa Fe: Bear and Company, 1985), 21.

71. Ibid., 22.

72. Ibid., 23.

73. E. Allison Peers, *Interior Castle: St. Teresa of Ávila*, 59.

74. Ibid., 73.

75. Ibid., 74.

76. Ibid., 86.

77. Saint Teresa of Ávila, *The Way of Perfection*. Translated and edited by E. Allison Peers (New York: Doubleday, Image Books, 1964), 204.

78. Kieran Kavanaugh, O.C.D., and Otilio Rodriguez, O.C.D., *The Collected Works*, Vol. 1, 141.

79. E. Allison Peers, *The Way of Perfection: St. Teresa of Ávila*, 206.

80. E. Allison Peers, *Interior Castle: St. Teresa of Ávila*, 88.

81. E. Allison Peers, *The Way of Perfection: St. Teresa of Ávila*, 204.

82. E. Allison Peers, *Interior Castle: St. Teresa of Ávila*, 104-107.

83. Kieran Kavanaugh, O.C.D., and Otilio Rodriguez, O.C.D., *The Collected Works*, Vol. 1, 147-149.

84. Ibid., 148.

85. E. Allison Peers, *Interior Castle: St. Teresa of Ávila*, 122.

86. Kieran Kavanaugh, O.C.D., and Otilio Rodriguez, O.C.D., *The Collected Works*, Vol. 1, 161.

87. Ibid., 179-180.

88. E. Allison Peers, *Interior Castle: St. Teresa of Ávila*, 160-161.

89. Kieran Kavanaugh, O.C.D., and Otilio Rodriguez, O.C.D., *The Collected Works*, Vol. 1, 430.

90. E. Allison Peers, *Interior Castle: St. Teresa of Ávila*, 197-199.

91. Kieran Kavanaugh, O.C.D., and Otilio Rodriguez, O.C.D., *The Collected Works*, Vol. 1, 260.

92. Father Julian of Ávila, *Depositions*, 60-61.

93. E. Allison Peers, *Interior Castle: St. Teresa of Ávila*, 209-210; (cf. St. John 14:23).

94. Ibid., 206-212.

95. Ibid., 219-225.

96. Ibid., 225.

97. Camille Campbell, *Meditations*, 140.

98. Kieran Kavanaugh, O.C.D., and Otilio Rodriguez, O.C.D., *The Collected Works*, Vol. 1, 211-212.

99. Letter 162 to Maria de San José.

100. Letter 350 to Gratian, 811.
101. Camille Campbell, *Meditations*, 142.

Glossary

ARCHETYPE: An unrepresentable, unconscious, pre-existent form that is part of the inherited structure of the psyche; images of the collective unconscious held in common by different people at different places and different times. The identification of archetypes is a major contribution of Carl Gustav Jung, Swiss psychiatrist (1875-1961).

CARMELITE: Religious Order to which Saint Teresa belonged. When she entered the Incarnation, there were eleven Carmelite monasteries for nuns in Spain. Each convent required nuns to recite the Divine Office but not to observe closure. In the summer of 1562, Teresa initiated reforms of the Carmelite Order with the founding of the Convent of Saint Joseph. Thirteen nuns wore grilles and veils and observed strict enclosure in order to practice contemplative, or mental prayer. Later, the reform movement spread with the founding of other monasteries of nuns, and eventually, Carmelite friars directed by Saint John of the Cross.

CATHERINE OF GENOA, SAINT (1447-1510): From the age of twenty-seven, she lived a life of practical devotion, taking the Eucharist almost daily (rare at this period for a member of the laity). In the experience of union, she says: "My Being is God, not by simple participation, but by a true transformation of my Being . . . "

CONSCIOUSNESS: The entire dimension of existence experienced in various levels as physical sensations, emotions and feelings, perceptions, knowledge (ideas, constructs, beliefs), life energy, and conscious and unconscious awareness.

CONTEMPLATION: Term used by Western Latin writers, while Eastern Greek writers prefer mysticism. The consciousness of I-hood and of the world disappear. The mystic is conscious of being in immediate relation with God Himself; of participating in divinity. Contemplation installs a method of being and knowing. The word contemplation has acquired different meanings over the centuries, but it is essentially, in Christianity, a level of communing beyond words, feelings, thoughts, and actions.

CONTEMPLATIVE PRAYER: Refers to silent, interior prayer (rather than "vocal" prayer that is recited, liturgical, ritual, prescribed, or formulaic) in search of a loving intimacy and encounter with God. Generally, contemplatives experience a difference in contemplation, or a loving encounter with God, which a person achieves through personal effort (reflection upon Scriptural passages, for example) and contemplation that is "supernatural" or "infused" in which a person is drawn into deeper degrees of loving union with God in ways one cannot control or cause. Infused contemplation is usually accompanied by mystical phenomena, or effects of God, but *always* is accompanied by a profound transformation of consciousness which is expressed in loving service.

CONVENT: A "monastery;" a dwelling in which Religious Order nuns and friars live and work "cloistered" or "enclosed" from "the world." The degree of seclusion varied widely from one Carmelite convent to another.

COSMIC CONSCIOUSNESS: This consciousness shows the cosmos to consist of an immaterial, spiritual universe in which everyone and everything has eternal life. The birth of cosmic consciousness in mankind is the next stage of evolutionary development after self-consciousness. All is not known of the cosmos, however, merely because one becomes conscious of it. It will take thousands of years for humanity to give birth to the new consciousness.

DARK NIGHT OF THE SOUL: Divided between the passive night of the senses in which the bodily senses, imagination, and emotions are purified and the passive night of the spirit in which the Divine further purifies the soul, conforms the will to divine will, and dying to self occurs.

DISCALCED: "Shoe-less" reform movement of the Carmelite order initiated by Saint Teresa of Ávila. Teresa's followers wore *alparagatos*, or hemp sandals, rather than leather shoes. Teresa discouraged her nuns and friars from actually going barefoot.

DISCURSIVE PRAYER: Vocal prayer with use of images, pictures, and relics to help a person still her mind and restless heart. Called discursive meditation, it is verbalized mental prayer. Saint Teresa recommended getting "an image or picture of this Lord . . . to use regularly when you talk to Him." Discursive prayer eventually leads, according to the Saint, to the beginning of contemplative prayer.

ECKHART, JOHANNES (1260-1327): Known as "Meister" Eckhart, he was a Dominican mystic and theologian of Germany; one of the giants of world mysticism.

ECSTASY: Temporary suspension, by divine action, of thinking and feeling faculties, sometimes including the external senses; facilitates experience of divine union.

EGO: As used in this book, the ego is the energy of self-will. The ego has different meanings among psychologies, East and West, and among different religions.

FALSE SELF: Lower or lesser self whose nature is self-centeredness; the mask we wear into the world and with which we identify.

FRANCIS OF ASSISI, SAINT (1182-1226): One of the most universally loved Catholic saints who lived with simplicity, love, and selfless service.

GURU: Spiritual teacher.

ILLUMINATION: In Christian mysticism, it is direct communication to the soul, bypassing the senses, which prepares us for union with God and the unitive state; wherever there is a point of contact between personal consciousness and universal consciousness, there is an extension of personal consciousness; not a single experience but a series of related spiritual discoveries; the effect of illumination is the sudden change of values and transfiguration of character when the Truth of the universe is revealed.

INTERIOR SILENCE: Quieting of imagination, feelings, faculties in the recollection process; loving attentiveness to God in pure faith.

JAMES, WILLIAM (1842-1910): American philosopher and psychologist. His book *The Varieties of Religious Experience* (1902) is a study of mystical and other religious experience.

JOHN OF THE CROSS, SAINT (1542-1591): A Spanish Carmelite mystic who was confessor and friend to Saint Teresa of Ávila. His books on the spiritual journey are classics in world mysticism: *The Ascent of Mount Carmel, The Dark Night of the Soul,* and *Spiritual Canticle.*

KARMA: The chain of cause and effect.

KURTA: Collarless, India-style shirt.

LAITY: Laypersons in the Catholic Church. In sixteenth century Spain, lay men and women had no authority in the Church and could not interpret or teach the faith. Deviation from church doctrine could result in penalties as a heretic.

LONGHI: Straight piece of cotton material, tied round the waist and reaching to the ankles.

MEDITATION: The process by which one achieves at-one-ment with God. It requires fixed concentration, whereby one is disconnected from the senses and is undisturbed by the outerworld. Eastern religions use the word "meditation" which is comparable to stages of "contemplation" in the Catholic tradition.

MENTAL PRAYER: Contemplative prayer as practiced and taught by Saint Teresa of Ávila.

MYSTICISM: The science of union with God; a supernatural state which of ourselves we are powerless to produce.

PRAYER OF QUIET: A state of infused prayer, according to Saint Teresa, "which is a quiet, deep and peaceful happiness in the will" (*Way of Perfection*); the soul is "captive," not free to love anything but God. The Prayer of Quiet is not created or controlled by a person's efforts, and may be experienced in differing degrees at various times for short or long periods.

RAJA YOGA: The "royal" or highest path to God-union. It teaches scientific meditation as the ultimate means for realizing God and includes the highest essentials from all other forms of Yoga.

RECOLLECTION: Gentle, infused awareness of God not produced by human effort. Senses and external things lose their hold on a person as God begins to draw one to Himself; accompanied by what Saint Teresa refers to as a desire to be "alone with the Alone."

SUFI: The "pathless path" to union with God. Originally called "blanket wearers," they were the Brotherhood of Purity who searched for Truth. Sufis are servants to humanity.

THERESE OF LISIEUX, SAINT (1873-1897): Though she only lived to the age of twenty-four, she was decreed by Pope Pius XI to be an equal patron with Saint Francis Xavier of all missions and the secondary patron of France with Saint Joan of Arc. She achieved such recognition so soon after her death because of her holiness. Her doctrine of sanctity is enshrined in her phrase, "the little way of spiritual childhood" which, as Christ did before, urges that we become "as little children." Saint Theresa emphasizes that great love, not great deeds, is the essence of sanctity.

THOMAS à KEMPIS (c. 1379-1471): Born near Cologne, as a member of the Brethren of the Common Life at Agnietenberg, he wrote, preached, and offered spiritual guidance for over seventy years. His greatest work: *The Imitation of Christ.*

TRANSFORMING UNION: The process in which we are purified, unified, and transformed by God's direct intervention in the soul; the cocoon stage; permanent state of union; abiding presence of God rather than particular experience(s).

TRUE SELF: Has been called higher or deeper self; the divine within each individual; image of God in which everyone is created.

TYAGA: Complete renunciation and surrender; called the path of love.

UNION WITH GOD: The revelation of our supernatural permanent oneness with God. It is not experienced by the emotions or intellect, but is at a deeper level of existence; a term describing a single experience of union of all faculties in God or the permanent state of union called transforming union.

UNITIVE STATE: The state following transforming union; represents the permanent state of unitive consciousness.

UPANISHADS: Mystical writings which are part of the Vedas, the record of spiritual discoveries of the sages of ancient India.

YOGA: From Sanskrit "yuji," meaning union with God through scientific methods of meditation.

YOGI: One who practices Yoga; anyone who practices scientific techniques for divine realization.

Bibliography

Alvarez, PP. Tomas CD., and Fernando Domingo, CD. *Saint Teresa of Ávila: A Spiritual Adventure.* Translated by Cristopher O'Mahony. Washington, D.C.: ICS Publications, 1982.

Auclair, Marcelle. *Teresa of Ávila.* New York: Doubleday, Image Books, 1961.

Bucke, Richard Maurice, M.D. *Cosmic Consciousness.* New York: E.P. Dutton, 1969.

Burrows, Elizabeth. *Harp of Destiny.* San Rafael, California: Cassandra Press, 1991.

Campbell, Camille. *Meditations with Teresa of Ávila.* Sante Fe: Bear and Company, 1985.

Catherine of Genoa, Saint. *Purgation and Purgatory: The Spiritual Dialogue.* Translated by Serge Hughes. *Classics of Western Spirituality: A Library of the Great Spiritual Masters.* New York: Paulist Press, 1980.

Doig, Desmond. *Mother Teresa: Her People and Her Work.* New York: Harper and Row Publishers, Inc., 1976.

Dubay, Thomas S.M. *Fire Within*. San Francisco: Ignatius Press, 1989.

Easwaran, Eknath. *Love Never Faileth*. Petaluma, California: Nilgiri Press, 1984.

_____. *Words To Live By: Inspiration for Every Day*. Petaluma, California: Nilgiri Press, 1990.

Eckhart, Meister. *Meister Eckhart: The Essential Sermons, Commentaries, Treatises, and Defense*. Translated by Edmund Colledge, O.S.A. and Bernard McGinn. *Classics of Western Spirituality: A Library of the Great Spiritual Masters*. New York: Paulist Press, 1981.

Egan, Eileen. *Such A Vision of the Street: Mother Teresa—The Spirit and the Work*. New York: Doubleday, Image Books, 1986.

Francis of Assisi, Saint. *The Little Flowers of Saint Francis*. New York: Doubleday, Image Books, 1958.

James, William. *The Varieties of Religious Experience*. New York: New American Library, Mentor Books, 1958.

John of the Cross, Saint. *Collected Works of St. John of the Cross*. Translated by Kieran Kavanaugh, O.C.D. and Otilio Rodriguez, O.C.D. Washington, D.C.: Institute of Carmelite Studies Publications, 1979.

_____. *Dark Night of the Soul: St. John of the Cross*. Translated and Edited by E. Allison Peers. Garden City, New York: Doubleday, Image Books, 1959.

_____. *John of the Cross: Selected Writings*. Edited by Kieran Kavanaugh, O.C.D. *Classics of Western Spirituality: A Library of the Great Spiritual Masters*. New York: Paulist Press, 1987.

Luti, Mary J. *Teresa of Ávila's Way*. Collegeville, Minnesota: The Liturgical Press, 1991.

Meister Eckhart: Teacher and Preacher. Edited by Bernard McGinn. Collaborators Frank Tobin and Elvira Borgstadt. *Classics of Western Spirituality: A Library of the Great Spiritual Masters.* New York: Paulist Press, 1986.

Mother Teresa. *A Gift for God: Prayers and Meditations.* San Francisco: Harper and Row Publishers, 1975.

——————. *Life in the Spirit: Reflections, Meditations, Prayers.* Edited by Kathryn Spink. San Francisco: Harper and Row Publishers, 1983.

——————. *The Love of Christ.* Edited by Georges Goree and Jean Barbier. San Francisco: Harper and Row Publishers, Inc., 1982.

——————. *My Life for the Poor: Mother Teresa of Calcutta.* Edited by José Luis González-Balado and Janet N. Playfoot. New York: Ballantine Books, 1985.

——————. *Prayer Times with Mother Teresa: A New Adventure in Prayer Involving Scriptures, Mother Teresa, and You.* Edited by Eileen Egan and Kathleen Egan, O.S.B. New York: Doubleday, Image Books, 1985.

Muggeridge, Malcolm. *Something Beautiful for God: Mother Teresa of Calcutta.* San Francisco: Harper and Row Publishers, Inc., 1971.

Peace Pilgrim: Her Life and Work in Her Own Words. Compiled by some of her friends. Santa Fe: Ocean Tree Books, 1983.

Porter, David. *Mother Teresa Early Years.* Grand Rapids, Michigan: Eerdman Publishing Company, 1986.

Roberts, Bernadette. *The Experience of No-Self: A Contemplative Journey.* Boston: Shambhala, 1985.

——————. *The Path to No-Self: Life at the Center.* Boston: Shambhala, 1985.

_____. *What is Self?: A Study of the Spiritual Journey in Terms of Consciousness.* Austin, Texas: M. Boens, Publisher, 1989.

Teresa of Ávila. *The Collected Works of St. Teresa of Ávila, Vol. 1.* Translated by Kieran Kavanaugh, O.C.D. and Otilio Rodriguez, O.C.D. Washington, D.C.: ICS Publications, 1976.

_____. *The Collected Works of St. Teresa of Ávila, Vol. 2.* Translated by Kieran Kavanaugh, O.C.D. and Otilio Rodriguez, O.C.D. Washington, D.C.: ICS Publications, 1980.

_____. *The Collected Works of St. Teresa of Ávila, Vol. 3.* Translated by Kieran Kavanaugh, O.C.D. and Otilio Rodriguez, O.C.D. Washington, D.C.: ICS Publications, 1985.

_____. *The Interior Castle.* Translated by Kieran Kavanaugh, O.C.D. and Otilio Rodriguez, O.C.D. *Classics of Western Spirituality: A Library of the Great Spiritual Masters.* New York: Paulist Press, 1979.

_____. *The Life of Saint Teresa of Ávila by Herself.* Translated by J. M. Cohen. New York: Penguin Books, 1957.

_____. *The Life of Teresa of Jesus: An Autobiography of Saint Teresa of Ávila.* Translated and Edited by E. Allison Peers. Garden City, New York: Doubleday, Image Books, 1960.

_____. *The Way of Perfection.* Translated and Edited by E. Allison Peers. Garden City, New York: Doubleday, Image Books, 1964.

Thérèse de Lisieux, Saint. *The Story of a Soul: An Autobiography.* Translated by John Bieners. Garden City, New York: Doubleday, Image Books, 1957.

Thomas à Kempis. *Imitation of Christ.* Translated by William Casey. Huntington, Indiana: Ave Maria Press, 1989.

Tweedie, Irina. *Daughter of Fire: A Diary of A Spiritual Training With a Sufi Master.* Nevada City, California: Blue Dolphin Publishing, 1986.

_____. *The Chasm of Fire: A Woman's Experience of Liberation Through the Teachings of a Sufi Master.* Dorset, England: Element Books, 1979.

Vaughan-Lee, Llewellyn. *The Lover and The Serpent: Dreamwork Within A Sufi Tradition.* Dorset, England: Element Books, 1990.

Notes

Notes

Notes

Notes

Notes

Notes